THE CHALLENGE OF FACTS
AND OTHER ESSAYS

AMS PRESS
NEW YORK

WILLIAM GRAHAM SUMNER
(1895)

THE
CHALLENGE OF FACTS
AND
OTHER ESSAYS

BY

WILLIAM GRAHAM SUMNER

EDITED BY

ALBERT GALLOWAY KELLER

NEW HAVEN: YALE UNIVERSITY PRESS
LONDON: HUMPHREY MILFORD
OXFORD UNIVERSITY PRESS
MDCCCCXIV

Reprinted from the edition of 1914, New Haven

First AMS EDITION published 1971

Manufactured in the United States of America

International Standard Book Number: 0-404-06303-9

Library of Congress Catalog Number: 74-126676

AMS PRESS INC.
NEW YORK, N.Y.   10003

PREFATORY NOTE

The New Haven Palladium: "For President?" *The Providence Evening Press:* "Democracy and Responsible Government." *The Chicago Tribune:* "Republican Government." *The Forum:* "Industrial War." *The Independent:* "The Demand for Men," "The Significance of the Demand for Men," "What the 'Social Question' Is," "What Emancipates," "Power and Progress," "Consequences of Increased Social Power," "What is the 'Proletariat?'" "Who Win by Progress?" "Federal Legislation on Railroads," "Legislation by Clamor," "The Shifting of Responsibility," "The State as an 'Ethical Person,'" "The New Social Issue," "Speculative Legislation," "The Concentration of Wealth: Its Economic Justification." *Messrs. D. Appleton & Company:* "What makes the Rich Richer and the Poor Poorer," "Sketch of William Graham Sumner." *The Reverend Peter Roberts and The Macmillan Company:* "Foreword to 'The Anthracite Coal Industry.'" *Messrs. P. F. Collier & Son, Inc.:* "Reply to a Socialist." *Professor James Elbert Cutler and Messrs. Longmans, Green, & Company:* "Foreword to 'Lynch-Law.'" *The University of Chicago Press:* "Sociology as a College Subject."

PREFACE

Of the essays collected in this volume the following are, so far as I know, now printed for the first time: the title-essay, "A Parable," "Advancing Social and Political Organization in the United States," the "Memorial Day Address," the "Introductory Lecture to Courses in Political and Social Science," and "The Predicament of Sociological Study." The titles of the first and last of these are not the ones which stood on the manuscripts. The first was called "Socialism," but I have taken the liberty of re-naming it in order to give both to it and to this volume a more distinctive title. The last was headed "Sociology" and required to be distinguished from the essay on Sociology in "War and Other Essays." The long essay on "Organization in the United States" is a find which should rejoice at least those former students of Sumner who pursued the study of American history with him. I should add to this list of new material the Memorial Addresses, which were included at request; that of Mr. Baldwin, however, has already been published among the records of the Yale class of 1885.

The presence of new Sumner essays in this volume, as in preceding ones, bears witness to the author's habit of withholding his writings from publication. Though I knew of this tendency I have been astonished at the amount, and also at the degree of elaboration, of the written manuscript found among his literary effects. Manuscripts were written and re-written, and then laid aside, apparently with no thought of publication. Meanwhile the eager mind of the author pressed on to other ranges, and time had its way with the work of his hand. Often it is from yellowing sheets that we have been able to present what here appears in print for the first time.

Perhaps Sumner would have made changes in these unpublished essays before they were allowed to fill the printed page; he may have had some conviction, in his scrupulous self-criticism, as to their state of incompleteness. But I have no apology for publishing them. They can stand for themselves. Now that the emending hand is still, there is no longer any hope of alteration except of inessential detail, and so no valid reason for longer withholding such a rare and characteristic product.

In spite of the fact, then, that some of the essays in this volume have not received the author's final touches in preparation for publication, and that certain of them are preserved only in newspaper reports of lectures, which may or may not have been written up from manuscript, the editor has been very chary about making any changes except those which were obviously necessary. Even where some slight repetition appears in bringing together utterances that were not designed to be together, I have thought it best to leave things as they stand. Where the only report was clearly a garbled one, as in that of an address on "The True Aim of Life," given in 1880 before the Seniors of Yale College, I have, with great regret, discarded the production altogether. Many also of Professor Sumner's best addresses seem to have been almost extemporaneous; nothing remains of these except small packets of slips with items of a more or less cryptic nature set down upon them. In a few instances I am convinced that Sumner later changed his position as to certain points; but I could scarcely try to alter such things. From his later writings it is easy to see what he came to believe. In general I have omitted much which would find a more appropriate place in a Life and Letters; and it is my conviction that such an enterprise should be sometime undertaken. If well done it could not but inure to the strengthening of hearts.

The dating of several of these essays is next to impossible. Sometimes the only clue to the time when they were written lies in the handwriting or the style. I judge, on these criteria, that the title-essay and "A Parable" belong to the eighties, and that the essay on "The Predicament of Sociological Study" is rather late — within a few years, one way or the other, of 1900.

The present intention of the publishers and editor is to bring out one more volume, which will include essays of a more technical character and will contain a full bibliography of Sumner's writings, in so far as such can now be assembled. This volume will probably be delayed for several years, in order to close the series definitively.

ALBERT GALLOWAY KELLER.

NEW HAVEN, September 17, 1914

CONTENTS

SKETCH OF WILLIAM GRAHAM SUMNER

SKETCH OF WILLIAM GRAHAM SUMNER [1]

[1889]

WILLIAM GRAHAM SUMNER was born at Paterson, New Jersey, October 30, 1840. He is the son of Thomas Sumner, who came to this country from England in 1836, and married here Sarah Graham, also of English birth. Thomas Sumner was a machinist, who worked at his trade until he was sixty years old, and never had any capital but what he saved out of a mechanic's wages. He was an entirely self-educated man, but always professed great obligations to mechanics' institutes and other associations of the kind, of whose opportunities he had made eager use in England. He was a man of the strictest integrity, a total abstainer, of domestic habits and indefatigable industry. He became enthusiastically interested in total abstinence when a young man in England, the method being that of persuasion and missionary effort. He used to describe his only attempt to make a speech in public, which was on this subject, when he completely failed. He had a great thirst for knowledge, and was thoroughly informed on modern English and American history and on the constitutional law of both countries. He made the education of his children his chief thought, and the only form of public affairs in which he took an active interest was that of schools. His contempt for demagogical arguments and for all the notions of the labor agitators, as well as for the entire gospel of gush, was that of a simple man with

[1] *The Popular Science Monthly,* Vol. XXXV, 1889.

sturdy common-sense, who had never been trained to entertain any kind of philosophical abstractions. His plan was, if things did not go to suit him, to examine the situation, see what could be done, take a new start, and try again. For instance, inasmuch as the custom in New Jersey was store pay, and he did not like store pay, he moved to New England, where he found that he could get cash. He had decisive influence on the convictions and tastes of the subject of this sketch.

Professor Sumner grew up at Hartford, Connecticut, and was educated in the public schools of that city. The High School was then under the charge of Mr. T. W. T. Curtis, and the classical department under Mr. S. M. Capron. These teachers were equally remarkable, although in different ways, for their excellent influence on the pupils under their care. There was an honesty and candor about both of them which were very healthful in example. They did very little "preaching," but their demeanor was in all respects such as to bear watching with the scrutiny of school-children and only gain by it. Mr. Curtis had great skill in the catechetical method, being able to lead a scholar by a series of questions over the track which must be followed to come to an understanding of the subject under discussion. Mr. Capron united dignity and geniality in a remarkable degree. The consequence was that he had the most admirable discipline, without the least feeling of the irksomeness of discipline on the part of his pupils. On the contrary, he possessed their tender and respectful affection. Mr. Capron was a man of remarkably few words, and he was a striking example of the power that may go forth from a man by what he is and does in the daily life of a schoolroom. Both these gentlemen employed in the schoolroom all the best methods of teaching now so much gloried in, without apparently knowing that they had any peculiar method at all. Professor Sumner has often declared in public that, as a teacher, he is deeply indebted to the sound traditions which he derived from these two men.

He graduated from Yale College in 1863, and in the summer of that year went to Europe. He spent the winter of 1863-1864 in Geneva, studying French and Hebrew with private instructors. He was at Göttingen for the next two years, studying ancient languages, history, especially church history, and biblical science. In answer to some questions, Professor Sumner has replied as follows:

"My first interest in political economy came from Harriet Martineau's 'Illustrations of Political Economy.' I came upon these by chance, in the library of the Young Men's Institute at Hartford, when I was thirteen or fourteen years old. I read them all through with the greatest avidity, some of them three or four times. There was very little literature at that time with which these books could connect. My teachers could not help me any, and there were no immediate relations between the topics of these books and any public interests of the time. We supposed then that free trade had sailed out upon the smooth sea, and was to go forward without further difficulty, so that what one learned of the fallacies of protection had only the same interest as what one learns about the fallacies of any old and abandoned error. In college we read and recited Wayland's 'Political Economy,' but I believe that my conceptions of capital, labor, money, and trade, were all formed by those books which I read in my boyhood. In college the interest was turned rather on the political than on the economic element. It seemed to me then, however, that the war, with the paper money and the high taxation, must certainly bring about immense social changes and social problems, especially making the rich richer and the poor poorer, and leaving behind us the old ante-war period as one of primitive simplicity which could never return. I used to put this notion into college compositions, and laid the foundation in that way for the career which afterward opened to me.

"I enjoyed intensely the two years which I spent at Göttingen. I had the sense of gaining all the time exactly what I wanted. The professors whom I knew there seemed to me bent on seeking a clear and comprehensive conception of the matter under study (what we call 'the truth') without regard to any consequences whatever. I have heard men elsewhere talk about the nobility of that spirit; but the only *body* of men whom I have ever known who really lived by it, sacrificing wealth, political distinction, church preferment, popularity, or anything else for the truth of science, were the professors of biblical science in Germany. That was precisely the range of subjects which in this country was then treated with a reserve in favor of tradition which was prejudicial to everything which a scholar should value. So far as those men infected me with their spirit, they have perhaps added to my usefulness but not to my happiness. They also taught me rigorous and pitiless methods of investigation and deduction. Their analysis was their strong point. Their negative attitude toward the poetic element, their indifference to sentiment, even religious sentiment, was a fault, seeing that they studied the Bible as a religious book and not for philology and history only; but their method of study was nobly scientific, and was worthy to rank, both for its results and its discipline, with the best of the natural science methods. I sometimes wonder whether there is any one else in exactly the same position as I am, having studied biblical science with the Germans, and then later social science, to mark the striking contrast in method between the two. The later social science of Germany is the complete inversion in its method of that of German philology, classical criticism, and biblical science. Its subjection to political exigencies works upon it as disastrously as subjection to dogmatic creeds has worked upon biblical science in this country.

"I went over to Oxford in the spring of 1866. Having given up all my time in Germany to German books, I wanted to read English literature on the same subjects. I expected to find it rich and independent. I found that it consisted of second-hand adaptation of what I had just been studying. I was then quite thoroughly Teutonized, as all our young men are likely to be after a time of study in Germany. I had not undergone the toning-down process which is necessary to bring a young American back to common sense, and I underrated the real services of many Englishmen to the Bible as a religious book — exactly the supplement which I then needed to my German education. Ullmann's 'Wesen des Christenthums,' which I had read at Göttingen, had steadied my religious faith, and I devoted myself at Oxford to the old Anglican divines and to the standard books of the Anglican communion. The only one of these which gave me any pleasure or profit was Hooker's 'Ecclesiastical Polity.' The first part of this book I studied with the greatest care, making an analysis of it and reviewing it repeatedly. It suited exactly those notions of constitutional order, adjustment of rights, constitutional authority, and historical continuity, in which I had been brought up, and it presented those doctrines of liberty under law applied both to church and state which commanded my enthusiastic acceptance. It also presented Anglicanism in exactly the aspect in which it was attractive to me. It re-awakened, however, all my love for political science, which was intensified by reading Buckle and also by another fact next to be mentioned.

"The most singular contrast between Göttingen and Oxford was this: at Göttingen everything one got came from the university, nothing from one's fellow-students. At Oxford it was not possible to get anything of great value from the university; but the education one could get from one's fellows was invaluable. There was a set of young fellows, or men reading for fellowships, there at that time, who were studying Hegel. I became intimate with several of them. Two or three of them have since died at an early age, disappointing hopes of useful careers. I never caught the Hegelian fever.

I had heard Lotze at Göttingen, and found his suggestions very convenient to hold on by, at least for the time. We used, however, in our conversations at Oxford, to talk about Buckle and the ideas which he had then set afloat, and the question which occupied us the most was whether there could be a science of society, and, if so, where it should begin and how it should be built. We had all been eager students of what was then called the 'philosophy of history,' and I had also felt great interest in the idea of God in history, with which my companions did not sympathize. We agreed, however, that social science must be an induction from history, that Buckle had started on the right track, and that the thing to do was to study history. The difficulty which arrested us was that we did not see how the mass of matter to be collected and arranged could ever be so mastered that the induction could actually be performed if the notion of an 'induction from history' should be construed strictly. Young as we were, we never took up this crude notion as a real program of work. I have often thought of it since, when I have seen the propositions of that sort which have been put forward within twenty years. I have lost sight of all my associates at Oxford who are still living. So far as I know, I am the only one of them who has become professionally occupied with social science."

Mr. Sumner returned to the United States in the autumn of 1866, having been elected to a tutorship in Yale College. Of this he says:

"The tutorship was a great advantage to me. I had expected to go to Egypt and Palestine in the next winter, but this gave me an opportunity to study further, and to acquaint myself with church affairs in the United States before a final decision as to a profession. I speedily found that there was no demand at all for 'biblical science'; that everybody was afraid of it, especially if it came with the German label on it. It was a case in which, if a man should work very hard and achieve remarkable results, the only consequence would be that he would ruin himself. At this time I undertook the translation of the volume of Lange's 'Commentary on Second Kings.' While I was tutor I read Herbert Spencer's 'First Principles' — at least the first part of it — but it made no impression upon me. The second part, as it dealt with evolution, did not then interest me. I also read his 'Social Statics' at that period. As I did not believe in natural rights, or in his 'fundamental principle,' this book had no effect on me."

Mr. Sumner was ordained deacon at New Haven in December, 1867, and priest at New York, July, 1869. He became assistant to Dr. Washburn at Calvary Church, New York, in March, 1869. He was also editor of a Broad Church paper, which Dr. Washburn and some other clergymen started at this time. In September, 1870, he became rector of the Church of the Redeemer at Morristown, New Jersey.

"When I came to write sermons, I found to what a degree my interest lay in topics of social science and political economy. There was then no public interest in the currency and only a little in the tariff. I thought that these were matters of the most urgent importance, which threatened all the interests, moral, social, and economic, of the nation; and I was young enough to believe that they would all be settled in the next four or five years. It was not possible to preach about them, but I got so near to it that I was detected sometimes, as, for instance, when a New Jersey banker came to me, as I came down from the pulpit, and said, 'There was a great deal of political economy in that sermon.'

"It was at this period that I read, in an English magazine, the first of those essays of Herbert Spencer which were afterward collected into the volume 'The Study of Sociology.' These essays immediately gave me the lead which I wanted, to bring into shape the crude notions which had been floating in my head for five or six years, especially since the Oxford days. The conception of society, of social forces, and of the

science of society there offered was just the one which I had
been groping after but had not been able to reduce for myself.
It solved the old difficulty about the relation of social science
to history, rescued social science from the dominion of the
cranks, and offered a definite and magnificent field for work,
from which we might hope at last to derive definite results for
the solution of social problems.

"It was at this juncture (1872) that I was offered the chair
of Political and Social Science at Yale. I had always been
very fond of teaching and knew that the best work I could
ever do in the world would be in that profession; also, that
I ought to be in an academical career. I had seen two or three
cases of men who, in that career, would have achieved distinguished usefulness, but who were wasted in the parish and
the pulpit."

Mr. Sumner returned to New Haven as professor in
September, 1872. Of the further development of his
opinions he says:

"I was definitely converted to evolution by Professor
Marsh's horses some time about 1875 or 1876. I had re-read
Spencer's 'Social Statics' and his 'First Principles,' the second
part of the latter now absorbing all my attention. I now read
all of Darwin, Huxley, Haeckel, and quite a series of the natural scientists. I greatly regretted that I had no education in
natural science, especially in biology; but I found that the
'philosophy of history' and the 'principles of philology,' as I
had learned them, speedily adjusted themselves to the new
conception, and won a new meaning and power from it. As
Spencer's 'Principles of Sociology' was now coming out in
numbers, I was constantly getting evidence that sociology, if
it borrowed the theory of evolution in the first place, would
speedily render it back again enriched by new and independent evidence. I formed a class to read Spencer's book in the
parts as they came out, and believe that I began to interest
men in this important department of study, and to prepare

them to follow its development, years before any such attempt was made at any other university in the world. I have followed the growth of the science of sociology in all its branches and have seen it far surpass all the hope and faith I ever had in it. I have spent an immense amount of work on it, which has been lost because misdirected. The only merit I can claim in that respect is that I have corrected my own mistakes. I have not published them for others to correct."

The above statement of the history of Professor Sumner's education shows the school of opinion to which he belongs. He adopts the conception of society according to which it is the seat of forces, and its phenomena are subject to laws which it is the business of science to investigate. He denies that there is anything arbitrary or accidental in social phenomena, or that there is any field in them for the arbitrary intervention of man. He therefore allows but very limited field for legislation. He holds that men must do with social laws what they do with physical laws — learn them, obey them, and conform to them. Hence he is opposed to state interference and socialism, and he advocates individualism and liberty. He has declared that bimetallism is an absurdity, involving a contradiction of economic laws, and his attacks on protectionism have been directed against it as a philosophy of wealth and prosperity for the nation. As to politics he says:

"My only excursion into active politics has been a term as alderman. In 1872 I was one of the voters who watched with interest and hope the movement which led up to the 'Liberal' Convention at Cincinnati, that ended by nominating Greeley and Brown. The platform of that convention was very outspoken in its declarations about the policy to be pursued toward the South. I did not approve of the reconstruction policy. I wanted the South let alone and treated with pa-

tience. I lost my vote by moving to New Haven, and was
contented to let it go that way. In 1876 I was of the same
opinion about the South. If I had been asked what I wanted
done, I should have tried to describe just what Mr. Hayes
did do after he got in. I therefore voted for Mr. Tilden for
President. In 1880 I did not vote. In 1884 I voted as a
Mugwump for Mr. Cleveland. In 1888 I voted for him on
the tariff issue."

A distinguished American economist, who is well
acquainted with Professor Sumner's work, has kindly
given us the following estimate of his method and
of his position and influence as a public teacher:

"For exact and comprehensive knowledge Professor Sumner
is entitled to take the first place in the ranks of American
economists; and as a teacher he has no superior. His leading
mental characteristic he has himself well stated in describing
the characteristics of his former teachers at Göttingen; namely,
as 'bent on seeking a clear and comprehensive conception of
the matter or "truth" under study, without regard to any
consequences whatever,' and further, when in his own mind
Professor Sumner is fully satisfied as to what the truth is, he
has no hesitation in boldly declaring it, on every fitting occasion, without regard to consequences. If the theory is a
'spade,' he calls it a spade, and not an implement of hus-
bandry. Sentimentalists, followers of precedent because it is
precedent, and superficial reasoners find little favor, therefore,
with Professor Sumner; and this trait of character has given
him a reputation for coldness and lack of what may be called
'humanitarianism,' and has rendered one of his best essays,
'What Social Classes Owe to Each Other,' almost repulsive in
respect to some of its conclusions. At the same time, the
representatives of such antagonisms, if they are candid, must
admit that Professor Sumner's logic can only be resisted by
making their reason subordinate to sentiment. Professor
Sumner is an earnest advocate of the utmost freedom in re-

spect to all commercial exchanges; and the results of his experiences in the discussion of the relative merits and advantages of the systems of free trade and protection have been such that probably no defender of the latter would now be willing to meet him in a public discussion of these topics."

THE CHALLENGE OF FACTS

THE CHALLENGE OF FACTS[1]

SOCIALISM is no new thing. In one form or another it is to be found throughout all history. It arises from an observation of certain harsh facts in the lot of man on earth, the concrete expression of which is poverty and misery. These facts challenge us. It is folly to try to shut our eyes to them. We have first to notice what they are, and then to face them squarely.

Man is born under the necessity of sustaining the existence he has received by an onerous struggle against nature, both to win what is essential to his life and to ward off what is prejudicial to it. He is born under a burden and a necessity. Nature holds what is essential to him, but she offers nothing gratuitously. He may win for his use what she holds, if he can. Only the most meager and inadequate supply for human needs can be obtained directly from nature. There are trees which may be used for fuel and for dwellings, but labor is required to fit them for this use. There are ores in the ground, but labor is necessary to get out the metals and make tools or weapons. For any real satisfaction, labor is necessary to fit the products of nature for human use. In this struggle every individual is under the pressure of the necessities for food, clothing, shelter, fuel, and every individual brings with him more or less energy for the conflict necessary to supply his needs. The relation, therefore, between each man's needs and each man's energy, or "individualism," is the first fact of human life.

[1] For approximate date, see preface.

It is not without reason, however, that we speak of a "man" as the individual in question, for women (mothers) and children have special disabilities for the struggle with nature, and these disabilities grow greater and last longer as civilization advances. The perpetuation of the race in health and vigor, and its success as a whole in its struggle to expand and develop human life on earth, therefore, require that the head of the family shall, by his energy, be able to supply not only his own needs, but those of the organisms which are dependent upon him. The history of the human race shows a great variety of experiments in the relation of the sexes and in the organization of the family. These experiments have been controlled by economic circumstances, but, as man has gained more and more control over economic circumstances, monogamy and the family education of children have been more and more sharply developed. If there is one thing in regard to which the student of history and sociology can affirm with confidence that social institutions have made "progress" or grown "better," it is in this arrangement of marriage and the family. All experience proves that monogamy, pure and strict, is the sex relation which conduces most to the vigor and intelligence of the race, and that the family education of children is the institution by which the race as a whole advances most rapidly, from generation to generation, in the struggle with nature. Love of man and wife, as we understand it, is a modern sentiment. The devotion and sacrifice of parents for children is a sentiment which has been developed steadily and is now more intense and far more widely practiced throughout society than in earlier times. The relation is also coming to be regarded in a light quite different from that in which it was formerly viewed. It used to be believed that the parent had unlimited claims on the child and rights over him. In a truer view of the matter, we are coming to see that the rights are on the side of the child and the duties on the side of the parent. Existence is not a boon for which the child owes all subjection to the parent. It is a responsibility assumed by the parent towards the child without the child's consent, and the consequence of it is that the parent owes all possible devotion to the child to enable him to make his existence happy and successful.

The value and importance of the family sentiments, from a social point of view, cannot be exaggerated. They impose self-control and prudence in their most important social bearings, and tend more than any other forces to hold the individual up to the virtues which make the sound man and the valuable member of society. The race is bound, from generation to generation, in an unbroken chain of vice and penalty, virtue and reward. The sins of the fathers are visited upon the children, while, on the other hand, health, vigor, talent, genius, and skill are, so far as we can discover, the results of high physical vigor and wise early training. The popular language bears witness to the universal observation of these facts, although general social and political dogmas have come into fashion which contradict or ignore them. There is no other such punishment for a life of vice and self-indulgence as to see children grow up cursed with the penalties of it, and no such reward for self-denial and virtue as to see children born and grow up vigorous in mind and body. It is time that the true import of these observations for moral and educational purposes was developed, and it may well be questioned whether we do not go too far in our reticence in regard to all these matters when we leave it to romances and poems to do almost all the educational work that is done in the way of spreading ideas about them. The defense of marriage and the family, if their sociological value were better understood, would be not only instinctive but rational. The struggle for existence with which we have to deal must be understood, then, to be that of a man for himself, his wife, and his children.

The next great fact we have to notice in regard to the struggle of human life is that labor which is spent in a direct struggle with nature is severe in the extreme and is but slightly productive. To subjugate nature, man needs weapons and tools. These, however, cannot be won unless the food and clothing and other prime and direct necessities are supplied in such amount that they can be consumed while tools and weapons are being made, for the tools and weapons themselves satisfy no needs directly. A man who tills the ground with his fingers or with a pointed stick picked up without labor will get a small crop. To fashion even the rudest spade or hoe will cost time, during which the laborer must still eat and drink and wear, but the tool, when obtained, will multiply immensely the power to produce. Such products of labor, used to assist production, have a function so peculiar in the nature of things that we need to distinguish them. We call them capital. A lever is capital, and the advantage of lifting a weight with a lever over lifting it by direct exertion is only a feeble illustration of the power of capital in production. The origin of capital lies in the darkness before history, and it is probably impossible for us to imagine the slow and painful steps by which the race began the formation of it. Since then it has gone on rising to higher and higher powers by a ceaseless involution, if I may use a mathematical expression.   Capital is labor raised to a higher power by being constantly multiplied into itself.   Nature has been more and more subjugated by the human race through the power of capital, and every human being now living shares the improved status of the race to a degree which neither he nor any one else can measure, and for which he pays nothing.

Let us understand this point, because our subject will require future reference to it.   It is the most short-sighted ignorance not to see that, in a civilized community, all the advantage of capital except a small fraction is gratuitously enjoyed by the community. For instance, suppose the case of a man utterly destitute of tools, who is trying to till the ground with a pointed stick.   He could get something out of it.   If now he should obtain a spade with which to till the ground, let us suppose, for illustration, that he could get twenty times as great a product.   Could, then, the owner of a spade in a civilized state demand, as its price, from the man who had no spade, nineteen-twentieths of the product which could be produced by the use of it? Certainly not.   The price of a spade is fixed by the supply and demand of products in the community.   A spade is bought for a dollar and the gain from the use of it is an inheritance of knowledge, experience, and skill which every man who lives in a civilized state gets for nothing.   What we pay for steam transportation is no trifle, but imagine, if you can, eastern Massachusetts cut off from steam connection with the rest of the world, turnpikes and sailing vessels remaining.   The cost of food would rise so high that a quarter of the population would starve to death and another quarter would have to emigrate. To-day every man here gets an enormous advantage from the status of a society on a level of steam transportation, telegraph, and machinery, for which he pays nothing.

So far as I have yet spoken, we have before us the struggle of man with nature, but the social problems, strictly speaking, arise at the next step. Each man carries on the struggle to win his support for himself, but there are others by his side engaged in the same struggle. If the stores of nature were unlimited, or if the last unit of the supply she offers could be won as easily as the first, there would be no social problem. If a square mile of land could support an indefinite number of human beings, or if it cost only twice as much labor to get forty bushels of wheat from an acre as to get twenty, we should have no social problem. If a square mile of land could support millions, no one would ever emigrate and there would be no trade or commerce. If it cost only twice as much labor to get forty bushels as twenty, there would be no advance in the arts. The fact is far otherwise. So long as the population is low in proportion to the amount of land, on a given stage of the arts, life is easy and the competition of man with man is weak. When more persons are trying to live on a square mile than it can support, on the existing stage of the arts, life is hard and the competition of man with man is intense. In the former case, industry and prudence may be on a low grade; the penalties are not severe, or certain, or speedy. In the latter case, each individual needs to exert on his own behalf every force, original or acquired, which he can command. In the former case, the average condition will be one of comfort and the population will be all nearly on the average. In the latter case, the average condition will not be one of comfort, but the population will cover wide extremes of comfort and misery. Each will find his place according to his ability and his effort. The former society will be democratic; the latter will be aristocratic.

The constant tendency of population to outstrip the means of subsistence is the force which has distributed population over the world, and produced all advance in civilization. To this day the two means of escape for an overpopulated country are emigration and an advance in the arts. The former wins more land for the same people; the latter makes the same land support more persons. If, however, either of these means opens a chance for an increase of population, it is evident that the advantage so won may be speedily exhausted if the increase takes place. The social difficulty has only undergone a temporary amelioration, and when the conditions of pressure and competition are renewed, misery and poverty reappear. The victims of them are those who have inherited disease and depraved appetites, or have been brought up in vice and ignorance, or have themselves yielded to vice, extravagance, idleness, and imprudence. In the last analysis, therefore, we come back to vice, in its original and hereditary forms, as the correlative of misery and poverty.

The condition for the complete and regular action of the force of competition is liberty. Liberty means the security given to each man that, if he employs his energies to sustain the struggle on behalf of himself and those he cares for, he shall dispose of the product exclusively as he chooses. It is impossible to know whence any definition or criterion of justice can be derived, if it is not deduced from this view of things; or if it is not the definition of justice that each shall enjoy the fruit of

his own labor and self-denial, and of injustice that the idle
and the industrious, the self-indulgent and the self-deny-
ing, shall share equally in the product.   Aside from the
a priori speculations of philosophers who have tried to
make equality an essential element in justice, the human
race has recognized, from the earliest times, the above
conception of justice as the true one, and has founded
upon it the right of property.   The right of property,
with marriage and the family, gives the right of
bequest.

Monogamic marriage, however, is the most exclusive
of social institutions.   It contains, as essential principles, preference, superiority, selection, devotion.   It
would not be at all what it is if it were not for these
characteristic traits, and it always degenerates when
these traits are not present.   For instance, if a man
should not have a distinct preference for the woman he
married, and if he did not select her as superior to
others, the marriage would be an imperfect one according to the standard of true monogamic marriage.   The
family under monogamy, also, is a closed group, having
special interests and estimating privacy and reserve as
valuable advantages for family development.   We grant
high prerogatives, in our society, to parents, although
our observation teaches us that thousands of human
beings are unfit to be parents or to be entrusted with
the care of children.   It follows, therefore, from the
organization of marriage and the family, under monogamy, that great inequalities must exist in a society
based on those institutions.   The son of wise parents
cannot start on a level with the son of foolish ones, and
the man who has had no home discipline cannot be
equal to the man who has had home discipline.   If
the contrary were true, we could rid ourselves at once

of the wearing labor of inculcating sound morals and manners in our children.

Private property, also, which we have seen to be a feature of society organized in accordance with the natural conditions of the struggle for existence produces inequalities between men. The struggle for existence is aimed against nature. It is from her niggardly hand that we have to wrest the satisfactions for our needs, but our fellow-men are our competitors for the meager supply. Competition, therefore, is a law of nature. Nature is entirely neutral; she submits to him who most energetically and resolutely assails her. She grants her rewards to the fittest, therefore, without regard to other considerations of any kind. If, then, there be liberty, men get from her just in proportion to their works, and their having and enjoying are just in proportion to their being and their doing. Such is the system of nature. If we do not like it, and if we try to amend it, there is only one way in which we can do it. We can take from the better and give to the worse. We can deflect the penalties of those who have done ill and throw them on those who have done better. We can take the rewards from those who have done better and give them to those who have done worse. We shall thus lessen the inequalities. We shall favor the survival of the unfittest, and we shall accomplish this by destroying liberty. Let it be understood that we cannot go outside of this alternative: liberty, inequality, survival of the fittest; not-liberty, equality, survival of the unfittest. The former carries society forward and favors all its best members; the latter carries society downwards and favors all its worst members.

For three hundred years now men have been trying

to understand and realize liberty. Liberty is not the right or chance to do what we choose; there is no such liberty as that on earth.   No man can do as he chooses: the autocrat of Russia or the King of Dahomey has limits to his arbitrary will; the savage in the wilderness, whom some people think free, is the slave of routine, tradition, and superstitious fears; the civilized man must earn his living, or take care of his property, or concede his own will to the rights and claims of his parents, his wife, his children, and all the persons with whom he is connected by the ties and contracts of civilized life.

What we mean by liberty is civil liberty, or liberty under law; and this means the guarantees of law that a man shall not be interfered with while using his own powers for his own welfare.   It is, therefore, a civil and political status; and that nation has the freest institutions in which the guarantees of peace for the laborer and security for the capitalist are the highest.   Liberty, therefore, does not by any means do away with the struggle for existence.   We might as well try to do away with the need of eating, for that would, in effect, be the same thing.   What civil liberty does is to turn the competition of man with man from violence and brute force into an industrial competition under which men vie with one another for the acquisition of material goods by industry, energy, skill, frugality, prudence, temperance, and other industrial virtues.   Under this changed order of things the inequalities are not done away with.   Nature still grants her rewards of having and enjoying, according to our being and doing, but it is now the man of the highest training and not the man of the heaviest fist who gains the highest reward.   It is impossible that the man with capital and the man without capital should be equal. To affirm that they are equal would be to say that a man who has no tool can get as much food out of the ground as the man who has a spade or a plough; or that the man who has no weapon can defend himself as well against hostile beasts or hostile men as the man who has a weapon. If that were so, none of us would work any more. We work and deny ourselves to get capital just because, other things being equal, the man who has it is superior, for attaining all the ends of life, to the man who has it not. Considering the eagerness with which we all seek capital and the estimate we put upon it, either in cherishing it if we have it, or envying others who have it while we have it not, it is very strange what platitudes pass current about it in our society so soon as we begin to generalize about it. If our young people really believed some of the teachings they hear, it would not be amiss to preach them a sermon once in a while to reassure them, setting forth that it is not wicked to be rich, nay even, that it is not wicked to be richer than your neighbor.

It follows from what we have observed that it is the utmost folly to denounce capital. To do so is to undermine civilization, for capital is the first requisite of every social gain, educational, ecclesiastical, political, æsthetic, or other.

It must also be noticed that the popular antithesis between persons and capital is very fallacious. Every law or institution which protects persons at the expense of capital makes it easier for persons to live and to increase the number of consumers of capital while lowering all the motives to prudence and frugality by which capital is created. Hence every such law or institution tends to produce a large population, sunk in misery.

All poor laws and all eleemosynary institutions and expenditures have this tendency. On the contrary, all laws and institutions which give security to capital against the interests of other persons than its owners, restrict numbers while preserving the means of subsistence. Hence every such law or institution tends to produce a small society on a high stage of comfort and well-being. It follows that the antithesis commonly thought to exist between the protection of persons and the protection of property is in reality only an antithesis between numbers and quality.

I must stop to notice, in passing, one other fallacy which is rather scientific than popular. The notion is attributed to certain economists that economic forces are self-correcting. I do not know of any economists who hold this view, but what is intended probably is that many economists, of whom I venture to be one, hold that economic forces act compensatingly, and that whenever economic forces have so acted as to produce an unfavorable situation, other economic forces are brought into action which correct the evil and restore the equilibrium. For instance, in Ireland overpopulation and exclusive devotion to agriculture, both of which are plainly traceable to unwise statesmanship in the past, have produced a situation of distress. Steam navigation on the ocean has introduced the competition of cheaper land with Irish agriculture. The result is a social and industrial crisis. There are, however, millions of acres of fertile land on earth which are unoccupied and which are open to the Irish, and the economic forces are compelling the direct corrective of the old evils, in the way of emigration or recourse to urban occupations by unskilled labor. Any number of economic and legal nostrums have been proposed for this situation, all of which propose to leave the original causes untouched. We are told that economic causes do not correct themselves. That is true. We are told that when an economic situation becomes very grave it goes on from worse to worse and that there is no cycle through which it returns. That is not true, without further limitation. We are told that moral forces alone can elevate any such people again. But it is plain that a people which has sunk below the reach of the economic forces of self-interest has certainly sunk below the reach of moral forces, and that this objection is superficial and short-sighted. What is true is that economic forces always go before moral forces. Men feel self-interest long before they feel prudence, self-control, and temperance. They lose the moral forces long before they lose the economic forces. If they can be regenerated at all, it must be first by distress appealing to self-interest and forcing recourse to some expedient for relief. Emigration is certainly an economic force for the relief of Irish distress. It is a palliative only, when considered in itself, but the virtue of it is that it gives the non-emigrating population a chance to rise to a level on which the moral forces can act upon them. Now it is terribly true that only the better ones emigrate, and only the better ones among those who remain are capable of having their ambition and energy awakened, but for the rest the solution is famine and death, with a social regeneration through decay and the elimination of that part of the society which is not capable of being restored to health and life. As Mr. Huxley once said, the method of nature is not even a word and a blow, with the blow first. No explanation is vouchsafed. We are left to find out for ourselves why our ears are boxed. If we do not find out, and find out correctly, what the error is for which we are being punished, the blow is repeated and poverty, distress, disease, and death finally remove the incorrigible ones. It behooves us men to study these terrible illustrations of the penalties which follow on bad statesmanship, and of the sanctions by which social laws are enforced. The economic cycle does complete itself; it must do so, unless the social group is to sink in permanent barbarism. A law may be passed which shall force somebody to support the hopelessly degenerate members of a society, but such a law can only perpetuate the evil and entail it on future generations with new accumulations of distress.

The economic forces work with moral forces and are their handmaidens, but the economic forces are far more primitive, original, and universal. The glib generalities in which we sometimes hear people talk, as if you could set moral and economic forces separate from and in antithesis to each other, and discard the one to accept and work by the other, gravely misconstrue the realities of the social order.

We have now before us the facts of human life out of which the social problem springs. These facts are in many respects hard and stern. It is by strenuous exertion only that each one of us can sustain himself against the destructive forces and the ever recurring needs of life; and the higher the degree to which we seek to carry our development the greater is the proportionate cost of every step. For help in the struggle we can only look back to those in the previous generation who are responsible for our existence. In the competition of life the son of wise and prudent ancestors has immense advantages over the son of vicious and imprudent ones. The man who has capital possesses immeasurable advantages for the struggle of life over him who has none. The more we break down privileges of class, or industry, and establish liberty, the greater will be the inequalities and the more exclusively will the vicious bear the penalties. Poverty and misery will exist in society just so long as vice exists in human nature.

I now go on to notice some modes of trying to deal with this problem. There is a modern philosophy which has never been taught systematically, but which has won the faith of vast masses of people in the modern civilized world. For want of a better name it may be called the sentimental philosophy. It has colored all modern ideas and institutions in politics, religion, education, charity, and industry, and is widely taught in popular literature, novels, and poetry, and in the pulpit. The first proposition of this sentimental philosophy is that nothing is true which is disagreeable. If, therefore, any facts of observation show that life is grim or hard, the sentimental philosophy steps over such facts with a genial platitude, a consoling commonplace, or a gratifying dogma. The effect is to spread an easy optimism, under the influence of which people spare themselves labor and trouble, reflection and forethought, pains and caution — all of which are hard things, and to admit the necessity for which would be to admit that the world is not all made smooth and easy, for us to pass through it surrounded by love, music, and flowers.

Under this philosophy, "progress" has been represented as a steadily increasing and unmixed good; as if the good steadily encroached on the evil without involving any new and other forms of evil; and as if we could plan great steps in progress in our academies and lyceums, and then realize them by resolution. To

minds trained to this way of looking at things, any
evil which exists is a reproach. We have only to consider it, hold some discussions about it, pass resolutions,
and have done with it. Every moment of delay is,
therefore, a social crime. It is monstrous to say that
misery and poverty are as constant as vice and evil
passions of men! People suffer so under misery and
poverty! Assuming, therefore, that we can solve all
these problems and eradicate all these evils by expend-
ing our ingenuity upon them, of course we cannot
hasten too soon to do it.

A social philosophy, consonant with this, has also
been taught for a century. It could not fail to be
popular, for it teaches that ignorance is as good as
knowledge, vulgarity as good as refinement, shiftless-
ness as good as painstaking, shirking as good as faithful
striving, poverty as good as wealth, filth as good as
cleanliness — in short, that quality goes for nothing in
the measurement of men, but only numbers. Culture,
knowledge, refinement, skill, and taste cost labor, but
we have been taught that they have only individual,
not social value, and that socially they are rather draw-
backs than otherwise. In public life we are taught to
admire roughness, illiteracy, and rowdyism. The ignorant, idle, and shiftless have been taught that they are
"the people," that the generalities inculcated at the
same time about the dignity, wisdom, and virtue of
"the people" are true of them, that they have nothing
to learn to be wise, but that, as they stand, they possess
a kind of infallibility, and that to their "opinion" the
wise must bow. It is not cause for wonder if whole
sections of these classes have begun to use the
powers and wisdom attributed to them for their
interests, as they construe them, and to trample on all

the excellence which marks civilization as on obsolete superstition.

Another development of the same philosophy is the doctrine that men come into the world endowed with "natural rights," or as joint inheritors of the "rights of man," which have been "declared" times without number during the last century. The divine rights of man have succeeded to the obsolete divine right of kings. If it is true, then, that a man is born with rights, he comes into the world with claims on somebody besides his parents. Against whom does he hold such rights? There can be no rights against nature or against God. A man may curse his fate because he is born of an inferior race, or with an hereditary disease, or blind, or, as some members of the race seem to do, because they are born females; but they get no answer to their imprecations. But, now, if men have rights by birth, these rights must hold against their fellow-men and must mean that somebody else is to spend his energy to sustain the existence of the persons so born. What then becomes of the natural rights of the one whose energies are to be diverted from his own interests? If it be said that we should all help each other, that means simply that the race as a whole should advance and expand as much and as fast as it can in its career on earth; and the experience on which we are now acting has shown that we shall do this best under liberty and under the organization which we are now developing, by leaving each to exert his energies for his own success. The notion of natural rights is destitute of sense, but it is captivating, and it is the more available on account of its vagueness. It lends itself to the most vicious kind of social dogmatism, for if a man has natural rights, then the reasoning is clear up to the finished

socialistic doctrine that a man has a natural right to
whatever he needs, and that the measure of his claims
is the wishes which he wants fulfilled. If, then, he
has a need, who is bound to satisfy it for him? Who
holds the obligation corresponding to his right? It
must be the one who possesses what will satisfy that
need, or else the state which can take the possession
from those who have earned and saved it, and give it
to him who needs it and who, by the hypothesis, has
not earned and saved it.

It is with the next step, however, that we come to
the complete and ruinous absurdity of this view. If a
man may demand from those who have a share of
what he needs and has not, may he demand the same
also for his wife and for his children, and for how many
children? The industrious and prudent man who takes
the course of labor and self-denial to secure capital,
finds that he must defer marriage, both in order to save
and to devote his life to the education of fewer children.
The man who can claim a share in another's product has
no such restraint. The consequence would be that the
industrious and prudent would labor and save, without families, to support the idle and improvident who
would increase and multiply, until universal destitution
forced a return to the principles of liberty and property;
and the man who started with the notion that the world
owed him a living would once more find, as he does
now, that the world pays him its debt in the state
prison.

The most specious application of the dogma of rights
is to labor. It is said that every man has a right to
work. The world is full of work to be done. Those
who are willing to work find that they have three days'
work to do in every day that comes. Work is the

necessity to which we are born. It is not a right, but an irksome necessity, and men escape it whenever they can get the fruits of labor without it. What they want is the fruits, or wages, not work. But wages are capital which some one has earned and saved. If he and the workman can agree on the terms on which he will part with his capital, there is no more to be said. If not, then the right must be set up in a new form. It is now not a right to work, nor even a right to wages, but a right to a certain rate of wages, and we have simply returned to the old doctrine of spoliation again. It is immaterial whether the demand for wages be addressed to an individual capitalist or to a civil body, for the latter can give no wages which it does not collect by taxes out of the capital of those who have labored and saved.

Another application is in the attempt to fix the hours of labor *per diem* by law. If a man is forbidden to labor over eight hours per day (and the law has no sense or utility for the purposes of those who want it until it takes this form), he is forbidden to exercise so much industry as he may be willing to expend in order to accumulate capital for the improvement of his circumstances.

A century ago there were very few wealthy men except owners of land. The extension of commerce, manufactures, and mining, the introduction of the factory system and machinery, the opening of new countries, and the great discoveries and inventions have created a new middle class, based on wealth, and developed out of the peasants, artisans, unskilled laborers, and small shop-keepers of a century ago. The consequence has been that the chance of acquiring capital and all which depends on capital has opened before classes which formerly passed their lives in a dull round of ignorance and drudgery. This chance has brought with it the same alternative which accompanies every other opportunity offered to mortals. Those who were wise and able to profit by the chance succeeded grandly; those who were negligent or unable to profit by it suffered proportionately. The result has been wide inequalities of wealth within the industrial classes. The net result, however, for all, has been the cheapening of luxuries and a vast extension of physical enjoyment. The appetite for enjoyment has been awakened and nourished in classes which formerly never missed what they never thought of, and it has produced eagerness for material good, discontent, and impatient ambition. This is the reverse side of that eager uprising of the industrial classes which is such a great force in modern life. The chance is opened to advance, by industry, prudence, economy, and emigration, to the possession of capital; but the way is long and tedious. The impatience for enjoyment and the thirst for luxury which we have mentioned are the greatest foes to the accumulation of capital; and there is a still darker side to the picture when we come to notice that those who yield to the impatience to enjoy, but who see others outstrip them, are led to malice and envy. Mobs arise which manifest the most savage and senseless disposition to burn and destroy what they cannot enjoy. We have already had evidence, in more than one country, that such a wild disposition exists and needs only opportunity to burst into activity.

The origin of socialism, which is the extreme development of the sentimental philosophy, lies in the undisputed facts which I described at the outset. The socialist regards this misery as the fault of society. He thinks that we can organize society as we like and that an organization can be devised in which poverty and misery shall disappear. He goes further even than this. He assumes that men have artificially organized society as it now exists. Hence if anything is disagreeable or hard in the present state of society it follows, on that view, that the task of organizing society has been imperfectly and badly performed, and that it needs to be done over again. These are the assumptions with which the socialist starts, and many socialists seem also to believe that if they can destroy belief in an Almighty God who is supposed to have made the world such as it is, they will then have overthrown the belief that there is a fixed order in human nature and human life which man can scarcely alter at all, and, if at all, only infinitesimally.

The truth is that the social order is fixed by laws of nature precisely analogous to those of the physical order. The most that man can do is by ignorance and self-conceit to mar the operation of social laws. The evils of society are to a great extent the result of the dogmatism and self-interest of statesmen, philosophers, and ecclesiastics who in past time have done just what the socialists now want to do. Instead of studying the natural laws of the social order, they assumed that they could organize society as they chose, they made up their minds what kind of a society they wanted to make, and they planned their little measures for the ends they had resolved upon. It will take centuries of scientific study of the facts of nature to eliminate from human society the mischievous institutions and traditions which the said statesmen, philosophers, and ecclesiastics have introduced into it. Let us not, however, even then delude ourselves with any impossible hopes. The

hardships of life would not be eliminated if the laws of
nature acted directly and without interference. The
task of right living forever changes its form, but let us
not imagine that that task will ever reach a final solution or that any race of men on this earth can ever be
emancipated from the necessity of industry, prudence,
continence, and temperance if they are to pass their
lives prosperously. If you believe the contrary you
must suppose that some men can come to exist who
shall know nothing of old age, disease, and death.

The socialist enterprise of reorganizing society in
order to change what is harsh and sad in it at present
is therefore as impossible, from the outset, as a plan
for changing the physical order. I read the other day
a story in which a man dreamt that somebody had
invented an application of electricity for eradicating
certain facts from the memory. Just think of it! What
an emancipation to the human race, if a man could so
emancipate himself from all those incidents in his past
life which he regrets! Let there no longer be such a
thing as remorse or vain regret! It would be half as
good as finding a fountain of eternal youth. Or invent
us a world in which two and two could make five. Two
two-dollar notes could then pay five dollars of debts.
They say that political economy is a dismal science and
that its doctrines are dark and cruel. I think the hardest
fact in human life is that two and two cannot make
five; but in sociology while people will agree that two
and two cannot make five, yet they think that it might
somehow be possible by adjusting two and two to one
another in some way or other to make two and two
equal to four and one-tenth.

I have shown how men emerge from barbarism only
by the use of capital and why it is that, as soon as they

begin to use capital, if there is liberty, there will be inequality. The socialist looking at these facts says that it is capital which produces the inequality. It is the inequality of men in what they get out of life which shocks the socialist. He finds enough to criticize in the products of past dogmatism and bad statesmanship to which I have alluded, and the program of reforms to be accomplished and abuses to be rectified which the socialists have set up have often been admirable. It is their analysis of the situation which is at fault. Their diagnosis of the social disease is founded on sectarian assumptions, not on the scientific study of the structure and functions of the social body. In attacking capital they are simply attacking the foundations of civilization, and every socialistic scheme which has ever been proposed, so far as it has lessened the motives to saving or the security of capital, is anti-social and anti-civilizing.

Rousseau, who is the great father of the modern socialism, laid accusation for the inequalities existing amongst men upon wheat and iron. What he meant was that wheat is a symbol of agriculture, and when men took to agriculture and wheat diet they broke up their old tribal relations, which were partly communistic, and developed individualism and private property. At the same time agriculture called for tools and machines, of which iron is a symbol; but these tools and machines are capital. Agriculture, individualism, tools, capital were, according to Rousseau's ideas, the causes of inequality. He was, in a certain way, correct, as we have already seen by our own analysis of the facts of the social order. When human society reached the agricultural stage machinery became necessary. Capital was far more important than on the hunting or pastoral stage, and the inequalities of men were devel-

oped with great rapidity, so that we have a Humboldt,
a Newton, or a Shakespeare at one end of the scale and
a Digger Indian at the other.   The Humboldt or Newton
is one of the highest products produced by the constant
selection and advance of the best part of the human
race, *viz.*, those who have seized every chance of advancing; and the Digger Indian is a specimen of that
part of the race which withdrew from the competition
clear back at the beginning and has consequently never
made any advance beyond the first superiority of man
to beasts.   Rousseau, following the logic of his own
explanation of the facts, offered distinctly as the cure
for inequality a return to the hunting stage of life as
practiced by the American Indians.   In this he was
plainly and distinctly right.   If you want equality you
must not look forward for it on the path of advancing
civilization.   You may go back to the mode of life of
the American Indian, and, although you will not then
reach equality, you will escape those glaring inequalities
of wealth and poverty by coming down to a comparative
equality, that is, to a status in which all are equally
miserable.   Even this, however, you cannot do without
submitting to other conditions which are far more
appalling than any sad facts in the existing order of
society.   The population of Massachusetts is about
two hundred to the square mile; on the hunting stage
Massachusetts could not probably support, at the
utmost, five to the square mile; hence to get back to
the hunting stage would cost the reduction of the
population to two and a half where there are now
one hundred.   In Rousseau's day people did not even
know that this question of the power of land to support
population was to be taken into account.

Socialists find it necessary to alter the definition of

capital in order to maintain their attacks upon it. Karl
Marx, for instance, regards capital as an accumulation
of the differences which a merchant makes between his
buying price and his selling price. It is, according to
him, an accumulation of the differences which the
employer gains between what he pays to the employees
for making the thing and what he obtains for it from
the consumer. In this view of the matter the capitalist
employer is a pure parasite, who has fastened on the
wage-receiving employee without need or reason and
is levying toll on industry. All socialistic writers
follow, in different degrees, this conception of capital.
If it is true, why do not I levy on some workers somewhere and steal this difference in the product of their
labor? Is it because I am more honest or magnanimous
than those who are capitalist-employers? I should
not trust myself to resist the chance if I had it. Or
again, let us ask why, if this conception of the origin
of capital is correct, the workmen submit to a pure
and unnecessary imposition. If this notion were true,
co-operation in production would not need any effort
to bring it about; it would take an army to keep it
down. The reason why it is not possible for the first
comer to start out as an employer of labor is that capital
is a prerequisite to all industry. So soon as men pass
beyond the stage of life in which they live, like beasts,
on the spontaneous fruits of the earth, capital must
precede every productive enterprise. It would lead
me too far away from my present subject to elaborate
this statement as it deserves and perhaps as it needs,
but I may say that there is no sound political economy
and especially no correct conception of wages which is
not based on a complete recognition of the character
of capital as necessarily going before every industrial

operation. The reason why co-operation in production is exceedingly difficult, and indeed is not possible except in the highest and rarest conditions of education and culture amongst artisans, is that workmen cannot undertake an enterprise without capital, and that capital always means the fruits of prudence and self-denial already accomplished. The capitalist's profits, therefore, are only the reward for the contribution he has made to a joint enterprise which could not go on without him, and his share is as legitimate as that of the hand-worker.

The socialist assails particularly the institution of bequest or hereditary property, by which some men come into life with special protection and advantage. The right of bequest rests on no other grounds than those of expediency. The love of children is the strongest motive to frugality and to the accumulation of capital. The state guarantees the power of bequest only because it thereby encourages the accumulation of capital on which the welfare of society depends. It is true enough that inherited capital often proves a curse. Wealth is like health, physical strength, education, or anything else which enhances the power of the individual; it is only a chance; its moral character depends entirely upon the use which is made of it. Any force which, when well used, is capable of elevating a man, will, if abused, debase him in the same proportion. This is true of education, which is often and incorrectly vaunted as a positive and purely beneficent instrumentality. An education ill used makes a man only a more mischievous scoundrel, just as an education well used makes him a more efficient, good citizen and producer. So it is with wealth; it is a means to all the higher developments of intellectual and moral culture.

A man of inherited wealth can gain in youth all the advantages which are essential to high culture, and which a man who must first earn the capital cannot attain until he is almost past the time of life for profiting by them. If one should believe the newspapers, one would be driven to a philosophy something like this: it is extremely praiseworthy for a man born in poverty to accumulate a fortune; the reason why he wants to secure a fortune is that he wants to secure the position of his children and start them with better advantages than he enjoyed himself; this is a noble desire on his part, but he really ought to doubt and hesitate about so doing because the chances are that he would do far better for his children to leave them poor.   The children who inherit his wealth are put under suspicion by it; it creates a presumption against them in all the activities of citizenship.

Now it is no doubt true that the struggle to win a fortune gives strength of character and a practical judgment and efficiency which a man who inherits wealth rarely gets, but hereditary wealth transmitted from generation to generation is the strongest instrument by which we keep up a steadily advancing civilization. In the absence of laws of entail and perpetuity it is inevitable that capital should speedily slip from the hold of the man who is not fit to possess it, back into the great stream of capital, and so find its way into the hands of those who can use it for the benefit of society.

The love of children is an instinct which, as I have said before, grows stronger with advancing civilization. All attacks on capital have, up to this time, been shipwrecked on this instinct. Consequently the most rigorous and logical socialists have always been led sooner or later to attack the family. For, if bequest should be abolished, parents would give their property to their children in their own life-time; and so it becomes a logical necessity to substitute some sort of communistic or socialistic life for family life, and to educate children in masses without the tie of parentage. Every socialistic theory which has been pursued energetically has led out to this consequence. I will not follow up this topic, but it is plain to see that the only equality which could be reached on this course would be that men should be all equal to each other when they were all equal to swine.

Socialists are filled with the enthusiasm of equality. Every scheme of theirs for securing equality has destroyed liberty. The student of political philosophy has the antagonism of equality and liberty constantly forced upon him. Equality of possession or of rights and equality before the law are diametrically opposed to each other. The object of equality before the law is to make the state entirely neutral. The state, under that theory, takes no cognizance of persons. It surrounds all, without distinctions, with the same conditions and guarantees. If it educates one, it educates all — black, white, red, or yellow; Jew or Gentile; native or alien. If it taxes one, it taxes all, by the same system and under the same conditions. If it exempts one from police regulations in home, church, and occupation, it exempts all. From this statement it is at once evident that pure equality before the law is impossible. Some occupations must be subjected to police regulation. Not all can be made subject to militia duty even for the same limited period. The exceptions and special cases furnish the chance for abuse. Equality before the law, however, is one of the cardinal principles of civil liberty, because it leaves each man to run the race of life for himself as best he can. The state stands neutral but benevolent. It does not undertake to aid some and handicap others at the outset in order to offset hereditary advantages and disadvantages, or to make them start equally. Such a notion would belong to the false and spurious theory of equality which is socialistic. If the state should attempt this it would make itself the servant of envy. I am entitled to make the most I can of myself without hindrance from anybody, but I am not entitled to any guarantee that I shall make as much of myself as somebody else makes of himself.

The modern thirst for equality of rights is explained by its historical origin. The mediaeval notion of rights was that rights were special privileges, exemptions, franchises, and powers given to individuals by the king; hence each man had just so many as he and his ancestors had been able to buy or beg by force or favor, and if a man had obtained no grants he had no rights. Hence no two persons were equal in rights and the mass of the population had none. The theory of natural rights and of equal rights was a revolt against the mediaeval theory. It was asserted that men did not have to wait for a king to grant them rights; they have them by nature, or in the nature of things, because they are men and members of civil society. If rights come from nature, it is inferred that they fall like air and light on all equally. It was an immense step in advance for the human race when this new doctrine was promulgated. Its own limitations and errors need not now be pointed out. Its significance is plain, and its limits are to some extent defined when we note its historical origin.

I have already shown that where these guarantees

exist and where there is liberty, the results cannot be equal, but with all liberty there must go responsibility. If I take my own way I must take my own consequences; if it proves that I have made a mistake, I cannot be allowed to throw the consequences on my neighbor. If my neighbor is a free man and resents interference from me he must not call on me to bear the consequences of his mistakes. Hence it is plain that liberty, equality before the law, responsibility, individualism, monogamy, and private property all hold together as consistent parts of the same structure of society, and that an assault on one part must sooner or later involve an assault on all the others.

To all this must be added the political element in socialism. The acquisition of some capital—the amount is of very subordinate importance — is the first and simplest proof that an individual possesses the industrial and civil virtues which make a good citizen and a useful member of society. Political power, a century ago, was associated more or less, even in the United States, with the possession of land. It has been gradually extended until the suffrage is to all intents and purposes universal in North and South America, in Australia, and in all Europe except Russia and Turkey. On this system political control belongs to the numerical majority, limited only by institutions. It may be doubted, if the terms are taken strictly and correctly, whether the non-capitalists outnumber the capitalists in any civilized country, but in many cities where capital is most collected they certainly do. The powers of government have been abused for ages by the classes who possessed them to enable kings, courtiers, nobles, politicians, demagogues, and their friends to live in exemption from labor and self-denial, that is, from the universal lot of man. It is only a continuation of the same abuse if the new possessors of power attempt to employ it to secure for themselves the selfish advantages which all possessors of power have taken. Such a course would, however, overthrow all that we think has been won in the way of making government an organ of justice, peace, order, and security, without respect of persons; and if those gains are not to be lost they will have to be defended, before this century closes, against popular majorities, especially in cities, just as they had to be won in a struggle with kings and nobles in the centuries past.

The newest socialism is, in its method, political. The essential feature of its latest phases is the attempt to use the power of the state to realize its plans and to secure its objects. These objects are to do away with poverty and misery, and there are no socialistic schemes yet proposed, of any sort, which do not, upon analysis, turn out to be projects for curing poverty and misery by making those who have share with those who have not. Whether they are paper-money schemes, tariff schemes, subsidy schemes, internal improvement schemes, or usury laws, they all have this in common with the most vulgar of the communistic projects, and the errors of this sort in the past which have been committed in the interest of the capitalist class now furnish precedents, illustration, and encouragement for the new category of demands. The latest socialism divides into two phases: one which aims at centralization and despotism—believing that political form more available for its purposes; the other, the anarchical, which prefers to split up the state into townships, or "communes," to the same end. The latter furnishes the true etymology and meaning of "communism" in its present use, but all socialism, in its second stage, merges into a division of property according to the old sense of communism.

It is impossible to notice socialism as it presents itself at the present moment without pointing out the immense mischief which has been done by sentimental economists and social philosophers who have thought it their professional duty, not to investigate and teach the truth, but to dabble in philanthropy. It is in Germany that this development has been most marked, and as a consequence of it the judgment and sense of the whole people in regard to political and social questions have been corrupted. It is remarkable that the country whose learned men have wrought so much for every other science, especially by virtue of their scientific method and rigorous critical processes, should have furnished a body of social philosophers without method, discipline, or severity of scholarship, who have led the nation in pursuit of whims and dreams and impossible desires. Amongst us there has been less of it, for our people still possess enough sterling sense to reject sentimental rubbish in its grosser forms, but we have had and still have abundance of the more subtle forms of socialistic doctrine, and these open the way to the others. We may already see the two developments forming a congenial alliance. We have also our writers and teachers who seem to think that "the weak" and "the poor" are terms of exact definition; that government exists, in some especial sense, for the sake of the classes so designated; and that the same classes (whoever they are) have some especial claim on the interest and attention of the economist and social philosopher. It may be believed that, in the opinion of these persons, the training of men is the only branch of human effort in which the labor and care should be spent, not on the best specimens but on the poorest.

It is a matter of course that a reactionary party should arise to declare that universal suffrage, popular education, machinery, free trade, and all the other innovations of the last hundred years are all a mistake. If any one ever believed that these innovations were so many clear strides towards the millennium, that they involve no evils or abuses of their own, that they tend to emancipate mankind from the need for prudence, caution, forethought, vigilance — in short, from the eternal struggle against evil — it is not strange that he should be disappointed. If any one ever believed that some "form of government" could be found which would run itself and turn out the pure results of abstract peace, justice, and righteousness without any trouble to anybody, he may well be dissatisfied. To talk of turning back, however, is only to enhance still further the confusion and danger of our position. The world cannot go back. Its destiny is to go forward and to meet the new problems which are continually arising. Under our so-called progress evil only alters its forms, and we must esteem it a grand advance if we can believe that, on the whole, and over a wide view of human affairs, good has gained a hair's breadth over evil in a century. Popular institutions have their own abuses and dangers just as much as monarchical or aristocratic institutions. We are only just finding out what they are. All the institutions which we have inherited were invented to guard liberty against the encroachments of a powerful monarch or aristocracy, when these classes possessed land and the possession of land was the greatest social power. Institutions must now be devised to guard civil liberty against popular majorities, and this necessity arises first in regard to the protection of property, the first and greatest function of government and element in civil liberty. There is no escape from any dangers involved in this or any other social struggle save in going forward and working out the development. It will cost a struggle and will demand the highest wisdom of this and the next generation. It is very probable that some nations — those, namely, which come up to this problem with the least preparation, with the least intelligent comprehension of the problem, and under the most inefficient leadership — will suffer a severe check in their development and prosperity; it is very probable that in some nations the development may lead through revolution and bloodshed; it is very probable that in some nations the consequence may be a reaction towards arbitrary power. In every view we take of it, it is clear that the general abolition of slavery has only cleared the way for a new social problem of far wider scope and far greater difficulty. It seems to me, in fact, that this must always be the case. The conquest of one difficulty will only open the way to another; the solution of one problem will only bring man face to face with another. Man wins by the fight, not by the victory, and therefore the possibilities of growth are unlimited, for the fight has no end.

The progress which men have made in developing the possibilities of human existence has never been made by jumps and strides. It has never resulted from the schemes of philosophers and reformers. It has never been guided through a set program by the wisdom of any sages, statesmen, or philanthropists. The progress which has been made has been won in minute stages by men who had a definite task before them, and who have dealt with it in detail, as it presented itself, without referring to general principles, or attempting to bring it into logical relations to an *a priori* system. In most cases the agents are unknown and cannot be found. New and better arrangements have grown up imperceptibly by the natural effort of all to make the best of actual circumstances. In this way, no doubt, the new problems arising in our modern society must be solved or must solve themselves. The chief safeguard and hope of such a development is in the sound instincts and strong sense of the people, which, although it may not reason closely, can reject instinctively. If there are laws — and there certainly are such — which permit the acquisition of property without industry, by cunning, force, gambling, swindling, favoritism, or corruption, such laws transfer property from those who have earned it to those who have not. Such laws contain the radical vice of socialism. They demand correction and offer an open field for reform because reform would lie in the direction of greater purity and security of the right of property. Whatever assails that right, or goes in the direction of making it still more uncertain whether the industrious man can dispose of the fruits of his industry for his own interests exclusively, tends directly towards violence, bloodshed, poverty, and misery. If any large section of modern society should rise against the rest for the purpose of attempting any such spoliation, either by violence or through the forms of law, it would destroy civilization as it was destroyed by the irruption of the barbarians into the Roman Empire.

The sound student of sociology can hold out to mankind, as individuals or as a race, only one hope of better and happier living. That hope lies in an enhancement of the industrial virtues and of the moral forces which thence arise. Industry, self-denial, and temperance are the laws of prosperity for men and states; without them advance in the arts and in wealth means only corruption and decay through luxury and vice. With them progress in the arts and increasing wealth are the prime conditions of an advancing civilization which is sound enough to endure. The power of the human race to-day over the conditions of prosperous and happy living are sufficient to banish poverty and misery if it were not for folly and vice. The earth does not begin to be populated up to its power to support population on the present stage of the arts; if the United States were as densely populated as the British Islands, we should have 1,000,000,000 people here. If, therefore, men were willing to set to work with energy and courage to subdue the outlying parts of the earth, all might live in plenty and prosperity. But if they insist on remaining in the slums of great cities or on the borders of an old society, and on a comparatively exhausted soil, there is no device of economist or statesman which can prevent them from falling victims to poverty and misery or from succumbing in the competition of life to those who have greater command of capital. The socialist or philanthropist who nourishes them in their situation and saves them from the distress of it is only cultivating the distress which he pretends to cure.

REPLY TO A SOCIALIST

REPLY TO A SOCIALIST[1]

[1904]

"ALWAYS dig out the major premise!" said an experienced teacher of logic and rhetoric. The major premise of Mr. Sinclair is that everybody ought to be happy, and that, if anybody is not so, those who stand near him are under obligations to make him so. He nowhere expresses this. The major premise is always most fallacious when it is suppressed. The statement of the woes of the garment workers is made on the assumption that it carries upon its face some significance. He deduces from the facts two inferences for which he appeals to common consent: (1) that such a state of things ought not to be allowed to continue forever, and (2) that somehow, somewhere, another "system" must be found. The latter inference is one which the socialists always affirm, and they seem to be satisfied that it has some value, both in philosophy and in practical effort. They criticize the "system," by which they mean the social world as it is. They do not perceive that the world of human society is what has resulted from thousands of years of life. It is not a system any more than a man sixty years old is a system. It is a product. To talk of making another system is like talking of making a man of sixty into something else than what his life has made him. As for the inference that some other industrial system must be found, it is as idle as anything which words can express. It leads

[1] *Collier's Weekly*, October 29, 1904.

to nothing and has no significance. The industrial system has changed often and it will change again. Nobody invented former forms. No one can invent others. It will change according to conditions and interests, just as the gilds and manors changed into modern phases. It is frightful to know of the poverty which some people endure. It is also frightful to know of disease, of physical defects, of accidents which cripple the body and wreck life, and of other ills by which human life is encompassed. Such facts appeal to human sympathy, and call for such help and amelioration as human effort can give. It is senseless to enumerate such facts, simply in order to create a state of mind in the hearer, and then to try to make him assent that "the system ought to be changed." All the hospitals, asylums, almshouses, and other eleemosynary institutions prove that the world is not made right. They prove the existence of people who have not "equal chances" with others. The inmates can not be happy. Generally the institutions also prove the very limited extent to which, with the best intentions and greatest efforts, the more fortunate can do anything to help the matter — that is, to "change the system."

The notion that everybody ought to be happy, and equally happy with all the rest, is the fine flower of the philosophy which has been winning popularity for two hundred years. All the petty demands of natural rights, liberty, equality, etc., are only stepping-stones toward this philosophy, which is really what is wanted. All through human history some have had good fortune and some ill fortune. For some the ills of life have taken all the joy and strength out of existence, while the fortunate have always been there to show how glorious life might be and to furnish dreams of bliss to tantalize those who

have failed and suffered.   So men have constructed in
philosophy theories of universal felicity.   They tell us
that every one has a natural right to be happy, to be
comfortable, to have health, to succeed, to have knowledge, family, political power, and all the rest of the
things which anybody can have.   They put it all into
the major premise.   Then they say that we all ought to
be equal.   That proposition abolishes luck.   In making
propositions we can imply that all ought to have equally
good luck, but, inasmuch as there is no way in which
we can turn bad luck into good, or misfortune into
good fortune, what the proposition means is that if
we can not all have good luck no one shall have it.
The unlucky will pull down the lucky.   That is all that
equality ever can mean.   The worst becomes the standard.   When we talk of "changing the system," we
ought to understand that that means abolishing luck
and all the ills of life.   We might as well talk of abolishing storms, excessive heat and cold, tornadoes, pes-
tilences, diseases, and other ills.   Poverty belongs to
the struggle for existence, and we are all born into that
struggle.   The human race began in utter destitution.
It had no physical or metaphysical endowment whatever.   The existing "system" is the outcome of the
efforts of men for thousands of years to work together,
so as to win in the struggle for existence.   Probably
socialists do not perceive what it means for any man
now to turn about and pass his high judgment on the
achievements of the human race in the way of civilization, and to propose to change it, by resolution, in about
"six years."   The result of the long effort has been that
we all, in a measure, live above the grade of savages,
and that some reach comfort and luxury and mental
and moral welfare.   Efforts to change the system have

not been wanting. They have all led back to savagery.
Mr. Sinclair thinks that the French Revolution issued
out in liberty. The French Revolution is open to
very many different interpretations and constructions;
but, on the whole, it left essential interests just about
where it found them. A million men lost their lives to
get Louis de Bourbon off the throne and Napoleon
Bonaparte on it, and by the spoils of Europe to make
rich nobles of his generals. That is the most definite
and indisputable result of the Revolution. Mr. Sinclair
also repeats the familiar warning or threat that those
who are not competent to win adequate success in the
struggle for existence will "rise." They are going to
"shoot," unless we let him and his associates redistribute property. It seems that it would be worth
while for them to consider that, by their own hypothesis, those-who-have will possess advantages in
"shooting": (1) they will have the guns; (2) they
will have the talent on their side because they can pay
for it; (3) they can hire an army out of the ranks of
their adversaries.

In all this declamation we hear a great deal about
votes and political power, "ballots or bullets." Of
course this is another outcome of the political and
social philosophy of the last two centuries. Mr. Sinclair says that "Democracy is an attitude of soul. It
has its basis in the spiritual nature of man, from which
it follows that all men are equal, or that, if they are
not, they must become so." Then Democracy is a
metaphysical religion or mythology. The age is not
friendly to metaphysics or mythology, but it falls under
the dominion of these old tyrants in its political philosophy. If anybody wants to put his soul in an attitude,
he ought to do it. The "system" allows that liberty,

and it is far safer than shooting. It is also permitted
to believe that, if men are not equal, they will become
so. If we wait a while they will all die, and then they
will all be equal, although they certainly will not be so
before that.

There are plenty of customs and institutions among
us which produce evil results. They need reform; and
propositions to that end are reasonable and useful. A
few years ago we heard of persons who wanted to abolish
poverty. They had no plan or scheme by which to do it;
in the meantime, however, people were working day by
day to overcome poverty as well as they could, each for
himself. The talk about abolishing poverty by some
resolution or construction has died out. The "industrial system" is just the organized effort which we are
all making to overcome poverty. We do not want to
change the system unless we can be convinced that we
can make a shift which will accomplish that purpose
better. Then, be it observed, the system will be
changed without waiting for any philosophers to propose it. It is being changed every day, just as quickly
as any detail in it can be altered so as to defeat poverty better. This is a world in which the rule is, "Root,
hog, or die," and it is also a world in which "the longest
pole knocks down the most persimmons." It is the
popular experience which has formulated these sayings.
How can we make them untrue? They contain immense tragedies. Those who believe that the problems
of human pain and ill are waiting for a speculative
solution in philosophy or ethics can dream of changing
the system; but to everybody else it must seem worse
than a waste of time to wrangle about such a thing. It
is not a proposition; it does not furnish either a thesis
to be tested or a project to be considered.

I am by no means arguing that "everything is for the best in the best of worlds," even in that part of it where the Stars and Stripes still float. I am, on the contrary, one of those who think that there is a great deal to be dissatisfied about. I may be asked what I think would be a remedy for the distress of the garment workers. I answer candidly that I do not know — that is why I have come forward with no proposition. My business now is to show how empty and false Mr. Sinclair's proposition is, and how harmful it would be to heed it. He only adds to our trouble and burden by putting forward erroneous ideas and helping to encourage bad thinking. The plan to rise and shoot has no promise of welfare in it for anybody.

Neither is there any practical sense or tangible project behind the suggestion to redistribute property. Some years ago I heard a socialist orator say[1] that he could get along with any audience except "these measly, mean-spirited workingmen, who have saved a few hundred dollars and built a cottage, with a savings bank mortgage, of which they rent the second story and live in the first. They," said he, "will get up and go out, a benchful at a time, when I begin to talk about rent." If he had been open to instruction from facts, he might have learned much from the conduct of those measly workingmen. They will fight far more ferociously for their cottages than the millionaires for their palaces. A redistribution of property means universal war. The final collapse of the French Revolution was due to the proposition to redistribute property. Property is the opposite of poverty; it is our bulwark against want and distress, but also against disease and

[1] This was one of Professor Sumner's pet anecdotes, and I risk its repetition here and elsewhere in the volume. — THE EDITOR.

all other ills, which, if it can not prevent them, it still holds at a distance. If we weaken the security of property or deprive people of it, we plunge into distress those who now are above it.

Property is the condition of civilization. It is just as essential to the state, to religion, and to education as it is to food and clothing. In the form of capital it is essential to industry, but if capital were not property it would not do its work in industry. If we negative or destroy property we arrest the whole life of civilized society and put men back on the level of beasts. The family depends on property; the two institutions have been correlative throughout the history of civilization. Property is the first interest of man in time and in importance. We can conceive of no time when property was not, and we can conceive of no social growth in which property was not the prime condition. The property interest is also the one which moves all men, including the socialists, more quickly and deeply than any other. Property is that feature of the existing "industrial system" which would most stubbornly resist change if it was threatened in its essential character and meaning. There is a disposition now to apologize for property, even while resisting attack upon it. This is wrong. Property ought to be defended on account of its reality and importance, and on account of its rank among the interests of men.

What the socialists complain of is that we have not yet got the work of civilization all done and that what has been done does not produce ideal results. The task is a big one — it may even be believed that it is infinite, because what we accomplish often only opens new vistas of trouble. At present we are working on with all the wisdom we have been able to win, and we hope to gain more. If the socialists could help by reasonable and practical suggestions, their aid would be welcome. When they propose to redistribute property, or to change the industrial system, they only disturb the work and introduce confusion and destruction. When they talk about rising and shooting, as if such acts would not be unreasonable or beyond possibility, they put themselves at the limit of the law, and may, before they know it, become favorers of crime.

WHAT MAKES THE RICH RICHER AND THE POOR POORER?

WHAT MAKES THE RICH RICHER AND THE POOR POORER?[1]

[1887]

KARL MARX says, "An accumulation of wealth at one pole of society indicates an accumulation of misery and overwork at the other."[2] In this assertion, Marx avoids the very common and mischievous fallacy of confusing causes, consequences, and symptoms. He suggests that what is found at one pole indicates, or is a symptom of what may be found at the other. In the development of his criticisms on political economy and the existing organization of society, however, Marx proceeds as if there were a relation of cause and effect in the proposition just quoted, and his followers and popularizers have assumed as an indisputable postulate that the wealth of some is a cause of the poverty of others. The question of priority or originality as between Marx, Rodbertus, and others is at best one of vanity between them and their disciples,[3] but it is of great interest and importance to notice that the doctrine that wealth at one pole makes misery at the other is the correct logical form of the notion that progress and poverty are correlative. This doctrine rests upon another and still more fundamental one, which is not often formulated,

[1] *Popular Science Monthly*, Vol. XXX, 1887, pp. 289–296.

[2] "Das Capital," I, 671.

[3] On this question see Anton Menger, "Das Recht auf den vollen Arbeitsertrag," Stuttgart, 1886. This writer traces back for a century the fundamental socialistic notions. He aims to develop the jural as distinguished from the economic aspect of socialism.

but which can be detected in most of the current socialistic discussions, *viz.*, that all the capital which is here
now would be here under any laws or institutions about
property, as if it were due to some independent cause;
and that some have got ahead of others and seized upon
the most of it, so that those who came later have not been
able to get any.   If this notion about the source of capital is not true, then wealth at one pole cannot cause
poverty at the other.   If it is true, then we can make
any regulations we like about the distribution of wealth,
without fear lest the measures which we adopt may prevent any wealth from being produced.

In Rome, under the empire, wealth at one pole was a
symptom of misery at the other, because Rome was not
an industrial state.   Its income came from plunder.
The wealth had a source independent of the production
of the society of Rome.   That part of the booty which
some got, others could not have.   No such thing is true
of an industrial society.   The wealth of the commercial
cities of Italy and southern Germany, in the Middle
Ages, was largely in the hands of merchant-princes.   If
one were told that some of these merchants were very
rich, he would have no ground of inference that others
in those cities must have been poor.   The rich were
those who developed the opportunities of commerce
which were, in the first instance, open to all.   What they
gained came out of nothing which anybody else ever had
or would have had.   The fact that there are wealthy
men in England, France, and the United States to-day
is no evidence that there must be poor men here.   The
riches of the rich are perfectly consistent with the high
condition of wealth of all, down to the last.   In fact,
the aggregations of wealth, both while being made and
after realization, develop and sustain the prosperity

of all. The forward movement of a strong population, with abundance of land and highly developed command by machinery over the forces of nature, must produce a state of society in which, misfortune and vice being left out of account, average and minimum comfort are high, while special aggregations may be enormous.

Whatever nexus there is between wealth at one pole and poverty at the other can be found only by turning the proposition into its converse — misery at one pole makes wealth at the other. If the mass at one pole should, through any form of industrial vice, fall into misery, they would offer to the few wise an opportunity to become rich by taking advantage of them. They would offer a large supply of labor at low wages, a high demand for capital at high rates of interest, and a fierce demand for land at high rent.

It is often affirmed, and it is true, that competition tends to disperse society over a wide range of unequal conditions. Competition develops all powers that exist according to their measure and degree. The more intense competition is, the more thoroughly are all the forces developed. If, then, there is liberty, the results can not be equal; they must correspond to the forces. Liberty of development and equality of result are therefore diametrically opposed to each other. If a group of men start on equal conditions, and compete in a common enterprise, the results which they attain must differ according to inherited powers, early advantages of training, personal courage, energy, enterprise, perseverance, good sense, etc., etc. Since these things differ through a wide range, and since their combinations may vary through a wide range, it is possible that the results may vary through a wide scale of degrees. Moreover, the more intense the competition, the greater are the prizes of success and the heavier are the penalties of failure. This is illustrated in the competition of a large city as compared with that of a small one. Competition can no more be done away with than gravitation. Its incidence can be changed. We can adopt as a social policy, "Woe to the successful!" We can take the prizes away from the successful and give them to the unsuccessful. It seems clear that there would soon be no prizes at all, but that inference is not universally accepted. In any event, it is plain that we have not got rid of competition — *i.e.*, of the struggle for existence and the competition of life. We have only decided that, if we cannot all have equally, we will all have nothing.

Competition does not guarantee results corresponding with merit, because hereditary conditions and good and bad fortune are always intermingled with merit, but competition secures to merit all the chances it can enjoy under circumstances for which none of one's fellowmen are to blame.

Now it seems to be believed that although competition produces wide grades of inequality, yet almsgiving, or forcible repartition of wealth, would not do so. Here we come to the real, great, and mischievous fallacy of the social philosophy which is in vogue. Whether there are great extremes of rich and poor in a society is a matter of very little significance; there is no ground for the importance which is attached to that fact in current discussion. It is constantly affirmed in one form or another that, although one man has in half a lifetime greatly improved his own position, and can put his children in a far better condition than that in which he started, nevertheless he has not got his fair share in the gains of civilization, because his neighbor, who started where he did, has become a millionaire. John, who is

eating a beefsteak off iron-stone china, finds that the taste
of it is spoiled because he knows that James is eating
pheasants off gold. William, who would have to walk
anyway, finds that his feet ache a great deal worse
because he learns that Peter has got a horse. Henry,
whose yacht is twenty feet long, is sure that there is
something wrong in society because Jacob has one a
hundred feet long. These are weaknesses of human
nature which have always been the fair game of the
satirists, but in our day they are made the basis of a
new philosophy and of a redistribution of rights and of
property. If the laws and institutions of the society
hinder any one from fighting out the battle of life on his
or her own behalf to the best of one's ability, especially
if they so hinder one to the advantage of another, the
field of effort for intelligent and fruitful reform is at
once marked out; but if examination should reveal
no such operation of laws and institutions, then the inequality of achievements is no indication of any social
disease, but the contrary.

The indication of social health or disease is to be
sought in quite another fact. The question whether the
society is formed of only two classes, the rich and the
poor, the strong and the weak, or whether all the intervening grades are represented in a sound and healthy
proportion, is a question which has importance because
it furnishes indications of the state and prospects of the
society. No society which consists of the two extreme
classes only is in a sound and healthy condition.

If we regard the society of a new country, with little
government regulation, free institutions, low taxes,
and insignificant military duty, as furnishing us with the
nearest example of a normal development of human
society under civilization, then we must infer that such

a society would not consist of two well-defined classes widely separated from each other, but that there would be no well-defined classes at all, although its members might, in their extremest range, be far apart in wealth, education, talent, and virtue. Such a society might, as it grew older, and its population became more dense, develop, under high competition, great extremes of economic power and social condition, but there is no reason to suppose that the whole middle range would not be filled up by the great mass of the population.

I have now cleared the ground for the proposition which it is my special purpose, in this paper, to offer:

It is the tendency of all social burdens to crush out the middle class, and to force the society into an organization of only two classes, one at each social extreme.

It is in the nature of the case impracticable to adjust social burdens proportionately to the power of individuals to support them. If this could be done, it is possible that the burdens might become great, even excessive, without producing the effect which I have stated. Since, however, it is impossible to so adjust them, and they must be laid on "equally" with reference to the unit of service, and not with reference to some unit of capacity to endure them, it follows that the effect must be as stated. So soon as the burden becomes so great that it surpasses the power of some part of the society, a division takes place between those who can and those who cannot endure it. At first, those who are close to this line, but just above it, are not far removed from those who are close to it, but just below it; but, as time goes on, and the pressure continues to operate, they are constantly separated from each other by a wider and wider interval.

Let us look at some of the historical facts which

show us this law. If we take early Roman history as Mommsen relates it to us, we observe the constant recurrence of the difficulty which arose from the tendency of the society toward two extreme classes. It was plainly the pressure of military duty and taxes which was constantly developing two classes, debtors and creditors. The demands of the state fell upon different men in very different severity according to circumstances.[1] One found himself just so well established that he could endure without being crushed. Another found that the time demanded, or the wound received, or the loss sustained by an inroad, or by being on an unsuccessful expedition, threw him back so that he fell into debt. The former, securing a foothold and gaining a little, bought a slave and established himself with a greater margin of security. Slavery, of course, mightily helped on the tendency. Twenty years later the second man was the bankrupt debtor and bondman of the first.

All insecurity of property has the same effect, above all, however, when the insecurity is produced by abuse of state power. In the later history of Rome, the Roman power, having conquered the world and dragged thousands born elsewhere into Italy as slaves, set to work to plunder its conquest. The booty taken by emperors, proconsuls, and freedmen-favorites, and by the sovereign city, was shared, through the largesses, with the proletariat of the city. The largesses and slavery worked together to divide the Romans into two classes. The plunder of the provinces intensified the wealth of the wealthy. The largesses pauperized and proletarianized the populace of the great city.[2] They drew away citi-

---

[1] As to the heavy burdens of Roman citizenship, see Merivale, VIII, 284.

[2] See Mommsen, book III, chapters XI, XII; book V, chapter XI; Pöhlmann, "Die Uebervölkerung der antiken Gross-Städte," Leipzig, 1884.

zens from the country and from honest industry, to swell the mob of the city. If a band of robbers should split into patricians and plebeians and divide the plunder unequally, it is plain that, as time went on, they must separate into two great factions, one immensely rich, the other miserably poor.[1] As for the victims, although at first the severity and security of Roman law and order were not too dear even at the price which they cost, nevertheless the inevitable effect of robbery came out at last, and the whole Roman world was impoverished.[2] Those only among the provincials could get or retain wealth who could gain favor with, or get on the side of the rulers. No satisfactory exposition of the political economy of the Roman commonwealth has yet been written. The effect of the Roman system on population, on the development of capital in the provinces, on the arts and sciences, on the distribution of the precious metals, on city population at Rome and Constantinople, on the development of talent and genius, offers lessons of profound importance, touching in many points on questions which now occupy us. The Roman Empire was a gigantic experiment in the way of a state which took from some to give to others. "At the beginning of the third century already the signs of a fatal loss of vitality manifested themselves with frightful distinctness, and spread with such rapidity that no sagacious observer

---

[1] See especially Friedländer, "Sittengeschichte," I, 22: "In the enjoyment of the extravagant abundance of advantages, excitements, and spectacles, which the metropolis offered, the highest and lowest classes were best off. The great majority of the free male inhabitants were fed partly or entirely at public expense. The great found there an opportunity and means for a royal existence as nowhere else on earth. The middle classes were most exposed to the disadvantages of life at Rome."

[2] See Merivale, VIII, 351; Gibbon, chapter XXXVI, at the end.

could deceive himself any longer as to the beginning dissolution of the gigantic body." [1]

All violence has the same effect. In the fifth and sixth centuries of our era, the general disorder and violence which prevailed gradually brought about a division of society on a line which, of course, wavered for a long time. A man who was strong enough in his circumstances to just maintain himself in such times became a lord; another, who could not maintain himself, sought safety by becoming the lord's man. As time went on, every retainer whom the former obtained made him seem a better man to be selected as lord; and, as time went on, any man who was weak but independent found his position more and more untenable. [2]

Taine's history shows distinctly that the middle class were the great sufferers by the French Revolution. Attention has always been arrested by the nobles who were robbed and guillotined. When, however, we get closer to the life of the period, we see that, taking the nation over for the years of the revolutionary disorder, the victims were those who had anything, from the peasant or small tradesman up to the well-to-do citizen. [3] The rich bought their way through, and the nobles were replaced by a new gang of social parasites enriched by plunder and extortion. These last come nearer than any others whom history presents to the type of what the

---

[1] Friedländer, I, preface. While reading the proof of this article, I have read Professor Boccardo's "Manuale di Storia del Comercio, delle Industrie e dell' Economia Politica" (Torino-Napoli, 1886), in which, pp. 74, 75, he expresses the same view as is above given more nearly than I have ever seen it elsewhere.

[2] See Gibbon, chapter XXXVIII; Duruy, "Histoire du Moyen Age," pp. 233, 234; Hallam's "Middle Ages," chapter I, part II; Seebohm, "The English Village Community," chapter VIII.

[3] See Taine, vol. III, book V, chapter I.

"committee" in a socialistic state may be expected to be.[1]

All almsgiving has the same effect, especially if it is forced by state authority. The Christian Church of the fourth and fifth centuries, by its indiscriminate almsgiving on a large scale, helped on the degeneration of the Roman state.[2] A poor-law is only another case. The poor-rates, as they become heavier, at last drive into the workhouses the poorest of those who have hitherto maintained independence and paid poor-rates. With this new burden the chance of the next section upward to maintain themselves is imperiled, and so on indefinitely.

All taxation has the same effect. It presses hardest on those who, under the conditions of their position in life and the demands which are made upon them, are trying to save capital and improve their circumstances. The heavier it becomes, the faster it crushes out this class of persons — that is, all the great middle class — and the greater the barrier it sets up against any efforts of persons of that class to begin accumulation. If the taxes have for their object to take from some and give to others, as is the case with all protective taxes, we have only a more intense and obvious action in the same direction, and one whose effects must be far greater and sooner realized. The effect of protective taxes in this country, to drive out the small men and to throw special lines of industry into the hands of a few large capitalists, has been noted often. It is only a case of the law which I am defining.

My generalization might even be made broader. It is the tendency of all the hardships of life to destroy the middle class. Capital, as it grows larger, takes on new

---

[1] See Taine, vol. III, book III, chapter III.　　[2] Pöhlmann, p. 62.

increments with greater and greater ease. It acquires
a kind of momentum. The rich man, therefore, can
endure the shocks of material calamity and misfortune
with less distress the richer he is. A bad season may
throw a small farmer into debt from which he can never
recover. It may not do more to a large farmer than
lessen one year's income. A few years of hard times may
drive into bankruptcy a great number of men of small
capital, while a man of large capital may tide over the
distress and put himself in a position to make great gains
when prosperity comes again.

The hardships and calamities which are strictly social
are such as come from disorder, violence, insecurity,
covetousness, envy, etc. The state has for its function
to repress all these. It appears from what I have said
that it is hard to maintain a middle class on a high stage
of civilization. If the state does not do its work properly, such classes, representing the wide distribution
of comfort and well-being, will die out. If the state
itself gives license to robbery and spoliation, or enforces
almsgiving, it is working to destroy the whole middle
class, and to divide society into two great classes, the
rich who are growing richer, not by industry but by spoliation, and the poor who are growing poorer, not by
industrial weakness but by oppression.

Now, a state which is in any degree socialistic is in
that degree on the line of policy whose disastrous effects
have here been described. The state, it cannot too
often be repeated, has nothing, and can give nothing,
which it does not take from somebody. Its victims must
be those who have earned and saved, and they must be
the broad, strong, middle classes, from whom alone any
important contributions can be drawn. They must be
impoverished. Its pets, whoever they may be, must

be pauperized and proletarianized.   Its agents alone —
that is, those who, in the name of the state, perform the
operation of taking from some to give to others — can
become rich, and if ever such a state should be organized they may realize wealth beyond the dreams of a
proconsul.

To people untrained in the study of social forces it
may appear the most obvious thing in the world that,
if we should confiscate the property of those who have
more than a determined amount, and divide the proceeds among those who have less than a certain amount,
we should strengthen the middle class, and do away with
the two extremes.   The effect would be exactly the
opposite.   We should diminish the middle classes and
strengthen the extremes.   The more we helped at the
bottom, the more we should have to help, not only on
account of the increase of the population and the influx
of eager members of "the house of want," but also on
account of the demoralization of the lowest sections of
the middle class who were excluded.   The more we
confiscated at the top, the more craft and fraud would
be brought into play to escape confiscation, and the wider
must be the scope of taxation over the upper middle
classes to obtain the necessary means.

The modern middle class has been developed with,
and in, an industrial civilization.   In turn they have
taken control of this civilization and developed social
and civil institutions to accord with it.   The organization which they have made is now called, in the cant of
a certain school, "capitalism" and a "capitalistic system."   It is the first organization of human society that
ever has existed based on rights.   By virtue of its own
institutions, it now puts itself on trial and stands open
to revision and correction whenever, on sober and ra-

tional grounds, revision can be shown to be necessary to guarantee the rights of any one. It is the first organization of human society that has ever tolerated dissent or criticism of itself. Nobles and peasants have never made anything but Poland and Russia. The proletariat has never made anything but revolution. The socialistic state holds out no promise that it will ever tolerate dissent. It will never consider the question of reform. It stands already on the same footing as all the old states. It knows that it is right, and *all* right. Of course, therefore, there is no place in it for reform. With extreme reconstructions of society, however, it may not be worth while to trouble ourselves; what we need to perceive is, that all socialistic measures, whatever their degree, have the same tendency and effect. It is they which may be always described as tending to make the rich richer and the poor poorer, and to extinguish the intervening classes.

THE CONCENTRATION OF WEALTH:
ITS ECONOMIC JUSTIFICATION

THE CONCENTRATION OF WEALTH: ITS ECONOMIC JUSTIFICATION[1]

[1902]

THE concentration of wealth I understand to include the aggregation of wealth into large masses and its concentration under the control of a few. In this sense the concentration of wealth is indispensable to the successful execution of the tasks which devolve upon society in our time. Every task of society requires the employment of capital, and involves an economic problem in the form of the most expedient application of material means to ends. Two features most prominently distinguish the present age from all which have preceded it: first, the great scale on which all societal undertakings must be carried out; and second, the transcendent importance of competent management, that is, of the personal element in direction and control.

I speak of "societal undertakings" because it is important to notice that the prevalent modes and forms are not confined to industrial undertakings, but are universal in all the institutions and devices which have for their purpose the satisfaction of any wants of society. A modern church is a congeries of institutions which seeks to nourish good things and repress evil ones; it has buildings, apparatus, a store of supplies, a staff of employees, and a treasury. A modern church (parish) will soon be as complex a system of institutions as a mediaeval monastery was. Contrast such an establishment with the corresponding one of fifty years ago.

[1] *Independent,* April–June, 1902.

A university now needs an immense "concentration of wealth" for its outfit and work. It is as restricted in its work as the corresponding institution of fifty years ago was, although it may command twenty times as much capital and revenue. Furthermore, when we see that all these and other societal institutions pay far higher salaries to executive officers than to workers, we must recognize the fact that the element of personal executive ability is in command of the market, and that means that it is the element which decides success. To a correct understanding of our subject it is essential to recognize the concentration of wealth and control as a universal societal phenomenon, not merely as a matter of industrial power, or social sentiment, or political policy.

Stated in the concisest terms, the phenomenon is that of a more perfect integration of all societal functions. The concentration of power (wealth), more dominant control, intenser discipline, and stricter methods are but modes of securing more perfect integration. When we perceive this we see that the concentration of wealth is but one feature of a grand step in societal evolution.

Some may admit that the concentration of wealth is indispensable, but may desire to distinguish between joint-stock aggregations on the one side and individual fortunes on the other. This distinction is a product of the current social prejudice and is not valid. The predominance of the individual and personal element in control is seen in the tendency of all joint-stock enterprises to come under the control of very few persons. Every age is befooled by the notions which are in fashion in it. Our age is befooled by "democracy"; we hear arguments about the industrial organization which are deductions from democratic dogmas or which appeal to prejudice by using analogies drawn from democracy to affect sentiment about industrial relations. Industry may be republican; it never can be democratic, so long as men differ in productive power and in industrial virtue. In our time joint-stock companies, which are in form republican, are drifting over into oligarchies or monarchies because one or a few get greater efficiency of control and greater vigor of administration. They direct the enterprise in a way which produces more, or more economically. This is the purpose for which the organization exists and success in it outweighs everything else. We see the competent men refuse to join in the enterprise, unless they can control it, and we see the stockholders willingly put their property into the hands of those who are, as they think, competent to manage it successfully. The strongest and most effective organizations for industrial purposes which are formed nowadays are those of a few great capitalists, who have great personal confidence in each other and who can bring together adequate means for whatever they desire to do. Some such nucleus of individuals controls all the great joint-stock companies.

It is obvious that "concentration of wealth" can never be anything but a relative term. Between 1820 and 1830 Stephen Girard was a proverb for great wealth; to-day a man equally rich would not be noticed in New York for his wealth. In 1848 John Jacob Astor stood alone in point of wealth; to-day a great number surpass him. A fortune of $300,000 was then regarded as constituting wealth; it was taken as a minimum above which men were "rich." It is certain that before long some man will have a billion. It is impossible to criticize such a moving notion. The concentration of capital is also necessarily relative to the task to be performed; we wondered lately to see a corporation formed which had a capital of a billion. No one will wonder at such a corporation twenty-five years hence.

There seems to be a great readiness in the public mind to take alarm at these phenomena of growth — there might rather seem to be reason for public congratulation. We want to be provided with things abundantly and cheaply; that means that we want increased economic power. All these enterprises are efforts to satisfy that want, and they promise to do it. The public seems to turn especially to the politician to preserve it from the captain of industry; but when has anybody ever seen a politician who was a match for a captain of industry? One of the latest phenomena is a competition of the legislatures of several states for the profit of granting acts of incorporation; this competition consists, of course, in granting greater and greater powers and exacting less and less responsibility.

It is not my duty in this place to make a judicial statement of the good and ill of the facts I mention — I leave to others to suggest the limitations and safeguards which are required. It is enough to say here that of course all power is liable to abuse; if anybody is dreaming about a millennial state of society in which all energy will be free, yet fully controlled by paradisaic virtue, argument with him is vain. If we want results we must get control of adequate power, and we must learn to use it with safeguards. If we want to make tunnels, and to make them rapidly, we have to concentrate supplies of dynamite; danger results; we minimize it, but we never get rid of it. In late years our streets have been filled with power-driven cars and vehicles; the risk and danger of going on the streets has been very greatly increased; the danger is licensed by law, and it is inseparable from the satisfaction of our desire to move about rapidly. It is in this light that we should view the evils (if there are any) from the concentration of wealth. I do not say that "he who desires the end desires the means," because I do not believe that that dictum is true; but he who will not forego the end must be patient with the incidental ills which attend the means. It is ridiculous to attempt to reach the end while making war on the means. In matters of societal policy the problem always is to use the means and reach the end as well as possible under the conditions. It is proper to propose checks and safeguards, but an onslaught on the concentration of wealth is absurd and a recapitulation of its "dangers" is idle.

In fact, there is a true correlation between (a) the great productiveness of modern industry and the consequent rapid accumulation of capital from one period of production to another and (b) the larger and larger aggregations of capital which are required by modern industry from one period of production to another. We see that the movement is constantly accelerated, that its scope is all the time widening, and that the masses of material with which it deals are greater and greater. The dominant cause of all this is the application of steam and electricity to transportation, and the communication of intelligence — things which we boast about as great triumphs of the nineteenth century. They have made it possible to extend efficient control, from a given central point, over operations which may be carried on at a great number of widely separated points, and to keep up a close, direct, and intimate action and reaction between the central control and the distributed agents. That means that it has become possible for the organization to be extended in its scope and complexity, and at the same time intensified in its activity. Now whenever such a change in the societal organization becomes possible it also becomes *inevitable*, because there is economy in it. If we confine our attention to industrial undertakings (although states, churches, universities, and other associations and institutions are subject to the same force and sooner or later will have to obey it) we see that the highest degree of organization which is possible is the one that offers the maximum of profit; in it the economic advantage is greatest. There is therefore a gravitation toward this degree of organization. To make an artificial opposition to this tendency from political or alleged moral, or religious, or other motives would be to have no longer any real rule of action; it would amount to submission to the control of warring motives without any real standards or tests.

It is a consequence of the principle just stated that at every point in the history of civilization it has always been necessary to concentrate capital in amounts large relatively to existing facts. In low civilization chiefs control what capital there is, and direct industry; they may be the full owners of all the wealth or only the representatives of a collective theory of ownership. This organization of industry was, at the time, the most efficient, and the tribes which had it prospered better than others. In the classical states with slavery and in the mediaeval states with serfdom, the great achievements which realized the utmost that the system was capable of were attained only where wealth was concentrated in productive enterprises in amounts, and under management, which were at the maximum of what the system and the possibilities of the time called for. If we could get rid of some of our notions about liberty and equality, and could lay aside this eighteenth century philosophy according to which human society is to be brought into a state of blessedness, we should get some insight into the might of the societal organization: what it does for us, and what it makes us do. Every day that passes brings us new phenomena of struggle and effort between parts of the societal organization. What do they all mean? They mean that all the individuals and groups are forced against each other in a ceaseless war of interests, by their selfish and mutual efforts to fulfill their career on earth within the conditions set for them by the state of the arts, the facts of the societal organization, and the current dogmas of world philosophy. As each must win his living, or his fortune, or keep his fortune, under these conditions, it is difficult to see what can be meant in the sphere of industrial or economic effort by a "free man." It is no wonder that we so often hear angry outcries about being "slaves" from persons who have had a little experience of the contrast between the current notions and the actual facts.

In fact, what we all need to do is to be taught by the facts in regard to the notions which we ought to adopt, instead of looking at the facts only in order to pass judgment on them and make up our minds how we will change them. If we are willing to be taught by the facts, then the phenomena of the concentration of wealth which we see about us will convince us that they are just what the situation calls for. They ought to be because they are, and because nothing else would serve the interests of society.

I am quite well aware that, in what I have said, I have not met the thoughts and feelings of people who are most troubled about the "concentration of wealth." I have tried to set forth the economic necessity for the concentration of wealth; and I maintain that this is the controlling consideration. Those who care most about the concentration of wealth are indifferent to this consideration; what strikes them most is the fact that there are some rich men. I will, therefore, try to show that this fact also is only another economic justification of the concentration of wealth.

I often see statements published, in which the objectors lay stress upon the great *inequalities* of fortune, and, having set forth the contrast between rich and poor, they rest their case. What law of nature, religion, ethics, or the state is violated by inequalities of fortune? The inequalities prove nothing. Others argue that great fortunes are won by privileges created by law and not by legitimate enterprise and ability. This statement is true, but it is entirely irrelevant; we have to discuss the concentration of wealth within the facts of the institutions, laws, usages, and customs which our ancestors have bequeathed to us and which we allow to stand. If it is proposed to change any of these parts of the societal order, that is a proper subject of discussion, but it is aside from the concentration of wealth. So long as tariffs, patents, etc., are part of the system in which we live, how can it be expected that people will not take advantage of them; what else are they for? As for franchises, a franchise is only an x until it has been developed. It never develops itself; it requires capital and skill to develop it. When the enterprise is in the full bloom of prosperity the objectors complain of it, as if the franchise, which never was anything but an empty place where something might be created, had been the completed enterprise. It is interesting to compare the exploitation of the telephone with that of the telegraph fifty years earlier. The latter was, in its day, a far more wonderful invention, but the time and labor required to render it generally available were far greater than what has been required for the telephone, and the fortunes which were won from the former were insignificant in comparison with those which have been won from the latter. Both the public and the promoters acted very differently in the two cases. In these later times promoters seize with avidity upon an enterprise which contains promise, and they push it with energy and ingenuity, while the public is receptive to "improvements"; hence the modern methods offer very great opportunities, and the rewards of those men who can "size up" a situation and develop its controlling elements with sagacity and good judgment, are very great. It is well that they are so, because these rewards stimulate to the utmost all the ambitious and able men, and they make it certain that great and useful inventions will not long remain unexploited as they did formerly. Here comes, then, a new reaction on the economic system; new energy is infused into it, with hope and confidence. We could not spare it and keep up the air of contentment and enthusiastic cheerfulness which characterizes our society. No man can acquire a million without helping a million men to increase their little fortunes all the way down through all the social grades. In some points of view it is an error that we fix our attention so much upon the very rich and overlook the prosperous mass, but the compensating advantage is that the great successes stimulate emulation the most powerfully.

What matters it then that some millionaires are idle, or silly, or vulgar; that their ideas are sometimes futile and their plans grotesque, when they turn aside from money-making? How do they differ in this from any other class? The millionaires are a product of natural selection, acting on the whole body of men to pick out those who can meet the requirement of certain work to be done. In this respect they are just like the great statesmen, or scientific men, or military men. It is because they are thus selected that wealth — both their own and that intrusted to them — aggregates under their hands. Let one of them make a mistake and see how quickly the concentration gives way to dispersion. They may fairly be regarded as the naturally selected agents of society for certain work. They get high wages and live in luxury, but the bargain is a good one for society. There is the intensest competition for their place and occupation. This assures us that all who are competent for this function will be employed in it, so that the cost of it will be reduced to the lowest terms; and furthermore that the competitors will study the proper conduct to be observed in their occupation. This will bring discipline and the correction of arrogance and masterfulness.

INDUSTRIAL LAW

INDUSTRIAL WAR [1]

[1886]

ANY ONE who has attentively read the discussion of the so-called labor question during the past few months, must have observed that a strict definition of terms and phrases is the first thing needed in the discussion, and the one thing that has most been wanting. The loose use of terms tolerated by the economists has been extended by the newspapers, adopted erroneously by the preachers, abused by the professional labor reformers, and finally entirely misunderstood by the employed, until the popular notion of the matter has become little else than a tangle of fallacies and misconceptions of social facts, relations, and possibilities. He who says "social," nowadays, takes license to promulgate vague and whimsical notions or projects, having for their general aim to bridge the traditional gulf between *meum* and *tuum*, or to take from one of his neighbors and give to another, according to his good judgment of what would be more "just." As an illustration of misuse of terms I mention the use of "capital and labor" to designate employer and employee, and as an illustration of the abuse of catch phrases I refer to the almost suicidal misuse of "An injury to one is an injury to all" in the south-western strike.

The only attempt I have met with, in this discussion, to define what the labor question is, formulated it in this way: "With the growth of democracy the political power has passed into the hands of a numerical majority, while

[1] *The Forum*, Vol. II, September, 1886.

property is in the hands of a minority.   There is therefore danger lest the former use the political power to plunder the latter, unless the latter conciliate the former by timely concessions."   If this were the question, it would, no doubt, be serious enough.   It would mean that political institutions are not the safeguard of liberty and property under democracy, any more than they were such under older political forms; but that they are still only convenient means for those who can control the institutions to violate liberty and property to their own advantage.   It would mean that all our boasted political progress was in question, for institutions that cannot guarantee property cannot be stable.   Democracy would either have to yield at once to communism, as the only realization of its own principles, or it would be overthrown by a monarchical reaction to secure property.   Furthermore, if the question were as stated, it would be one that would arise amongst the property classes, and would be suggested by alarm for their interests; it would not be a question raised amongst the employed, and bearing on their struggle for their interests.   The question would therefore be a political question and a property question; it would not be a labor question.

If I attempt, out of the vague, sentimental, and declamatory expressions of the parties interested, and their friends, to formulate the question they try to raise, it seems to me to be this: How can those who have neither land nor capital, and who must therefore enter the organization of society as wage-workers, get their living, or get a better living, or get more than they now get out of the stock of goods in society, for the productive effort which they put into the work of society?   The socialists answer this question by saying that a committee should be appointed to apportion the work of society, and distribute the product, according to some standards which each school of socialists says can easily be defined, but upon which no two schools are agreed. The professorial socialists say that some more "just" distribution ought to be found, that supply and demand will not do, that the socialistic schemes will not do, and that "ethics" must be asked to decide. The press, the pulpit, the politicians — all who solicit the power that the wages-class, by virtue of numbers, now possesses — stand eagerly ready to flatter and cajole it by any proposal or proposition that will please it.

Is the question above stated properly raised, or properly forced upon public attention? I venture to maintain that it is not. The question of how we shall get our living is common to all of us but that insignificant minority which has inherited land or capital enough to support a family without work. The question is no more anxious and perplexing to artisans or handicraftsmen than it is to the mass of the farmers, lawyers, doctors, clergymen, teachers, book-keepers, merchants, and editors, or to the aged, invalid, women, and others who depend upon small investments. It is constantly alleged in vague and declamatory terms that artisans and unskilled laborers are in distress and misery or are under oppression. No facts to bear out these assertions are offered. The wages-class is not a pauper class. It is not a petitioner for bounty nor a social burden. The problem how that part of society is to earn its living is not a public question; it is not a class question. The question how to earn one's living, or the best living possible in one's circumstances, is the most distinctly individual question that can be raised. A great deal might be done, by instruction and exhortation, to inform the individual mind and conscience — especially of parents — so that this question might be more wisely solved than it now is.   Such would be a legitimate field for discussion, and the social consequences of foresight and early self-denial, such as are now employed by the best parents and young people amongst us, would be incalculable; but no public question can properly be raised as to how some shall make it easier for others to get a living, when the first are already fully burdened with the task of getting a living for themselves.   Here, as at every other point in any unbiased attempt to deal with this subject, it is found that the real question is whether we shall maintain or abandon liberty with responsibility.

It is sometimes said to be a shocking doctrine that the employee enters into a contract to dispose of his energies, because this would put him on the same plane with commodities.   This objection has been current amongst the German professorial socialists for years, and it has recently been made much of here by those who catch eagerly at the sentimental aspects of this subject.   Every man who earns his living uses up his vital energy.   He may till his own land and live on his own product, or he may raise a product and contract it away in exchange for what he wants, or he may contract away his time, or his productive energies, or "himself," for the commodities that he needs for his maintenance.   In the first case, there is no social relation at all.   In the last two cases, no distinction can be made affecting the dignity or the interests of the man which is anything more than a dialectical refinement.   The lawyer, doctor, clergyman, teacher, and editor each makes a commodity of himself just as much as the handicraftsman does; each renders services that wear him out; each takes pay for his services; each is "exploited" just as much by those who pay as the handicraftsman is. We men have a way of inflating ourselves with big words on this earth, as if we thus gained dignity or were any the less bound down to toil and suffering. If wages were abolished, or if the socialistic state were established, not a feature of the case would be altered. Men would be worn out in maintaining their existence, and the only question would be just what it is now: Can each one get more maintenance for a given expenditure of himself by living in isolation, or by joining other men in mutual services?

The wages system, then, is part of the industrial organization. An American farmer is his own landlord, tenant, and laborer; if he finds it hard to get a living, he has no employer against whom he can strike; he may curse the ground, or shake his fist in the face of heaven, but that will not help him. He must either work harder or cut down his enjoyments to the measure of his production. If, however, the three interests are separated in a higher organization of society — if the farmer makes a contract by which he yields the use of his land to another, and himself becomes a landlord, and if the new tenant employs a laborer, then the personal rights and interests of three men come into play, and impinge upon each other at every change which before would have affected different interests of the same person. The first farmer could not as employee strike against himself as employer, but the three new parties have antagonistic interests which must be adjusted and readjusted from time to time by some force or other. If, then, we regard the economic forces of supply and demand as the only, the proper, and the inevitable regulators of the complex and highly refined interests that arise between the members of a highly organized society, then "justice" can mean nothing but the unrestricted play of supply and demand. Nobody will be bound to cease grumbling at the result, but each will accept it as the best that he could get in a world of toil and disappointment. He will be satisfied that his neighbors have not robbed him. If, on the other hand, we do not believe that there are any economic forces at work in the matter, or that, if there are any, they work under any necessary laws, then we must regard the adjustment of interests as a product of arbitrary effort. There can then be no right and no justice at all; the only thing to be expected is war, industrial war, carried on by the parties in interest each for himself and to the utmost. Such is the only result to which we can come, and the socialists have generally reached it. There is no doubt that it is a clear issue between two schools of political economy which are diametrically opposed to each other. If there are economic laws, then it behooves us to find them out and submit to them; for they must control all economic interests, and only under them can we establish peace, order, and justice. If there are no economic laws, then war is the normal and only possible condition of society, unless we take refuge under the pitiless despotism of the socialistic state, with its hierarchy of voluptuaries at the top and the stolid barbarism of its brutish masses at the bottom. To reject the economic laws, accept the condition of industrial war, and then look to "ethics" to rule the social tempest, is beneath discussion.

An industrial war is not like a military combat. It is an extension of the old commercial war, which consisted in inflicting a positive harm on one's self in the hope of causing a contingent harm to one's enemy. It is at best like the schoolboy game known as "cutting jackets."

The industrial war simply aims to see who can stand it longest. It is currently asserted that a man has a right to strike. That assertion involves one of the incorrect uses of the word "right," which are so common in this discussion. When a man "strikes" he exercises his will under liberty, that is to say, he exercises a prerogative, for it is the first prerogative of a free man to make or unmake contracts. He is also at liberty under our institutions, as at present existing, to combine with others of the same interest and the same way of thinking. However the other party to the contract has the same liberty. Hence, when both employers and employees combine, the battle is set for the industrial war.

There is a form of strike that would not be irrational, and would be in accordance with sound political economy; that is, if the employees should all stop work, maintaining that the employer could not fill their places except on the terms demanded by them, and should put their contention to the test by waiting to see whether he could or not. A lockout would be rational in the converse and corresponding case. It would then cost loss of time to the parties interested, but nothing more to them and nothing to anybody else. A strike, in which the employees take possession of the plant and hinder others from taking their places, is inconsistent with the peace and order of a modern civilized state. Such a device having once been employed, must inevitably be developed and elaborated in the effort to make it succeed. It could only produce anger and retaliation. It is an effort to coerce one of the parties to a bargain. Undoubtedly a man who has a bargain to make will do wisely to strengthen himself by all means in his power for the negotiation; but the man who pays wages parts with his capital, and, if he parts with it on terms to which he is coerced, he is wronged. He, in his turn, then, will defend his interests to the utmost.

The two chief extensions of the strike which have been made in the way of perfecting the methods of industrial war are the more intense organization and discipline of the employees and the boycott. The former has produced a conflict of organized with unorganized labor, and would, if it could be carried out, outlaw any employee who should choose to preserve his independence and liberty. The employees, while denouncing monopoly, have here employed the monopoly principle in its most outrageous form, and they seek to raise wages by crushing any one who will not come into the close combination which they regard as essential to the coercion they hope to exercise. In reaching about for means of this coercion, they have employed the strike to compel the employer to become their ally and discharge any one who stays out of their organization.

The boycott is a further attempt to find a point of re-action for the coercive apparatus. The original case of boycotting, from which the device got its name, was very generally approved, or at least not condemned, because it was set in operation against an Irish landlord. It was plain in that case, however, what the device was, and how monstrous an innovation it was in a civilized society. If, without process of law, a man can be so extruded from human society that he cannot buy or sell, hire, let, beg, borrow, lend, employ, or be employed, what becomes of the security of life, liberty, or property? Of course no such result could be brought about unless the boycotters could bring terrorism to bear on the whole community, including, at last, jurors, judges, and witnesses, to force people who are not parties to the quarrel to depart from the legal and peaceful enjoyment of their own will and pleasure to take part in the boycott. It is the severest trial to which our institutions have yet been put, to see whether they can protect in his rights a man who has incurred for any reason unpopularity amongst a considerable number of his neighbors, or whether democratic institutions are as powerless in this case as aristocratic institutions were when a man incurred the hostility of a great noble.

The doctrines that are preached about the relations of employer and employee would go to make that relationship one of status and not of contract, with the rights and duties unevenly divided. The relationship would then be one like marriage, entered by contract, but, when once entered upon, not solvable except by some process of divorce, and, while it lasts, having its rights and duties defined by law. It is very remarkable that just when all feudal relations between landlord and tenant are treated with disdain and eagerly assailed, there should be an attempt to establish feudal relations between employer and employee. An employer has no obligation whatever to an employee outside of the contract, any more than an editor has to his subscribers, or a merchant to his customers, or a house-owner to his tenants, or a banker to his depositors. In a free democratic state employees are not wards of the state; they are not like Indians, or freedmen, or women, or children. If it can be shown that any law or custom of our society keeps down the man who is struggling for himself, every fair-minded man could and would join the agitation for its removal; but when we are asked to create privileges or tolerate encroachments, resistance is equally a social duty.

These extravagant and cruel measures, therefore, produce war inside of our society. Industrial factions arise,

which are organized under monarchical or oligarchic
forms, and which threaten to carry out their program
at all cost to the community.   They are doomed to fail.
They will not be overcome by conciliation and concession because they are not animated by the spirit from
which any concession will secure peace, but only larger
demands.   They will fail because they will come into
collision with the sober sense of the community.   It is
indeed a great experiment to grant the fullest liberty
and the greatest political equality, in the faith that the
unsuccessful will not only regard without envy the prosperity of the successful, but also will help to secure and
defend it; but it is a fallacy in every point of view that,
because those-who-have-not outnumber those-who-have,
therefore those-who-have-not will plunder those-who-
have.   Still more certainly, the measures that have been
used to assist the employed class against the employers
will fail, because they are irrational and at war with
economic forces.   There are a great many cases in sociology where the sum of the parts is not the whole, but
is zero.   The trades-union is one of them; a national
trades-union, or an international trades-union, of all
employees, instead of being invincible would be nil.   If
by all going out to-day all could force an advance in
wages, by all going back to-morrow all would restore
the old rate.   The human race cannot lift itself by the
boot-straps in this way any more than in any other.   If
we want more wages, the only way to get them is by
working, not by not working.

A PARABLE

A PARABLE[1]

A CERTAIN respectable man had three sons, who grew up, lived, and died in the same city.

The oldest one turned his back at an early age on study. Being eager to earn something at once, he obtained employment driving a grocer's delivery wagon. He never acquired a trade, but was a teamster or driver all his life. In his youth he spent all his spare time with idle companions and devoted his earnings to beer, tobacco, and amusement. At twenty-two he fell in love and married. He had six children who scrambled part way through the public grammar school after a negligent fashion, but cost as much money and more of the teachers' time than if they had been regular and studious. This son never earned over two dollars a day except on election day, when he earned five or more, according to circumstances. He never had ten dollars in his possession over and above his debts.

The second son was the scholar of the family. By energy, perseverance, and self-denial he managed to get a professional education. He married at thirty, being in the receipt of an adequate income from his profession, but not yet having accumulated any capital. He had three children who were all educated in the public grammar and high schools, and his son went to the university, which was a state institution supported by taxation. His wife had strong social ambition, and, although he had early trained himself in habits of frugality and prudence, he found himself forced to enlarge his expendi-

[1] For approximate date, see preface.

[105]

tures quite as rapidly as his income increased; so that, although he earned at last several thousand dollars a year, he left no property when he died.

The third son had no taste for professional study, but he had good sense and industry. He was apprenticed to a carpenter. He spent his leisure time in reading and formed no expensive habits. As soon as he began to receive wages he began to save. On account of his care, diligence, and good behavior, he was made an under-foreman. The highest earnings he ever obtained were $1,500 per year. At thirty years of age he had saved $2,000. He then married. He invested his savings in a homestead, but was obliged to incur a debt which it took him years of patient struggle to pay. He had three children who went through the public grammar school, but he was not able to support them through the high school and college. When he died he left the homestead clear of debt and nothing more.

The oldest son never paid a cent of local or direct tax in his life. The second son never paid any. The third paid taxes from the time he was twenty-two, when he first began to save, and while the mortgage rested on his homestead, he paid taxes on his debt as well as on his property. The taxes which he paid went to pay for police, lights, sewers, public schools, public charity, state university, public prison, public park, and public library, and also for soldiers' monuments, public celebrations, and all forms of occasional public expenditure. His brothers and his brothers' children all enjoyed these things as much as, or, as we have seen, more than he and his children.

The oldest brother borrowed constantly of the two others, and he and his children availed themselves freely of the privileges of relationship. Inasmuch as the second brother, in spite of his large income, was constantly in pecuniary straits, it was the youngest who was the largest creditor of the oldest. The oldest was an earnest greenbacker with socialistic tendencies, and the only payment he ever made to the youngest was in the way of lectures on the crimes of capital, the meanness of capitalists, and the equality of all men. The oldest died first. Two of his children were still small and the older ones were a cause of anxiety to their relatives on account of careless habits and unformed character. The second son, or to be more accurate, his wife, would not, for social reasons, take charge of the orphans, and they fell to the care of the youngest brother, although the second, while he lived, contributed to their maintenance.

The neighbors differed greatly in their views of this family. Some called the oldest poor and the other two rich. Some called the two oldest poor and the other rich. Some called the oldest and youngest poor and the second rich. As the facts were all known throughout the neighborhood, it was found to be a very interesting and inexhaustible subject of debate. Some people compared the first and second and moralized on the inequality of the distribution of wealth — one living in poverty and the other in luxury. This state of things was generally regarded as very "unjust" to the oldest brother. He was fond of demonstrating that it was so to anyone who would listen. Nobody ever was known to refer to the youngest brother as the victim of any injustice. The oldest brother was liked and pitied by everybody. The second was very popular in his circle. The third was not very well known and was not popular with anybody.

THE DEMAND FOR MEN

THE DEMAND FOR MEN [1]

To every individual the history of the world begins and ends in himself. Each man finds it hard, if not impossible, to imagine the world without himself, that is, to imagine that he had never been born. Our way of looking at history is to treat all which has been done here as a preparation for us, and our current construction of the life of the world is that the sufferings of the past, and its achievements, have their sense through their utility in contributing to our welfare. Once in a while we do also speak about our obligations to posterity, as if we did feel that our way of thinking about the past brought with it a corollary that we are only links in the chain of preparation for others yet farther on; at this point, however, there is a notable drop in the intensity of interest and conviction with which the idea is pursued. Further, in all our speculations about the future we probably conceive of ourselves as present and as part of the future, and rarely, if ever, does the speaker himself realize that he will drop out of the host in its march and disappear from its activity, lost and forgotten like a thistle-down which floated for a moment on the summer breeze.

To the individual, therefore, it is hard to realize that he is not needed here; that his existence, however interesting and important to himself, is of no consequence to the world; that if he had never been born he never would have been missed; that the men in all history who

[1] The following fourteen essays come from the *Independent* of various dates between 1887 and 1891.

have proved by their life and works that the world did
need them and could illy have spared them, are not more
than a score or two.

Much more is it a remarkable idea that men in general should ever be in demand. If we do not go beyond
current habits of thought, we think that the world was
made for men, that it has no significance without men;
that its existence is, as it were, a call or demand for
men; that of course we all ought to be here, and, having
come, that we ought to be made welcome and honorably
provided for. Our complaints are for the most part complaints of those very conditions of earthly life by virtue
of which it is possible that we may be here. If there is
any "banquet of life" offered, by the fact that the world
is here, we find that there are a great number of us who
have come to be guests at it and that there is a hungry
crowd of other animals, upon whom we look down as
not fit to dispute the banquet with us, but who defend
their possession of it with as much ferocity and tenacity
as if they were revolutionists and could declaim about
natural rights. Our assumption is that we should all
be here, under any circumstances whatever, and that
the provision for us here is, or ought to be, somewhere
on hand.

Unfortunately none of these ideas can be verified by
an examination of the facts. We are not needed here at
all; the world existed no one knows how long without
any men on it. They were never missed by the other
forms of nature, who absorbed, enjoyed, and gave back
again into the cosmos the energy and the material of
organized existence, generation after generation; and
there is no room for any idea that the universe suffered
any lack or fell short of anything which was necessary
to keep it going on in a round of transformations and

repetitions which were adequate to the maintenance of all there was. There is no need for man and no demand for man, in nature; it is complete without him.

When he appears on earth he does not appear as one needed, but as another competitor for a place here. He is infinitely interesting to himself, and he has constructed for the gratification of his vanity whole systems of mythology and philosophy to prove to himself that the rest has sense only as used up by him. In truth he is here like the rest, on the tenure of sustaining himself if he can. The curse of the self-glorification of the human species is that it blinds them to the truth of their situation, keeps them from intelligent effort to make the best of it, and sets them to rending each other when their demands are not satisfied.

It is therefore a most extraordinary state of things on earth — a revolution — when men are in demand, that is, not only welcome, but subject to economic demand, so that their presence will be paid for; and the social consequences of such a state of affairs, when it occurs, stand in such contrast to the state when men are in excessive supply that the mind of man is astounded to contemplate the difference. It will be found that the glorification of modern progress, modern ideas, and so on, resolves itself into this "revolution" which causes all the others.

It must be noticed that the demand for men is not a demand for human beings; this distinction cannot be passed over, since the neglect of it has helped to prevent an understanding of the point we are now presenting. The human race reproduces and increases, but unfortunately its new-born members are a burden, the heaviest one which society has to bear. Between initial helplessness and capacity for self-maintenance lies a period of cost, or outlay, by the adult generation. Here again we come on the same fact, that there is no demand for men in the sense of human beings, since cost and outlay are never an object of demand but are in the nature of a penalty or sacrifice for a good not otherwise attainable. When savage races practice infanticide, it is because they rate the cost higher than the return; the self-centered view of the adult, mentioned above, then predominates entirely. For him the world begins and ends in himself, and the sacrifice he must endure to perpetuate the species, being just so much reduction from the individual enjoyment which he might get out of life (which is the case always touching the sacrifices of parents for offspring), seems to him to present no consideration.

It is therefore only when there is a demand for adults that there arises a demand for human beings which makes the cost of rearing them sink into comparative unimportance. When children are welcome as new power, instead of being unwelcome as new burdens, the real social revolution is accomplished. The book of Genesis presents, in the case of the patriarchs, a state of things in which more children meant more power, and the texts which express that fact in the social situation of that time have sometimes been used as giving an absolute religious sanction to special views of the significance of the increase of the species.

An economic demand is one which is backed up by an equivalent offered in reward for a satisfaction of it, and the demand for men is subject to the same interpretation, or it is a fiction. The payment which must be brought into the labor market as an equivalent to support the demand for men is means of subsistence; if men are wanted they must be subsisted, and they must be subsisted in such rich measure that they can sustain not only themselves but also wives and little ones to maintain the increase. Means of subsistence, however, are not raw land, for the latter, like the infants, is a long stage from the labor market. If raw land were a demand for men, that would mean that nature demands men — which, as we saw at the outset, is not true. Nature does not come into the market; she offers no equivalents in exchange; she presents no means of subsistence which are capable of sustaining more than the scantiest numbers in the lowest misery. The terms of the case in no wise apply to her, and all those who, when discussing these matters, allow themselves to philosophize about "boons of nature," and "banquets of life" are only spinning delusions.

The means of subsistence are capital-products which men who are already here have made and are ready to share with new-comers, as a means to persuade others to come. This is the demand for men. We are accustomed to call it "demand for labor," and this phrase, blinding us to the facts by a technical relation put in place of the real one, is the great cause of some of the foolish notions about wages which have been set afloat, and which have become the prolific cause of social and industrial fallacies. The case which is new, anomalous, astounding, is the one in which the men who are already here not only do not dread new-comers or treat them with hostility, but even pay them, out of the products of their own previous labor, to come. That is a true demand for men. When it arises, men rise in market value, with consequences which are next to be noted.

Here it remains only to point out that the reason why those already here will hire others to come, continually raising their bid, is that by bringing in more human labor they can raise the industrial organization to a higher grade and increase the production per man from the land at their disposal, so that the increase in numbers will increase, not diminish, the average rate of comfort for all.

This last remark exposes the fallacy of the arguments which are made against immigration, for immigration supplies the men, and without cost of production on them, for the community which gets them.

THE SIGNIFICANCE OF THE DEMAND FOR MEN

THE SIGNIFICANCE OF THE DEMAND
FOR MEN

To some people it appears a shame to say that men are subject to supply and demand; to others it seems that we want to know the facts about man and the world in which he lives, just as they are, without regard to anything else whatsoever. To the latter, therefore, it seems irrelevant and idle to talk about what is consonant with, or what is hostile to man's notions of his own dignity. It will be found that men are subject to supply and demand, that the whole industrial organization is regulated by supply and demand, and that any correct comprehension of the existing industrial system must proceed from supply and demand.

After Gracchus conquered Sardinia, slaves were so abundant at Rome that "cheap as a Sardinian" passed into a proverb; Roman slavery owed its peculiar harshness and cold-heartedness to the fact that slaves were so abundant at Rome in the last century of the Republic that it did not pay to spare them. The policy in regard to slave marriage was such as to prevent their natural increase. When, later, conquest declined and slaves were fewer, their treatment became far more humane, not because Romans were less cold-hearted (they were, in fact, more so), but because slaves grew rarer and more valuable. Probably this state of things also helped to convert slaves into *coloni*.

Sir Henry Maine says that want and distress converted men into beasts of burden in the later days of the Carlovingians. The reason for this seems clear. It

was that the conditions of existence in the society of
the time were such that men were reduced again to the
first necessities, with only the most meager means of
satisfying them.   The population was, therefore, declining, and the wretched men who were living struggled
with each other in desperate agony, or endeavored to
win subsistence from nature under the hardest conceivable exertion.   Any one, therefore, who at that
time, by any means whatsoever, possessed a store of
means of subsistence or could command resources, could
have men under his control without number.

At those times human life was held most cheap, and
physical pain or distress was scarcely noticed.   When
a thousand men could be sent to death at a Roman
feast, how could Romans be expected to hold human
life dear or to shudder at bloodshed?   When fist-law
prevailed, and every man's hand was against every
other man, when any one who had anything could be
sure of it only so long as he could command force to
defend it, it is not strange that torture and cruelty were
practised in this world and that the current conceptions
of punishment in the other world should make the blood
of the modern man run cold.

In general, then, when the men are too numerous for
the means of subsistence, the struggle for existence is
fierce.   The finer sentiments decline; selfishness comes
out again from the repression under which culture binds
it; the social tie is loosened; all the dark sufferings of
which humanity is capable become familiar phenomena.
Men are habituated to see distorted bodies, harsh and
frightful diseases, famine and pestilence; they find out
what depths of debasement humanity is capable of.
Hideous crimes are perpetrated; monstrous supersti-
tions are embraced even by the most cultivated members

of society; vices otherwise inconceivable become common, and fester in the mass of society; culture is lost; education dies out; the arts and sciences decline. All this follows for the most simple and obvious of all reasons: because a man whose whole soul is absorbed in a struggle to get enough to eat, will give up his manners, his morals, his education, or that of his children, and will thus, step by step, withdraw from and surrender everything else in order simply to maintain existence. Indeed, it is a fact of familiar knowledge that, under the stress of misery, all the finer acquisitions and sentiments slowly but steadily perish.

The converse of this statement, however, is true; and it is for the sake of the converse that we have now set forth what has already been said. If the subsistence of men is in excess of the number of men, all the opposite results are produced, for in that case the demand is in excess of the supply. The all-important thing under supply and demand is to know how the conjuncture stands. The party in the market whose demand for the goods of others is low while their demand for his goods is high, has command of the market, and the conjuncture is said to be in his favor; on the other hand, he whose demand for the products of others is high, while their demand for his products is low, is at a disadvantage in the market, and the conjuncture is against him. He, therefore, who brings only his natural, unskilled powers to market, when many others are offering the same thing, will win but meager subsistence from the stock of food, clothing, etc., in the market; on the other hand, he who brings personal services to market, when human energy is eagerly wanted to develop land and apply capital at the hand of those who possess land and capital, will be able to demand large quotas of the existing stock of subsistence in return for a day's time spent in supplying the thing which is in demand and without which the other conditions of abundance and prosperity cannot be made available.

With this observation we strike out and lay aside nearly all the so-called labor question, and nearly all the mystery of the alleged conflict of labor and capital. The conjuncture is in favor of the laborer, technically so-called; accordingly he can, to a great degree, have his own way with the other parties in the market.

We have not, however, developed our proposition merely for the sake of this negative and controversial result. On the contrary, its importance lies in the deduction yet to be made of the sense and significance of a state of the labor market, continuing for centuries, in which the conjuncture is in favor of the unskilled laborers. Such has been the case, if we take the terms of the proposition in their broadest and most liberal sense, since the great discoveries of the sixteenth century which opened the outlying continents to the masses of the population of Europe.

Whenever a period in which men are in demand supervenes upon a period in which they have been present in excess, the struggle for existence is softened. The disregard of human life and human suffering gives place to the contrary sentiments. It might seem to be logical that when all were suffering, all would sympathize with each other and that when many were well off, they would become inwrapped in selfish indifference to the few who, by exception, were suffering; but this is one of the cases, of which there are so many in social science, in which observation corrects the easy inference. It warns us again that what seems a simple and easy deduction is not even presumptively true. It is when all are suffering that men become callous to suffering; each sees in it what may be his own fate a moment later; it comes to be regarded as usual, natural, a part of the human lot. On the other hand, when most are in comfort and prosperity, misery pains them; it seems to be exceptional, unreasonable, unnecessary; their sympathies are painfully excited and for their own relief they seek to do away with it.

When men are in demand the average comfort is high; the grinding labor which distorts the body and superinduces diseases is avoided; the diet is good; the worst maladies from poor food, unwholesome crowding, unsanitary modes of living, and the like are done away with. Our discussions run on as if unsanitary arrangements in our homes and cities were totally unnecessary; but we ought to understand that nothing but the possession of capital in a certain degree of abundance enables us to take up the question of sanitary arrangements at all. If we had unlimited means we could absolutely set aside all danger from unsanitary conditions. If we were poor, we should have to submit to the perils and fatalities of unsanitary arrangements without remedy.

Other illustrations on the same line of thought will follow.

WHAT THE "SOCIAL QUESTION" IS

WHAT THE "SOCIAL QUESTION" IS

We have before us the idea that no social effect can be produced without an adequate cause; there can be no result which we may not account for, upon suitable study, by the forces which were at work behind it. It is a favorite notion that "ideas" are causes, that "thought" is a force, and that sentiment, or feeling, may control society. Intellectual affections of any kind whatsoever may determine the direction in which force shall be exerted; but they are not forces which are efficient to produce results. It is impossible to stir a step in any direction which has been selected without capital: we cannot subsist men, *i.e.*, laborers, without it; we cannot sustain study or science without it; we cannot recruit the wasted energies of the race without it; we cannot win leisure for deliberation without it; we cannot, therefore, undertake greater tasks, that is, make progress, without it.

It is the possession of an abundance of capital which sets us free to write and wrangle about "social questions"; it is the possession of abundance of capital which enables us to maintain "progress," and spend largely upon philanthropy, and increase our numbers at the same time. This point is worth a little more elucidation; when we get a social science this will be one of the controlling points of view in it.

The first task of men is self-maintenance, or nutrition; the second is the maintenance of the race. The two tasks are in antagonism with each other, for they are both demands on one source of power, *viz.*, the pro-

ductive power of the individual.   The interplay of these
two in the family has been touched upon before, and it
is by no means limited to the family; this interplay
extends through the whole social domain.   If the
social body undertakes more social burdens, it increases
the second demand on the individual, and contracts his
power of self-maintenance.   From this there is no
possible escape, and it may readily be seen how far much
of our current social discussion is from touching the
merits of the social questions, because it fails to run
upon the lines which are laid down for all discussion by
this observation of the conditions of the case.   What is
true, and what helps to explain the current modes of
thought, is the fact that the capital at the disposal of
society is so great that the diminutions of individual
well-being by social burdens all fall upon an outside
margin of superfluity, and so do not reach to the limits
of actual necessity or crush the producer down to
misery.

If the social burdens of government, public philanthropy, public defense, public entertainment and amusement, public glory, public education, did subtract from
the product of the society to such an extent as to produce
misery, this would react upon the numbers, and it
would do it in different ways.   It would make the
producer less able to support children and bring them
to maturity, and it would force the society to give up
part of the effort by which it now maintains indigent
and defective classes.

Therefore there has never been a period of civilization in which there has not been a social question, and
it is safe to say that no time ever will come when there
will not be a social question.   In a state of barbarism
the social question consists in this: whether the tribe

can maintain its numbers, or fighting strength, and at the same time do its fighting. The competition of life is then between tribe and tribe. The Zulus, for instance, solved it by stealing all their wives, that is, they let others bear the expense of bringing up the wives for them; they also were forbidden to marry except by permission of the king, which he never gave except to a meritorious warrior who had served ten or fifteen years. Other organizations equally remarkable have been devised for solving the problem, but my point now is, that there is a problem, and that it cannot be solved except by some adequate and appropriate application of industrial force. The current notion is that there is not, or need not be, or ought not to be any such problem, and that if there is such an apparent problem, all that is necessary is to "pass a law" such as some social speculator will easily devise.

In the higher forms of civilization there always has been a "social question." The modern democratic temper is irritated by a mention of social classes; I have heard it indignantly denied that there are classes among us. The mediaeval classes were defined by status, that is, by rank and birth; the one heterogeneous social element was the middle class population of the towns. That class was industrial by its definition; its power came from capital, of which it was the maker and possessor. The other classes needed capital more and more — hence the strife of land and city, of noble and bourgeoisie, of rank and capital. The social questions of the last five hundred years have turned on these antagonisms. They are by no means reduced to peaceful harmony yet, and they play a large part in the expositions of the socialists, especially when the latter take an historical turn.

The middle class, having substantially won its victory, has begun, by the inevitable tendency of all such massive social movements, to break up into sections which quarrel with each other. Of course new differentiations have begun inside of it. Peasants, artisans, and bourgeoisie allied with each other against a common foe, *viz.*, hereditary right; but, having broken the power of that tradition, they must of course put another notion in its place. They introduced free contract and competition. This is no sooner done, however, than new groups are formed having antagonistic interests inside of the new society. The result is industrial classes, or social groupings formed upon economic and industrial relations.

This new grouping is, in fact, a grand advance, for it is a new and higher organization and it signifies increased industrial power; but it is inevitably attended by a new "social question," produced by the struggle of these classes. The great question about which the whole struggle turns is, of course, this: whether some one class is getting its share of the fruits of the common victory. The victory has been social so far as it has meant the emancipation of classes and the endowment of all with equal rights before the law; it has been a victory over the ills of life so far as it has consisted in the acquisition of capital as power to have and do. This power of capital has been becoming constantly more valuable both for luxury, leisure, and enjoyment, and also for social control. The social question appears in the form of a complaint that the non-capitalists have been put off with "liberty" and "equal rights" in order that they might have no share in the capital, that is, in the leisure and luxury for which the age is athirst.

Our current literature bears ample testimony to the correctness of what is here asserted about the social question. If we should deny that there are classes in our society we should only prove our inability to recognize constant social elements under the changed phases in which they present themselves.

The point which I now beg to emphasize is this: if there had been no victory, there would be no social question in its present form. If there had not been an immense enhancement of luxury, culture, and power, the classes and the masses would never have come into antagonism to each other. The popular conception of it is that a common victory has been won (that is, the victory over nature by the acquisition of more industrial power) and that some have taken all the fruits, leaving to others nothing. Hence the demand for justice and equality and the passionate assertion of the obligation of classes to each other. Hence, also, the attempt to use the other victory (that over class privilege in the domain of civil institutions) to rectify the wrong done in the industrial domain.

If it were true that a part of those who have won the social and industrial victories had been deprived of their share in the fruits thereof, then they would have no hope of compelling any attention to their complaints, for they would have no force at their disposal. The fact that they can raise a social question and push on the fight over it proves that they have some power at their command. Mediaeval peasants had very few rights and scarcely any property; they could defend themselves only by some wild outbreak, like the Jacquerie, which did no good. The modern non-capital classes are in no such condition as that.

What force have they then? It is no doubt promptly answered, "Numbers." Numbers, however, are a source of weakness, not of strength, unless there is ample capital for their support. If there were here large numbers of men who were on the verge of starvation, they would submit to any terms in order to get food. Men who had capital (which we must always remember is subsistence, weapons, and tools) could hire armies of them to do any work which was demanded of them. It is, therefore, only because we all do share in the fruits of the industrial victory and in the power of the capital which has been won, that we have extra power with which to maintain our social conflicts. Democracy constantly vaunts itself against capital, and sets the power of numbers against the power of "money," but democracy, the power of the masses, is the greatest proof of the power of capital, for democracy cannot exist in any society unless the physical conditions of social power are present there in such abundance, and in such general distribution, that all the mass of the population is maintained up to the level below which they can not perform the operations which democracy assumes that they can and will perform.

It is, therefore, the demand for men, consisting in the capital and tools on hand, ready for their support and use, which maintains a number of men on a level where they can struggle to get all the material welfare which the labor market really holds for them, and where they can be democrats and win both full civil rights and a share, perhaps a predominant share, in political power. This is the only correct explanation of the power of the masses in politics and in the labor market; for it is the only one which refers the phenomena to an adequate and appropriate cause whose due connection with the

phenomena can be perceived through the social relations. Of course this explanation is in direct contradiction to such explanations as refer the phenomena to
sentimental, ethical, doctrinal, or political causes, consisting in the tenets of this or that social philosophy.

WHAT EMANCIPATES

WHAT EMANCIPATES

It is an incident of the tendency to realism of our time that historical studies have won in esteem. This is undoubtedly a great gain; but it is attended by a series of affectations such as are apparently inseparable from a new movement. We must have a new code of historical study before the abuses of history can be set aside; nowhere is this need more apparent than in economic history and in the history of social institutions. It is hardly too much to say that the received opinions about the historical development of social forces are all incorrect; that is to say, they are one-sided, imperfect, colored by prejudices of various schools of philosophy, or so stated as to support pet notions of our time. The student of history, therefore, finds himself constantly forced to modify the most currently received statements of fact, or he finds that the historical facts, when correctly understood, take on very different significance even if the formal statement of them is allowed to stand.

No history is good for anything except as it is interpreted correctly; and it is in the interpretation that the chance is offered for all the old arbitrary elements of philosophy and personal prejudice to come in, as well as some new ones peculiar to this field of study. Especially when the interpretations are wide, and step over great periods of history in grand strides, is it safe to say that they are worthless, because it is impossible to verify them. Almost any generalization can find a color of truth, if the historical scope of it is wide enough. It is a very school-boy notion that historical generalizations have any less peril in them than philosophical generalizations.

These remarks are especially worthy of affirmation whenever our attention is invited to alleged interpretations of the social developments of modern times, and when assertions are made about the causes and significance of the phases through which civilization has passed during the last five hundred years. The contrast of the Middle Ages with our time; the status of classes then and now; the effect of machinery; the rise of the captain of industry; the alleged advancing inequality of fortunes — such are topics which invite to the easiest possible generalization. Within twenty-five years there have been put in circulation, and are to be found now in current use as established facts, assertions on all these points which are really no better than myths.

I submit that nothing but power can account for results and that, therefore, if men have been emancipated from any ills, it must be that they have been emancipated by virtue of new power of some kind, over which they have obtained disposal. Therefore explanations of the expansion of human well-being may be offered which are "historical" in the sense of referring to notions which were once in fashion, or to acts, ordinances, and resolutions which were once upon a time adopted; but such explanations win no value from their pretended "historical" character. They do not allege an adequate cause. No men have ever emancipated themselves from slavery, poverty, ignorance, vice, or any other ill, by simply resolving to do so. No men, so far as I can learn, have ever reached the point of adopting a grand resolution to emancipate themselves from distress, unless they had some new power at their disposal, which raised them to a new plane on which such new adjustment of themselves to their past and their future was possible.

It is an easy assumption, and one which seems to be adopted without discussion, that men who break into revolt must be worse off than other men. There are no facts to support such an opinion. Men who are low, and are falling, do not revolt; it is men who, although they may be low, are rising, who revolt. Men who are on the verge of starvation do not strike for higher wages; it is only men who have strength to spare who spend any of it on a strike. It is the man who is rising whose ambition is awakened; it is he before whose mind new hopes arise, for, having won something, a man's mind always opens to the idea of winning more. On the contrary, he who has always lost ground or has never been able to win any, has neither energy nor will to engage in a contest which involves more than the satisfaction of the moment. How could it be otherwise? We must learn to observe and to think in social matters as we do in others. An extra expenditure of energy is an incontrovertible proof that there is extra energy to expend; therefore it cannot be a proof of decline or decay. Labor disputes and labor organizations are the best possible proof that the "laboring classes," technically so-called, are well off and gaining; but the advancing comfort of the mass of mankind, during any period, is a proof that they have won new physical and social power. No explanation of the increase in comfort can be correct, therefore, unless it is given in terms of this new power.

I therefore make bold to doubt whether there is any truth in the notion that new institutions have been produced by new ideas, and whether any new philosophies have ever become original molding forces in social development. To me it seems, on the contrary, that the new social power makes the new ideas, and that the command of new power of sustaining life on earth gives birth to new philosophies.

Acts, ordinances, and resolutions fall dead unless there is a social field fit for them; history is full of the skeletons of such still-born enactments. The same may be said of institutions. Institutions have had immeasurable importance in human history, but nowadays institution has become a word to juggle with. There have been all sorts of institutions, and those of them which have been invented by human wit have only served to bring human wit into scorn. Institutions which have been strong and effective have grown, we scarcely know how, because the soil and the seed were present. If that is so, then behind institutions we must seek the causes and conditions which brought them into being and nourished their growth. That brings us to social forces again.

In civil affairs it is most commonly believed that we can make constitutions as we choose, and that the wisdom of constitution-makers shapes the destinies of peoples. Is this so? Have we a republic because the men of 1787 voted so? Are our institutions democratic because those men disliked aristocracy and loved democracy? I do not so read history, although the current expressions in our literature all imply that such is the case. It was the industrial and social power of the masses of the population in a new country with unlimited land which made us democratic. It is the reflex influence of the new countries on the old centers of civilization which is breaking down aristocracy, and making them democratic too; but it is because the opening of the new continents has made a demand for men — it has brought about a call for more population. The consequence is that those who are here can marry, can support a family, and can at the same time save capital, or, if they like it better, they can work fewer hours a day. Hence we find our age full of discussion on these matters; but does any one suppose that men could discuss emigration, family comfort, politics, wages, rates, and eight-hour laws, unless there were conditions which brought these things within the range of possibility? The great question then is, what are those conditions? But in the discussion it hardly seems to be noted that they exist and that in them lies the key of the whole matter. If this view is correct, a social science which investigates those conditions is the only social science which has value; history will have its use as serving that science, and if it does not do so it only degenerates into a new form of scholasticism.

The acquisition and use of unlimited supplies of new land has made living easy; it has taken all terror from the increase of population — in fact, has made it a help and a blessing; it has made it easy to accumulate capital and has produced leisure for invention. This increase of power has, consequently, produced expansion of being in every direction and in every form.

The extension of acreage lowers the value of land and of land products against all other things, including services; it increases food products and raw materials, that is, subsistence and materials for laborers. Inventions increase the power of machines and multiply through them all the forms of clothing, furniture, fuel, lights, literature, etc. All this makes capital abundant and interest low; it also makes real wages high, and, by reducing prices, increases the purchasing power of money wages. The conjuncture is, therefore, all in favor of wage-earners and non-capitalists. They have the social power; they, therefore, take the political power. We may invent such institutions as we choose, but they will all speedily change into forms consistent with this distribution of social forces, or die. All the tendencies of the time are sure to stream toward the focus of the great predominating force, in the system, for the time; and the masters of this force are sure to be flattered and courted.

POWER AND PROGRESS

POWER AND PROGRESS

In its simplest and most concrete form, social power consists in the power of an individual man to produce by his labor, from the ground, more than the subsistence of one man. Its grades and degrees follow the increasing ratio of the product to the labor. If one man can produce subsistence for a number, the population rapidly increases, a society grows up, and increases soon to great numbers. The men are "in demand," as we have expressed it before; the surplus product of those already here constitutes a supply of subsistence all ready for others, and thus measures the demand for them as an economic quantity. The greater the productive power of the members of society the more luxurious will be the life in it; existence will be broad and ample in its comfort, and all the social capital will be rapidly multiplied. The members of the society all participate in the advantage of the social capital where liberty exists, and imperfectly even where it does not exist, for not even slaves could be prevented from sharing in those facilities and advantages which are public and general in a highly civilized state. Thus the power of the individual to produce much turns into a social power.

It is a painful disillusion to find that increasing social power does not tend toward a final social condition in which rest and contentment would be found after a task finished and executed, but that the problem has only changed its form. If the society, after taking up new elements, tends toward a new equilibrium in which those new elements are to be absorbed and assimilated, the

period of change and transition is found to be the period
of prosperity, expansion, and happiness. Rest and peace
would mean, not quiet and unruffled enjoyment, but
stagnation, routine, and decay. A new measure of
energy and strength is won, but it drives us on again;
we make new achievements, and get once more all the
exhilaration of advancing motion; but we throw aside
and lose much of our old winnings. It is never in the
quiet enjoyment of rest, or in exhausting the enjoyment
which comes from consuming the achievements of the
past that either power or happiness is won — it is in the
work of achievement, in the sense of gain and progress,
in the movement and transition from one plane to
another. How then is it possible to imagine that the
human race will ever get its work done? If it ever stops
to rest it will retrograde. It will then have its work to
begin all over again. Poverty, if ever conquered and
banished, will come again through the vices engendered
in a world without poverty, and so the conflict with it
must begin again.

The Egyptians owed their power and civilization to
the fact that the Nile mud so enriched the valley every
season that one man's labor could produce subsistence
for many. When the population increased, the power
of social maintenance was not diminished but increased.
When there was a great population there, using the land
with very painstaking labor according to the stage of
the arts, an immense surplus was produced which raised
war, statecraft, fine arts, science, and religion up to
a very high plane. Then they tried to satisfy the demand for men by slaves, that is, persons who contributed
to the social power to their utmost yet shared in it only
under the narrowest limitations. The system, after
reaching the full flower of prosperity of which it was

capable, became rigid, chiefly, as it appears, because the sanction of religion was given to the traditional and stereotyped forms. Also the power of social support which lay in the fertility of the soil had been exploited to its utmost. The arts by which more product might have been won advanced only very slowly — scarcely at all. There was hardly any emigration to new land. Hence a culmination was reached, after which there must be decline and decay. The achievements of the Egyptians were made in the period when they were growing up to the measure of the chances which they possessed.

In their case we can see a nation pass through the stages from the first to the last. Other nations, which are in full contact with the rest of the human race, undergo constantly renewed impulses to advance and they undergo periods of reaction. The phenomena are broken and confused and it is not easy to interpret them.

In the case of the individual also it is emphatically true that it is not the man who is rich who is happy; it is the man who is growing richer than he has been. Hence this great happiness is possible to all, for it is just as intense for a man who has been used to five hundred a year and is now winning eight hundred as it is to the man who has been having twenty thousand and is now winning twenty-five thousand.

Progress, therefore, means winning more social power; it goes along with increase of power and is the proof and the realization of such increase. The arts of life all contribute to the increase. Although it has been said that social power means power of an individual to produce, from the land, a surplus of subsistence beyond his own needs, yet it will not be understood that this power is increased by agricultural improvements only; it is increased by all improvements in any department of industrial effort; it is especially increased by the extension of the cultivated area of the globe, that is, by settling new countries. This last mode of increasing social power is also the easiest.

From the increase of industrial power there follows advance in science, fine arts, literature, and education, which react again on the social power to stimulate it and accelerate the rate of its activity, thus increasing its efficiency.

The point which here seems most important is to keep the sequence and relation of things distinct and clear. The notion that progress proceeds in the first instance from intellectual or moral stimuli, or that progress is really something in the world of thought, and not of sense, has led to the most disappointing and abortive efforts to teach and "elevate" inferior races or neglected classes. The ancestors of the present civilized races did not win their civilization by any such path; they built it up through centuries of toil from a foundation of surplus material means, which they won through improvements in the industrial arts and in the economic organization.

In this connection also we are brought to another question which must be regarded as one of the most important to be clearly answered for successful discussion of social problems. It is assumed to be the task of political economy or social science to account for "the degradation of mankind," or to find out the reasons for degradation of mankind as a preliminary step toward the cure of that degradation — which latter is taken to be the task of those sciences. But we are met at once by the question: Is the degradation of

mankind a problem? There have been many schools
of philosophers who have believed that men once were
pure and elevated and that they have fallen into degradation; the old theologians, the classical peoples, the
believers in a state of nature in which all was pure,
simple, and good, all held this notion in one form or another. For any of these schools it was undoubtedly a
reasonable question as to how the primitive bliss had
been lost.

At present, however, we no longer start from any assumptions of that kind at all. We know as a matter
of fact that mankind has never lived in any primitive
golden age or stage of nature; its earliest state was a
state of degradation, which was almost universal. If
we could trace the history of the race further back we
must believe that we should find the degradation universal. The question is not, therefore, how the race
ever fell into degradation, measuring degradation from
some ideal state of elevation; but, how the race ever
escaped from degradation as far as it has done so, reckon-
ing its present condition from what we know about the
primitive condition of the race. The mystery is not that
there is still a measure of degradation, but that there are
any men who have emerged from the primitive degradation.

It is evident that the difference in these two points
of view is as wide as any which could be imagined in this
domain. The latter is the only one which has any warrant in the facts of our knowledge. If it is true, then
all social discussion which proceeds from the other point
of view is mere fiction — and if we do not know which
is true, then we cannot yet make any fruitful discussion
at all.

For our present purpose, then, we observe that the

possession of social power in any society or in any generation, produces social movement, with expansion, reiterated new achievement, social hope and enthusiasm, with all that we call progress; and that this movement is so directed that degradation is behind it. The problem is not to account for degradation, because if we relax our efforts we shall fall back into it. The problem is how to maintain the effort and develop the power so as to keep up the movement away from it. It is true that the movement is by no means in a direct line away from primitive barbarism, and that it is subject to retrograde movements toward degradation; also that, even on its line of advance, it meets with and seems even to produce new forms of social degradation. But the fact that the primitive barbarism is to any degree left behind, or that it is even transformed, is the commanding fact which sets our point of view for us, and determines the interpretation which we must give to all the phenomena and to all the smaller and narrower movements. If we do not master the point which is here presented we can have no social science at all.

CONSEQUENCES OF INCREASED SOCIAL POWER

CONSEQUENCES OF INCREASED SOCIAL POWER

LET us ask what are some of the consequences of advancing social power. We ought, by taking up that question, to find out whether some of the social phenomena which interest us most are due to exuberant social power or are products of philosophy.

Social force is won by advance in the mechanic arts, or in science, or by the acquisition of more land. The history of inventions and discoveries, however, teaches us that they are never won arbitrarily, but always appear upon the lines of effort which lie directly in the path of human advance for the time being. Take the case of the two most important inventions which helped to break up the mediaeval order — those of gunpowder and printing. The invention of gunpowder came at the end of a series of efforts and experiments which had been continued for centuries for the purpose of attaining some more effective means of carrying on war, the chief business of the time. The invention of printing was produced out of the effort to find cheaper means of multiplying religious books, so as to meet the religious sentiment which was the most powerful sentiment of the time.

The discovery of America opened immense tracts of new land to settlement and use by the crowded populations of Western Europe. This latter gain was for a long time not available; it was necessary that the mechanic arts should go through a long development and come up to the point where they could assist in reaching the new land, before the latter could really affect the situation. The last hundred years have seen a prodigious advance in the mechanic arts which has made the new land of America and other continents easily available. The use of the new land has reacted upon the old population; it has made food cheap and abundant and this has, as it were, won wider space and given leisure. It has increased capital and thus made it possible to push on inventions; for it must be noticed that no man and no society can push on discovery and invention when the utmost powers are all the time strained to win means of subsistence from day to day; it is only when there is some surplus power already at one's disposal that time can be spent on science and invention, which do nothing for the time being for the support of the worker. The great advance in invention during the last hundred years is itself one consequence of increased social power.

The increase of social power and of capital has far outstripped the growth of population, and the inevitable result, as has already been said, has been to cause a demand for more men. An increase in numbers only increases the power, for the existing resources are by no means exploited to the utmost; more men mean more help, more accomplishment, greater well-being for all.

The United States is the country in which the two great elements of advancing industrial power, the new land and the improvements in the mechanic arts, have combined. It is therefore small marvel "that America marks the highest level not only of material well-being, but of intelligence and happiness, which the race has yet attained." Whether the causes of that fact have been correctly observed or the inferences from it have been correctly drawn, is another question.

The first consequence worth noticing, then, as following from the possession of exuberant social power, is that the elasticity and vitality of the society are high and that it can afford to take political and social risks. The field for social experimentation is very wide; as the society is going ahead all the time, its circumstances and surroundings are changing all the time. The "wisdom of the past" easily comes to be a by-word; prescription and precedent are odious, for they appear, not as protection and support, but as trammels. The sacrifice of past achievements goes on constantly and deserves no regret because the gain of the new creations is so very great. Is there any merit of men or institutions in this state of facts? There certainly is not. The men are easily wise when ignorance bears scarcely any penalties; the institutions easily win the credit of social effectiveness when their evil results, if they have any that are evil and hindering, are lost and overwhelmed in the great onward tide of power. If the real social tide is one of swelling and expanding creation or renovation, what can stop it? What can do it any great harm? How do we know, then, whether a given institution is assisting the advance or is hindering it? We certainly can get no light on that point by simply noting that the institution in question constitutes a part of the social aggregate which is moving on.

Another consequence of exuberant social power is that the sort of liberty which consists in pursuing one's own will without restraint becomes in a large measure possible, and that, of course, men are educated to believe in that kind of liberty. That kind of liberty is only possible in a society which possesses a large surplus of social power, very widely distributed — in that case each man is free with respect to nature, and then all are easily free with respect to each other. All men are easily equal when all are substantially well off, because the social pressure is slight; it is intense social pressure which draws the society out into ranks and classes. The relaxation of social pressure lets the ranks and classes come together again.

The three classes which form the skeleton of any aristocratic system, that is, of a system in which classes are widely separated from each other, are landlords, tenants, and laborers. The landlords are the holders of the land. The tenants are the holders of capital, because the land must be intensively cultivated, which cannot be done without capital. The laborers are those who have neither capital nor land and who seek a livelihood by putting personal services into the industrial organization.

If the population is dense and the land is all occupied, the possession of it is the possession of a natural monopoly of a thing which is in high demand. The landowners, therefore, possess an immense social advantage. The tenants and the whole middle capitalist class, which stands on the same social plane with them, possess the second social advantage. The laborers are those who possess neither. The three, therefore, are widely separated one from the other as respects the conditions of material well-being and earthly happinesss.

Suppose then that new social power is won — let it be assumed that some new mechanical force is obtained or that new areas of land are made accessible — what is the effect on the position of classes and on the relative difference in the status of classes? Plainly the social pressure is relaxed. The landlord finds that his monopoly is no longer worth as much as before, because the supply of it has been greatly increased. His rents decline and his tenants refuse any longer to be tenants because it is so easy to obtain land and become their own landlords. In their turn they find it harder to hire laborers; for when land is abundant intensive cultivation is no longer necessary and no longer pays. Capital is no longer indispensable for the cultivation, or a small amount of it will suffice. The laborer, therefore, is no longer differentiated from the other classes. He can easily obtain land and also the minimum of capital necessary to cultivate it. Thus the landlord comes down to be his own tenant and his own laborer. The tenant owns his own land and is his own laborer. The laborer becomes his own landlord and his own employer. The three classes have melted into one. It is no longer worth while to own a large estate in land, for the owner could not economically exploit it. A substantial equality of all on the middle rank is the inevitable social consequence, with democracy and all the other cognate political results.

At the same time, since capital is no longer so necessary to cultivate the ground, since the accumulation of capital goes on with constantly greater rapidity on account of the large proportion of the product to the labor under the new state of social power, and since the capital cannot be made productive without new supplies of labor, the men are on all accounts in demand and are worth more and more when measured in capital. The class, therefore, which was, under the first supposition, the worst off, obtains under the second supposition the command of the situation.

Is not this the correct interpretation of what we see going on about us? If it is, then the dogmatic or philosophical theorems, instead of being the cause of our social arrangements, are only the metaphysical dress which we have amused ourselves by imagining upon them. We are not free and equal because Jefferson put it into the Declaration of Independence that we were born so; but Jefferson could put it into the Declaration of Independence that all men are born free and equal because the economic relations existing in America made the members of society to all intents and purposes free and equal. It makes some difference to him who desires to attain to a correct social philosophy which of these ways of looking at the matter is true to the facts.

WHAT IS THE "PROLETARIAT"?

WHAT IS THE "PROLETARIAT"?

THE latest social agitation is marked by a fondness for big words and high-sounding phrases. The words which are most in favor are not those which are especially sonorous but those which have a philosophical clink and are a little pedantic; and as for the phrases, it is interesting and remarkable to notice in what mouths one may find a forlorn tatter of Hegelian philosophy. The leaders of the movement have created a dialect all their own, which has a strange and foreign sound to the uninitiated, and which suggests far-reaching observations on social philosophy to those who can find the occult significance of the phraseology. It is certain that it becomes a fashion and an affectation among the adherents of the movement to use the terms and bandy the catch phrases of the sect. They are largely the victims of the "phrase."

The dialect of a movement, however, is never a matter to be treated with indifference; in its origin, and in the mouths of the leaders, it had a motive and a logical sense. No American artisan can understand what he means when he talks about the "bourgeoisie" or the "proletariat." The former word certainly is entirely exotic; if it be explained to mean the middle class, it has no application to American society, and it has lost all the side signification which gives it its importance in Europe, when it is so explained. Such words are a part of the foreign dress of a set of ideas which are not yet naturalized. The word, however, cannot be given up by the leaders because the essence of their cause is in it with its acquired and historical side significations.

Proletariat should be a term of reproach. A proletarian at Rome was a man, who, having no property, could serve the state only with his offspring (*proles*), whom he gave to military service. No class in any modern state could correspond to that class at Rome. The only persons in a modern state to whom the name might perhaps have been transferred with some convenience are tramps and vagabonds, men without homes, family, calling, property, or reputation. The name has, however, been adopted and accepted without any dislike. It is a grand, foreign, classical, pedantic, and mysterious term, into which it is easy to distil all the side significations of class hatred and social rancor which any one may wish to transmit. After all it means nothing but what we used to call the masses, and it has just the same lack of definition and the same vagueness of limit in its social application. The new term, however, already begins to give precision to the social body which it specializes as a fighting faction. Such is the purpose and the utility of it.

If we try to define the limits of the class so named according to the present usage of language, it appears, in the first place, that there is no exclusion at the bottom. The term is most significant when used politically, and there are none who have political standing who are not available allies. Hence the proletariat includes all the dependent and delinquent classes so far as they have not lost political privileges.

It is the upper limit which is vague and undefined. Not all wage-receivers are in the proletariat, for those who get more than some vague limit or whose wages are paid at longer intervals (highly skilled laborers and salaried men) are not included. Not all the employed are in it, for high officials would not be recognized as belonging to it; not all laborers are in it, for we are all laborers except the little group of people of leisure. The President of the United States is an employee and a laborer. Not all capitalists are excluded from it, for many of its members have important savings. Here, however, we undoubtedly come nearest to a definition; for those who have savings would almost all break loose from the proletariat as soon as they recognized the sense of many of its propositions. This fact is so well known that those among the artisan and manual labor classes who have savings are regarded with peculiar dislike in the circles of proletarian agitation. The great millionaires are not denounced with such vigor as the "mean, sneaking workingman who has saved a few dollars which he has laid away in the savings bank, or who has built a little house and rents it for seven or eight dollars a month." "I have seen that class of men," said one orator, "march out by the bench-full as soon as I began to talk about interest and rent. I can talk to great capitalists and employers, but I can do nothing with those men." Still, on the other hand, not all who have not capital would be included; for there are plenty of people who have good incomes, all of which they spend, whose style of life would prevent them from being recognized as members of the proletariat. Peasants in Europe and farmers here do not belong to it; it is a city class quite as much as the bourgeoisie.

At the end of the last century a great revolution took place in which the bourgeoisie wrested political power from the nobles. The peasants and the town mob shared in the revolution and the latter finally got control of it. When the excesses had provoked reaction and order was restored, the bourgeoisie, as the most intelligent and capable section of the population, took control and secured, to some extent, their own ideal of civil liberty and economic prosperity. Their writers have generally agreed, therefore, in regarding the revolution as a great blessing, attended by some most lamentable, but perhaps inevitable excesses. It may yet be necessary to pay a heavy price for the revision of this opinion, for it is now claimed that revolution is a proper and, in fact, the only true and possible mode of social reform; that the bourgeoisie have arrogated to themselves all the gains of the last great revolution, and that another is needed to wrest from them, in turn, what they wrested from the nobles. The proletariat is, in fact, the faction which is formed for this assault. It finds its recruits where it can get them — among the discontented, the hot-headed, the ill-balanced, the ambitious, those who have nothing to lose, the flatterers of rising power, and other such persons who naturally gravitate toward a revolutionary party. It is plain that the thing to be struggled for is political power, not reform; in all great political struggles this is the real object, to gain political power and control of the force of the state.

The government of the bourgeoisie has been faulty enough, and there would be no reason to look with apprehension upon a transfer of the power of the state, if it were sought with the object of more thoroughly doing justice to all. The bourgeois government has threatened, and threatens now more than ever, to degenerate into a plutocracy. If sober and intelligent citizens could see some new power rising in the state, able and intelligently determined to correct and restrain this tendency, they could only welcome its coming.

So far, however, the proletariat has uttered nothing but truculent assertions about what it intends to do for itself against every other interest in the state. It seems to have noted all the sins and shortcomings of the bourgeoisie; but when we look to see what promise of reform it holds out, we find that it only cites the misdoings of the bourgeoisie as excuses and precedents for what it intends to do.

All the forces which gave the bourgeoisie the victory over the nobles are working in favor of the proletariat. The real question of moment is: What will they do with the state when they get control of it? That they will be utterly disappointed in the hopes which their leaders are now encouraging as to what they can do, is certain; but before they find it out society may go through a period of confusion and strife in which all the achievements of civilization will be put in jeopardy. Two parties are already taking shape for that contest. Mr. George recently called them, with the felicity which is his chief power, the House of Have and the House of Want; he defined them as those who are satisfied as things are and those who want to reform. Others have understood them to mean that the "land ought to belong, not to those who own it, but to those who want it." If it should appear upon due study that the latter is the more correct definition according to the facts, it will be another case in which Mr. George's felicity of expression far surpasses his power of analysis. We are indebted to him at least for an excellent terminology, which does away with the old clumsiness of "those-who-have" and "those-who-have-not."

WHO WIN BY PROGRESS?

WHO WIN BY PROGRESS?

In a former article I endeavored to show that the word proletariat, which is now coming into use as a name by which the wages-class is designated by itself and its friends, ought properly to be applied only to persons who live from hand to mouth, who have no definite industrial reliance for support, who have no capital and no reasonable chance of ever getting any, who touch elbows all the time with crime and occasionally fall into its power, and who increase the population through vice. No such class of persons as this exists in modern society, all assertions to the contrary notwithstanding.

Not even in the slums of great modern cities is there any class of persons who could be called proletarians and yet be distinguished from the dangerous and criminal class; for any honest man who finds himself there and is discontented can make his way, by moderate effort, to other places where the conditions are easier.

It is true that a poor man who is fond of the life of a great city cannot secure health, virtue, and capital for his children there at as easy a rate as he could in the country. What then? Shall his fellow-citizens, many of whom have fled to the country, not because they like it but because they can do better for their children in that way, be called upon to enable him to enjoy the delights of the city on the easy terms of the country? It has been asked whether there is not some remedy for the harsh contrasts of wealth and poverty in great cities. There is; it consists in a voluntary disruption of the city and a scattering of its population over the country. Now let us see who will go first — it is safe to predict that among the last to go will be the inhabitants of the slums.

In general, there is no man who is honest and industrious who cannot put himself in a way to maintain himself and his family, misfortune apart, in a condition of substantial comfort. We have any amount of reckless assertion to the contrary; it is asserted that the wages-class is in misery, and suffers from a great number of grievances; but no statement of this kind has ever been made in terms which could be subjected to examination.

It is also asserted that the wages-class have not shared in the advantages of progress. Here it should be noticed, in the first place, that so soon as a member of the non-capitalist class wins capital, he is reckoned with the capitalist class. What we should really need in order to test the question as to what chances the non-capitalists have had for a century past would be a census of the capitalists and non-capitalists a century ago, a similar census now, and a census of those who, in the meantime, have gone over from the latter to the former. The usual method of argument is to show that comparative poverty still exists, and this mode of argument is often extended still further, so that it amounts to arguing that our civilization has accomplished nothing at all because it can be shown that it has not yet got everything done.

In opposition to all this I maintain that the progress of the arts and sciences in the last hundred years has inured most of all to the benefit of the non-capitalists and that the social agitation which we are now witnessing is a proof of the strength, not of the weakness, of that class. If any one wants to see how weak classes have been treated in all ages of the world, let him note how landlords are treated now.

It is a common opinion that the effect of the extension of capital, especially in the form of machinery, is to displace human labor. That opinion is superficial and erroneous; the more complex the tools or machines, the more dependent the owner is on hired help to work them for him. The railroads do not employ fewer men than the canals and stage coaches which they displaced; the sewing machine does not give work to fewer women than the old hand sewing; a new loom calls for more help at another point or the number of new looms is multiplied until they need as much labor as the old ones. All these changes raise the social organization to higher power. We need more men and can support more men, and the machines set free those who are needed to sustain the higher organization by a more refined division of labor. The greater the power of the machines, the greater is the abundance of means of subsistence which the machines produce, and the greater, therefore, is the demand for productive services.

The effect of our progress in the arts and sciences within a century has, therefore, been:

1. That the civilized part of the earth, to say nothing of the other part, is able to support a greater population than ever before; the improvements in transportation have brought within the reach of civilized man vast areas of the earth's surface which were not available a century ago. This fact in itself, for those who can appreciate its significance, is enough to show what class of the population must be chiefly benefited.

2. It has been made cheap and easy for those who had nothing but strong hands and good will to get away

from the crowded centers of population to acquire almost without cost land which would richly repay their labor, and to send their products to those markets, however distant, which would return them the largest amount of other products in exchange. Hence the accumulation of capital has outstripped the growth of population, great as the latter has been. It certainly would be a strange social phenomenon if the century which has seen the new continents of America, Australia, and Africa opened to the use of civilized man had also seen the mass of civilized men reduced to lower comfort than they previously enjoyed. The economists and social philosophers who have given countenance to this notion have not only made a professional blunder but also incurred a great responsibility.

3. It is said, however, that the gains have all been won by landlords and capitalists. In truth the vast increase in the production of means of subsistence, won at constantly diminishing outlay of labor and capital, has lowered money prices and made money wages worth more, and has, at the same time, lowered the rate of interest on capital and increased the demand for labor. It is not at all astonishing that the results have combined and accumulated so as to produce a crisis.

4. It is the fact, also, that the improvements have lowered the pressure of population at the old centers and have, therefore, lowered the rent of land, so that landlords are in the way of being ruined and the old landed aristocracies seem doomed to extinction.

It seems to be believed that we can have all these changes, and that the non-capitalist class can win all the benefit from them without any correlative inconvenience; but that is impossible in the nature of things. The changes which have come about have made life

more stringent and exacting for everybody. The rewards of prudence and intelligence are more ample
and the penalties of heedlessness and adherence to
routine are greater than ever before; every one is
forced to "keep up." The more the machines do, the
more the rational animal, man, needs to bring brains
to bear to rise above the machines. In a sense, our
whole society is machine-ridden; it is our fate; it is
the price we pay for living in an age of steam, with all
the glories of which we boast. The man who has won
most of all from the progress is the man who possesses
executive power and organizing ability. We get together vast masses of capital and hundreds of laborers,
and the happiness or misery of thousands comes to
depend on the man whose judgment and knowledge
decide what shall be done, and how. We cannot break
out of this intense and exacting social organization
without sacrificing our means of comfort and throwing
thousands into distress; hence we pay the man who
can manage the organization a monopoly price for his
rare and indispensable abilities.

Next to these, however, who are not capitalists and
who are so few that they can hardly be spoken of as a
class, the wage-earners have won. They run a greater
risk than formerly of interruptions of work and of being
compelled to sacrifice routine knowledge which they have
acquired. These are weighty risks, and they are weightier
in proportion as the organization is more intense, because
the higher the organization the harder it is, having once
fallen out of it, to get into it again. What the landlords
and capitalists will do under the strain which the changes
have thrown on them remains to be seen.

The new position of the wage-earner, economically
speaking, is the cause of his gain in political power.

It is the reason why flatterers and sycophants cluster about him; it is the reason why the laws are warped in his favor, to give him privileges and to force others to yield to him. In our own experience within a year it has been evident that the wage-earners could win their demands when they limited them to a certain measure, that is to say, it has appeared that they were the strong party in the market. They are so, and until the population increases or the land is all taken up they will remain so. As between that which has been achieved and the struggle to achieve, the odds are now largely in favor of the latter.

FEDERAL LEGISLATION ON RAILROADS

FEDERAL LEGISLATION ON RAILROADS

DANIEL WEBSTER once said: "A strong conviction that something must be done is the parent of many bad measures." He made the observation early in his career; but it was a sign of his statesmanlike power to detect the common element in heterogeneous incidents of public life that he should have made it; scarcely a year passes which does not give us a new illustration of its truth. The next instance of headlong legislation with which this country is threatened is an act regulating railroads.

Two fallacies are of constant repetition in propositions for more government regulation. The first and widest is to argue that competition is not perfect in its action and does not satisfactorily solve the problem; it is inferred that we must have some form of government regulation. Plainly this inference is a *non sequitur*, unless it can be shown that government regulation will produce perfect and satisfactory results; or that regulation, although imperfect, will just complement and make up for the imperfections of competition. The second fallacy is illustrated when, after trying for a long time to solve a problem of the social order without success, we declare, in despair, that the state will have to take it in hand and legislate about it. This is a worse *non sequitur* than the other.

Both these fallacies are involved in the current arguments for the proposed legislation about railroads. Railroads are still new and still in their infancy. It seems reasonable to believe that they are capable of

great development beyond what any one can now foresee; new inventions are reasonably sure to cause transformations in railroad business and methods.   We have
only just reached the point where a few men are competent to manage great lines of railroad on their technical
side; we have only just begun to educate men for the
railroad business as a profession.   Railroad men do not
seem yet to have any code of right behavior or right
management between themselves — people often deride
the professional code of lawyers or doctors, but the
value of such a code is seen if we take a case like the one
before us, where a new profession has not yet developed
a code.   The social and economic questions raised by
railroads and about railroads are extremely difficult and
complicated; we have not, so far, accomplished much
of anything toward solving them by experience or theory.
The discussion, so far as it has yet gone, has shown only
that we have the task yet before us and that, so far, all
has been a struggle of various interests to use railroads
for their own advantage.   The true solution of the only
proper legislative problem, *viz.*, how to adjust all the interests so that no one of them can encroach upon the
others, has scarcely been furthered at all.   It is only
necessary to take up a volume of the evidence taken by
one of the Congressional committees on this subject, or
any debate about it which has arisen in Congress, to see
how true it is that conflicting interests are struggling
for advantage over each other.

The railroad question is far wider than the scope of
any proposed legislation with regard to it; it is so wide
that in any period of five or ten years new phases of it
come to the front and occupy public attention.   Just
now the prominent phase is the effect of competition on
a weak market; for the time being, the means of trans-

portation seem to have been multiplied in excess of the demand. The railroad monopoly is in the position of any monopoly which has overproduced its market. Pooling would be the mode of applying combination and restriction of production to this business; that pooling would suit the condition of things just at this moment, and would be a corrective for the evils which just now command public attention, is very probable. But the country is undoubtedly destined to enter on a new period of expanding a hitherto unknown prosperity, and what would be the effects of pooling on a strong and rising market under great demand for transportation? If a law is passed it becomes a rigid and unavoidable constraint. It is not, however, my purpose to argue that pooling is a good thing or a bad thing; the arguments upon that point are so strong upon either side that a case is made out for neither. Under such circumstances, to legislate is to decide, and to commit the interests at stake to a decision which is immature and is founded on nothing but the notion that something must be done. Competition has borne not only upon the rates but also upon the quality of cars and stations, upon speed and punctuality, upon parlor car and other conveniences. What would be the effect of strict pooling upon these?

The second point which seems now to occupy attention is the effect of railroads upon natural distances; it is assumed that it must be wrong that railroads should make a place which is near further off than one which is remote. It is a matter of familiar experience that railroads do invert relations of distance and make places which are two hundred miles off economically nearer than places one hundred miles off; and in doing this they also invert the interests of a great many people. It is a rash and mischievous undertaking to try to offset or correct this by arbitrary legislation. It is not possible to draft an intelligible and workable regulation to do it. The short-haul clause in the bill now before the Senate is already a subject of disputed interpretation, and whenever the courts come to act upon it they will interpret it as its language seems to require, not as anybody now says that it is intended to mean. The interests of the extreme West constantly demand that the full power of railroads to annihilate distance and time shall be exerted in their favor; during the last summer, Senator Edmunds pointed out to his Vermont constituents their grievance, in the fact that railroads pour into the Eastern market, in competition with them, all the products of the West — *i.e.*, do just what the West demands. Cheap freights westward benefit Eastern manufacturers and Western consumers while they injure Western manufacturers; cheap freights eastward favor Western farmers and cattle raisers and Eastern consumers while they injure Eastern farmers. How can the legislator meddle in this great complex of interests without doing harm to everybody, especially when he goes about it without any theoretical or practical principles to guide him, with nothing but the conviction that many things in the existing order are not as we should like them to be and that something must be done?

The railroad question, properly speaking, I repeat, goes far beyond the points which are now attracting attention. The railroad company has relations to its employees, to the state which taxes its property, to the municipalities whose streets its line crosses, to adjoining real-estate owners, to the legislators and editors who want free passes, etc., etc. In all these relations there are two parties, for even a railroad company has rights. Competing lines have relations to each other, and these often raise questions in which there is no simple "justice" — the competing lines may not be subject to the same legislative regulations. A country three thousand miles in extent is not much troubled by the extra prejudice which is imported into the question of long and short haul when it seems to include favor to foreigners at the expense of citizens; but if there is anything real in the latter grievance it is difficult to see why it should not also exist in a concealed form here. Finally, it cannot be forgotten that the railroad issue includes the question as to how those who have contributed the capital to build the road are to obtain their remuneration. If the state undertakes to regulate all the rest, it will see itself forced at last to regulate this also. Hitherto the stockholders have been left to get their remuneration out of their own enterprise if they could; if they could not, they have been left to make the best of it. If, however, the state interferes with the whole management of their enterprise, how will it at last escape the justice of the demand that it compensate them or secure them a return on their investment?

In the present state of the case it behooves us to remember that, in the varying phases of the industrial world of our time, first one interest gets a chance and then another; it is not in human wit to stand over this system and correct or adjust it so as to offset all the special combinations of industrial advantage and disadvantage. It is no question whether we like living in an age of steam or not; the steam-engine was invented in the course of time, just when all the antecedents which were necessary for it had been provided; it has come to stay and we must learn to live with it. We have sung a great many paeans over it, but it may be doubted whether we have found out yet what an uncomfortable social comrade it may prove to be when it is full grown. Many of its workings are very capricious in the chances which they throw in the way of one man or which they take away from another. Can we do anything wiser than to take the good chances and the ill chances over a period of years and make the best of them?

What we need most in regard to all social problems, if we want to solve them either by voluntary action or by legislation, is knowledge. If we could have a commission to study railroads, if its powers were only such as are required to enable it to get information and to investigate cases, and if its *personnel* were such as to inspire confidence that it was capable of conducting the investigation and that it would conduct it disinterestedly from the standpoint of justice to all interests, the commission might be very useful. It is very probable that legislation might ultimately prove necessary or expedient, but it would not then be an embodiment of anybody's whim or view of the matter but would be guided by experience and observation. Blundering experiments in legislation cannot be simply abandoned if they do not work well; even if they are set aside, they leave their effects behind; and they create vested interests which make it difficult to set them aside.

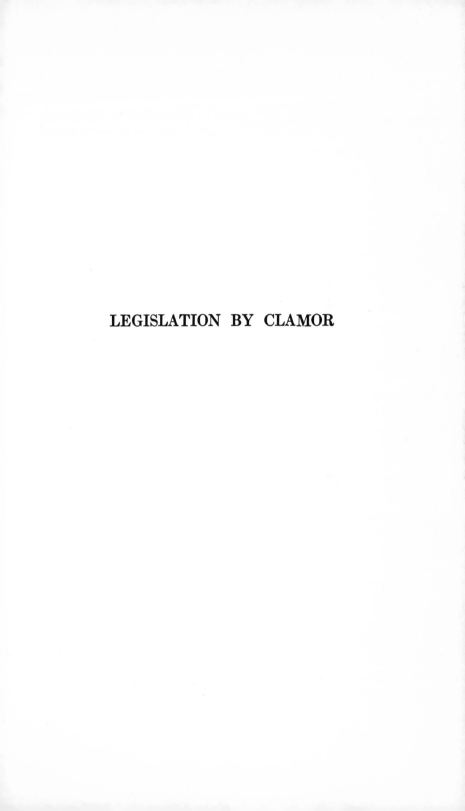

LEGISLATION BY CLAMOR

LEGISLATION BY CLAMOR

It is already evident that one feature of the "new time" into which we are hastening will be the subjection of legislatures to the pressure of groups of persons who are capable of controlling newspapers or combining votes. Under the old notions of legislation, the duty of legislators was to study carefully the details of proposed legislation, to debate and discuss measures, and so, by deliberation, to arrive at decisions as to what should be enacted. The notion was that the statesman should know what he intended to do and should consider the proper means of reaching the desired result. This theory of legislation never has been very thoroughly put into practice anywhere, but now the idea seems to be that it is antiquated, that we do not intend to seek a more complete realization of it as a reform in legislation, but that we abandon it altogether. At the same time, therefore, that there is a vast extension of the field of legislation, we abandon all sound traditions as to the method of legislative activity. Legislative bodies not only lay themselves open to be acted upon by outside influences, but they submit to clamor more than to any other influence. The tendency can be traced through the legislation of France, England, and the United States, during the last twenty years. If a faction of any kind assails the legislature with sufficient determination, they carry their point although the sincere opinion of nearly all who vote for the measure may be that it is foolish, or idle, or mischievous, or crude, or irrational, or extravagant, or otherwise improper.

Opinions differ greatly as to what it is that is "falling" or "going to decay" just at present. These phenomena support the notion that it is "the state" which is passing away. On the one hand, the highest wisdom of those who want anything now is to practice terrorism, to make themselves as disagreeable as possible, so that it shall be necessary to conciliate them, and those who appeal to reason find themselves disregarded. On the other hand, the public men seek peace and quiet by sacrificing any one who cannot or does not know enough to make a great clamor in order to appease a clamorous faction. It is thought to be the triumph of practical statesmanship to give the clamorers something which will quiet them, and a new and special kind of legislative finesse has been developed, *viz.*, to devise projects which shall seem to the clamorous petitioners to meet their demands, yet shall not really do it.

The most important case of legislation of this kind which has been passed in this country is the Bland Silver Bill. It contains no rational plan for accomplishing any purpose whatever. It never had any purpose which could be stated intelligibly. It does not introduce the double standard, does not help debtors, and if it favors silver-miners at all, does so in an insignificant degree. It satisfies the vanity of a few public men, quiets the clamor of a very noisy faction who did not know what they wanted and do not know whether they have got it or not, complicates the monetary system of the country, and contains possibilities of great mischief or great loss. It was passed as a patched-up compromise under the most rhythmical and best sustained clamor ever brought to bear on a public question. Those who raised the clamor went off content because they thought that they had obtained *something*, and they now resist the repeal of the law because they would feel that they had lost *something*.

The oleomargarine law is another case. The scientific evidence submitted to the committee of Congress was clear and uniform, that oleomargarine is a substitute for butter, just as maple sugar is a substitute for cane sugar; that it is not adulterated and not unwholesome. If it had been regarded as unwholesome, in spite of this evidence, or if it had been the purpose to make it recognizable, measures having these purposes in view, however ridiculous (like Senator Blair's proposition to color it red or blue), or however mischievous, would at least have been rational. The law to tax it two cents a pound was not rational, even with the object of practicing protectionism in favor of the dairymen. If the assertions made about the profits of the manufacture, and about the supply and demand of butter in the market, are even approximately true, then the tax comes out of the manufacturers, and is simply a toll levied by the state on the manufacture of a new commodity. It cannot avail to limit the production; the state simply mulcts the producers of a part of their profits. The enactment was a case of sacrificing to a clamorous faction the rights and interests of others who were absent.

The doctors of the Koran, at Mecca and Medina, were told that coffee, when the plant was yet new to them, was deleterious. They straightway forbade the faithful to drink it, and obedience or disobedience to this law embittered the strife of sects. History is full of similar prejudice against what is new and similar state interposition against improvement. If anybody

who finds butter beyond his means wants to use oleomargarine, it is an improvement to give him the chance
to do so.

The laws about convict labor are other instances.
The Illinois Bureau of Labor Statistics says that the
clamor is a proof that something is wrong, and that the
clamorers are not bound to solve the problem or propose a remedy; that they need only present their objections to what is and demand that the powers that be
find a remedy. The labor bureaus themselves might be
offered as a case of legislation by clamor; the necessity
of justifying their own existence, and of conciliating the
laborers, makes labor bureau literature one of the trials
of the day. The doctrine that clamor is a proof of a
grievance is so easy and summary that it is sure to be
popular, and its broad availability for the purposes of
the world-betterers need not be pointed out. It is also
characteristic of this school of thought that the legislature is commanded to find a remedy for the alleged
grievance. A legislature, if it acts rightly, has to recon-
cile interests and adjust rights. In so doing it can
rarely give to any one interest a clear and prompt remedy
for what that interest chooses to consider a grievance.
Are convicts to be idle? Are the tax-payers to be indefinitely burdened? These are parts of the problem
of convict labor; but, so far from having made a comprehensive solution of the convict labor question, including
these elements of it, the people who have assumed to
direct legislation show that they have not even mastered
the comparison of the three plans proposed for using
prison labor.

The Illinois Commissioner says that a wrong ought
not to be overlooked because it is a little wrong. That
is a thoroughly sound doctrine, and it would be easy

to bring from labor bureau literature illustrations of the wrong of neglecting it; but business competition is not a wrong at all, and convict labor legislation is not based on any established grievance of free laborers, nor is it adapted to remedy any grievance, if one existed.

The latest case of legislation by clamor is the Inter-State Railroad Act. Clamor has forced through a crude measure. What does it aim at? What are the means by which it attempts to attain its object? These are the questions which should go before legislation. No one can answer them in regard to this bill. *Something* has been done, and the clamor subsides. To act in this way is to set all reason and common sense at defiance. Thousands of voters would no doubt have been incensed at Congress if it had done nothing. They will not read the bill, and could not understand it if they did; but they are satisfied that something has been done. To do a bad thing in legislation is far worse than to do nothing.

People who study the railroad law, and who cannot understand it, say that it will be all right if the President only appoints a good commission, and that the law will mean whatever the commission interprets it to mean. We have come very far away from old and sound traditions of good government if we pin our faith for the adjustment of rights on the wisdom and integrity of men, and not on impersonal institutions. Where has the President this reserve of wise, good, and competent men? Where did he get them? Where does he keep them? The railroads, banks, insurance companies, and factory owners of the country are all eagerly looking for just that kind of men, and are ready to pay them from ten to thirty thousand dollars a year. The President must keep them close, therefore, for the state only pays from three to eight or ten thousand. To read the cur-

rent discussion of this law one would think that our railroad system only needed to be put into the hands of five
men whom the President can pick out in a few weeks and
who will be able to solve all the problems, when the fact
is that the railroads have expended energy and money
without stint for years to do just that very thing, and
have themselves employed commissioners at high salaries to try to solve their problems for them. It is true
that they did not look for their commissioners among
ex-members of Congress.

In all these cases it is immaterial what opinion one may
hold as to the subject matter of the legislation or what
view one may think correct about the questions involved.
The point is that this legislation by clamor fits no consistent idea of the matter, proceeds on no rational plan,
settles no question, but only produces new confusion
and new evils, carrying the difficulties forward in constantly increasing magnitude as the consequences of
legislative blunders are added to the original ills.

THE SHIFTING OF RESPONSIBILITY

THE SHIFTING OF RESPONSIBILITY

IF there are any ethical propositions which may be accepted as reasonably established, the following are among the number: to every one his own; that responsibility should be equal to liberty; that rights and duties are correlative; and that those should reap the consequences who have set in action the causes. The socialistic and semi-socialistic propositions which are before the public are immoral in that they all sin against these ethical principles.

We are using, at the same time, two weights and measures. We have at the same time two sets of dogmas, one for politics and the other for social matters. We affirm that all men are equal. If they are so, and if a state can be founded on the assumption that they are so, then each one of them must take his share in the burdens of the society; especially must each one take the responsibility for himself. No sooner, however, is this inference drawn than we are told that there are some people who are not equal to others and who cannot be held to the same duties or responsibilities. They are weak, ignorant, undisciplined, poor, vicious, or otherwise unfit. It is asserted that the strong, learned, well-trained, rich, and virtuous are bound to take care of the aforesaid persons. The democratic doctrine in politics is that wisdom resides in the masses; that it is a false and aristocratic doctrine to maintain that the educated or trained men are better fitted to direct common public interests than the uneducated; that, in fact, the educated men fail conspicuously whenever they undertake to

lead, and that there is a resource of strong, untrained
common sense in the masses on which a state may be
built in complete security.

No sooner, however, have we accepted this doctrine
as orthodox and indisputable matter of political faith,
than we are told that educated men and others who have
enjoyed exceptional advantages, or who have acquired
any of those forms of training which make men better
— not than other men, but than they would themselves
have been without the expenditure of capital and labor
— have a duty to perform: to lead, guide, and instruct
the real rulers.   It is asserted that when the masses
go astray it is the fault of the educated classes who did
not instruct them.   Therefore we arrive at this doctrine:
if a young man desires to fit himself to discharge the
duties of life well, he needs to spend his youth in study
and work, he needs to accumulate capital and to subject
himself to discipline.   This is a duty which is incumbent
on all and is enjoined on all, without exception.   If,
however, some conform to it and some do not, let it
not be maintained that the former shall have wealth and
honor and power in the society.   On the contrary, only
the latter shall have those things; for, since all the things
which improve men are hard and irksome, and the mass
of mankind shirk them, and the power rests with the
mass, the "minority" receive as their share the function
of persuading the "majority" to do right, if they can,
and if they do not succeed, they bear the responsibility
for whatever goes wrong.   Such a doctrine is profoundly
immoral, for there is a dislocation involved in it between
work and reward.

We encourage our children to earn and save and we
stimulate them to look forward to the accumulation of
wealth.   We explain to them the advantages of capital.

We point out| to them the woes of poverty, the con-
sequences of improvidence, the penalties of idleness;
the better parents we are the more we do this.   We
try to make them understand the world in which they
live, so that they may hold sound principles and direct
their energies wisely.   The motive and purpose is to
avoid the penalties which they see unwise men suffer, and
to attain to the material prosperity and comfort which
all men need and desire.   Some obey;   some do not.
Those who obey might think that they are justified,
then, in having, holding, and enjoying what they have
earned.   They might say that wealth is a reward for
duty done, and that the faithful workman is entitled
to sit down and enjoy the fruits of his labor.

If one of them draws any such inference he will be
immediately corrected by the new philosophy.   He will
be told that wealth is a duty and a responsibility;   that
he holds it not for himself, but for others;   and if he asks
for whom, he will be told that he is only a trustee for
those who did not obey the teachings of boyhood about
industry, temperance, prudence, and frugality.   He
tried to take his own course and let others take theirs;
he tried to do right and prosper and let others do ill and
suffer if they preferred;   but he finds, as a result of his
course, that he has made himself responsible for those
who took the other course, while they are not responsible
for anybody, not even for themselves.   This new kind of
trustee also is not allowed to administer his trust for the
benefit of the beneficiaries, according to his own judgment;   that is done for him by the doctors of the new
philosophy.   His function is limited to producing and
saving.

If a man, in the organization of labor, employs other
men to assist in an industrial enterprise, it was formerly

thought that the rights and duties of the parties were defined by the contract which they made with each other. The new doctrine is that the employer becomes responsible for the welfare of the employees in a number of respects. They do not each remain what they were before this contract, independent members of society, each pursuing happiness in his own way according to his own ideas of it. The employee is not held to any new responsibility for the welfare of the employer; the duties are all held to lie on the other side. The employer must assure the employed against the risks of his calling, and even against his own negligence; the employee is not held to assure himself, as a free man with all his own responsibilities, although the scheme may be so devised that the assurance is paid for out of his wages; he is released from responsibility for himself. The common law recognizes the only true and rational liability of employers, *viz.*, that which is deducible from the responsibilities which the employer has assumed in the relation. The new doctrines which are preached and which have been embodied in the legislation of some countries, are not based on any rational responsibility of the employer but on the fact that the employee may sometimes find himself in a very hard case, either through his own negligence or through unavoidable mischances of life, and that there is nobody else who can be made to take care of him but his employer.

In the advance of the industrial organization it has come about that interests have been subdivided and rights have been created in the various interests. The most important of these divisions is that between a specific interest, like that of the mortgagees or bond-holders, and a contingent interest, like that of the title-holder or the stock-holder. The tendency to separate these interests, and to define the rights corresponding to them, is rich in advantage to different classes in the community and in advantage to the industrial development. The specific interest in the gains of the enterprise is that of the landlord, mortgagee, bondholder, or employee; the contingent interest in the gains is that of the title-holder, stock-holder, tenant, or employer. The specific interest is always free from risk and excluded from control. The maintenance of this separation of interests is not possible unless there is the most firm enforcement of contracts. In some of the cases the difficulty is that the specific interest tries to get a share in the contingent gains, when it is found out that there are such. In other cases, the contingent gain not having been realized, those who own it try to encroach upon the specific or guaranteed interest. If it is possible for either to succeed, then a contract relation is transformed into a relation of "heads I win, tails you lose." The responsibilities of the parties are made to vary from the engagements into which they have entered. The current attacks on landlords and creditors are, therefore, radically unjust, and the insecurity for the more refined relations and interests which arises from the weakening of the contract relation is injurious to the whole industrial organization.

In short, the policy which we are invited to accept is one in which every duty which a man accomplishes is made the basis, not for rights and rewards, but for new duties and subjection to new demands. Every duty which is neglected becomes a ground for new rights and claims. The well-to-do man is to do without things which his means might buy for himself in order that he may pay taxes to provide those same things in a public way for people who have not earned them. The man who by toil has tried to get the knowledge which alone enables men to judge, is not to have the deciding voice, but is to stand behind the man who has neglected to get knowledge while the latter gives the deciding voice, and to take or avert the consequences. All this is preached to us on the ground that it is public-spirited, unselfish, and altruistic. It is immoral to the very last degree and opposed to the simplest common sense. It cannot fail to avenge itself in social consequences of the most serious character.

THE STATE AS AN "ETHICAL PERSON"

THE STATE AS AN "ETHICAL PERSON"

WE meet often, in current social discussion, with the assertion that "the state is an ethical person." This is not a proposition concerning a relation of things, which is said to be true, nor is it an observation of fact which can be verified by a new examination; it is an assertion in regard to the standpoint which should be adopted or the mode of conceiving of the matter which should be accepted. Such assertions are, no doubt, extremely useful and fruitful when they are correct; but they are also very easily made, which implies that they are very liable to be incorrect, and they furnish broad ground for fallacious deductions. Let us examine this one.

The student of social welfare finds that the limit of social well-being of the society in the progress of time depends on the possibility of increasing the capital faster than the numbers increase. But so soon as he comes to consider the increase of capital, he finds himself face to face with ethical facts and forces. Capital is the fruit of industry, temperance, prudence, frugality, and other industrial virtues. Here then the welfare of society is found to be rooted in moral forces, and the relation between ethical and social phenomena is given in terms of actual facts and not of rhetorical abstractions. It comes to this: that the question how well off we can be depends at last on the question how rational, virtuous, and enlightened we are. Hence the student of society finds that if the society has developed all the social and economic welfare which its existing moral development will justify or support, then there is no way to get any more welfare, save by advancing the moral development. It is possible that there may be obstacles in the political or social organization which prevent the actual moral power of the people from attaining its maximum result in social and material welfare. In any existing society there are such obstacles, and the field of reform lies in dealing with them. But if we may imagine such obstacles to be removed and all the social machinery to be perfect, we should then have distinctly before us the fact that for every increase of social well-being we must provide by ourselves becoming better men.

It is only putting the same statement in another form to say that whatever deficiencies there are in our society which are important or radical — that is to say, which surpass in magnitude the harm which comes from defects in the social machinery — are due to deficiencies in our moral development. We are as well off as we deserve to be. We are as well off as such moral creatures as we are can be. The solidarity of society holds us together so that, although some of us are better than others in industrial virtue, we must all go together.

Now arises the interesting question: Where can we get any more moral power? Where is there any spring or source of it which we have not yet used? What new stimulus can be applied to the development of moral energy to quicken or intensify it? When, therefore, we are told that the state is an ethical person, the question we have to ask is this: Is the state a source of moral energy which can contribute what is needed? Can it bring to us from some outside source that which, by the facts of the case, we lack? If it can, then indeed it is the most beneficent patron we possess; it has a function which is on the same plane with that ascribed by some theological doctrines to the Holy Spirit. Or, if not that, then it has a function similar to that of the church and the school, only far more elevated and incomparably more direct and effective; and it executes this function, not by acting on the minds and hearts of men, but by mechanical operations, regulations, and ceremonial activities. If the assertion that the state is an ethical person does not mean this, if it does not mean that, in the midst of our social struggles and perplexities, the state is an independent source of power which can be called in to help, by contributing the ethical energy which we need, then that assertion is an empty jingle of words, or, at most, it refers vaguely to the general advantage of the association and co-operation of men with each other. It appears, therefore, that the assertion that we ought to conceive of the state as an ethical person does not rest upon any such solid analysis of the facts of life and the nature of the state as would make it a useful and fruitful proposition for further study of social phenomena, but that it is a product of the phrase-mill. It is one of those mischievous dicta which seem to say something profound; but, upon examination, prove to say nothing which will bear analysis. In current discussion, especially of state interference, this proposition is always invoked just when the real crisis of discussion comes, and it serves to cover the lack of true analysis and sound thinking.

If we turn aside from the special field of social discussion for a moment to call up accepted principles of ethics and of sound thinking, we shall find it undisputed that the source of ethical energy is in the hearts and minds of human beings and not anywhere else. Institutions of which the family, the church, and the school are the chief, which have for their purpose the development of ethical energy in the rising generation, cost energy and give it back. The institution itself produces nothing. It is like any other machine; it only gives direction and combination or division to the forces which are put into it. It is the moral force of the parent and teacher which develops the moral force of the child; the institution is only a convenient arrangement or apparatus for bringing the one to bear on the other. The institution is at its best when it allows this personal contact and relationship to be most direct and simple — that is, when the institution itself counts for the least possible. When we turn to the state, we find that it is not even in nature and purpose, or pretence, an institution like those mentioned. It has its purposes, which are high and important, and for these it needs moral power and consumes moral power. The family, the church, and the school are preparing men and women of moral power for the service of the state; they hand them over, such as they are, to be citizens and members of the commonwealth. In that position their moral capacities are drawn upon; speaking of the society as a whole, we must say that they are used up. The practice of virtue increases virtue, whether it be in the state or the store, the profession or the handicraft; but there is no more reason on that account to call the state an ethical person than there is to apply the same high-sounding epithet to trades or professions. There is no sense in which it may be properly used in the one case in which it would not equally well apply to the other.

THE NEW SOCIAL ISSUE

THE NEW SOCIAL ISSUE

THE effect of the great improvements in the arts during the last century is to produce a social and economic order which is controlled by tremendous forces, and which comprehends the whole human race; which is automatic in the mode of its activity; which is delicate and refined in its susceptibility to the influence of interferences. It is therefore at once too vast in its magnitude and scope for us to comprehend it, and too delicate in its operation for us to follow out and master its details.

Under such circumstances the conservative position in social discussion is the only sound position. We do not need to resist all change or discussion — that is not conservatism. We may, however, be sure that the only possible good for society must come of evolution not of revolution. We have a right to condemn, and to refuse our attention to flippant and ignorant criticisms or propositions of reform; we can rule out at once all plans to reconstruct society, on anybody's system, from the bottom up. We may refuse to act to-day under the motive of redressing some wrong done, ignorantly perhaps, one or two or more centuries ago; or under the motive of bringing in a golden age which we think men can attain to, one or two or more centuries in the future. We may refuse to listen to any propositions which are put forward with menaces and may demand that all who avail themselves of the right of free discussion shall remain upon the field of discussion and refrain from all acts until they have duly and fairly convinced the reason and conscience of the community.

We may demand that no strain shall be put on any of
our institutions, such as majority rule, by a rash determination to override dissent and remonstrance and to
realize something for which there has been collected a
hasty majority, animated by heterogeneous motives and
purposes.

The institutions which we possess have cost something.
Few people seem to know how much — it is one of the
great defects in our education that we are not in a position to teach the history of civilization in such a way as
to train even educated men to know the cost at which
everything which to-day separates us from the brutes
has been bought by the generations which have preceded
us.   As time goes on we can win more, but we shall win
it only in the same way, that is, by slow and painful toil
and sacrifice, not by adopting some prophet's scheme of
the universe; therefore we have a right to ask that all
social propositions which demand our attention shall be
practical in the best sense, that is, that they shall aim
to go forward in the limits and on the lines of sound
development out of the past, and that none of our interests shall be put in jeopardy on the chance that
Comte, or Spencer, or George, or anybody else has solved
the world-problem aright.   If anybody has a grievance
against the social order, it is, on the simplest principles
of common sense, the right of busy men whose attention
he demands that he shall set forth in the sharpest and
precisest manner what it is; any allegation of injustice
which is vague is, by its own tenor, undeserving of
attention.

Finally, we each have a right to have our liberty re-
spected in such form as we have inherited it under the
laws and institutions of our country.   The fashion of
the day is to sneer at this demand and to propose to make

short work of it so soon as enough power shall have been collected to carry out the projects of certain social sects. Let us, however, give a moment's calm attention to it; the point is worth it, for here is where the tendencies now at work in society are to meet in collision. I do not mean by liberty any power of self-determination which all should allow to each or which each may demand of God, or nature, or society; I mean by it the aggregate of rights, privileges, and prerogatives which the laws and institutions of this country secure to each one of us to-day as conditions under which he may fight out the struggle for existence and the competition of life in this society. I call this liberty a thing which we have a "right" to demand, because, as a fact, the laws give us that right now; when I speak of rights and liberty, therefore, I wish to be understood as standing upon the law of the land and not on any platform of metaphysical or ethical deduction.

Such being the notion of liberty, it is plain that it stands on the line where right and might meet; where war passes over into peace, the guarantees of rights under law taking the place of the domination of might under lawlessness, and the limitation of rights by other rights taking the place of the limitation of powers by other powers. Many of the proposed changes in society aim to alter the demarcation of rights, and they aim to do this, not for a fuller realization of peace, order, liberty, and security, by a nicer adjustment of rights, but they avowedly aim to do it in the interest of certain groups and classes of persons. At this point, therefore, parties must be formed and issues must be joined. On one side is liberty under law, rights and interests being adjusted by the struggle of the parties under the natural laws of the social and industrial order and within

barriers set by impersonal and "equal" legislation; on
the other, state regulation, consisting of legislation
planned to warp rights and interests in favor of selected
groups under some *a priori* and arbitrary notion of
justice, and administered by persons who, by the fundamental principle of the system, must assume to be competent to decide what ought to be done with us all and
who must at the same time themselves be above the
most fundamental weaknesses of human nature. There
is room for a vast range and variety of opinion and sentiment on either side of this issue, but it is the issue which
is upon us and on which every man must take sides.

One of the world-improvers said: "We must know
how to do violence to mankind in general, in order to
make them happy." He naïvely expressed the sentiment which animates the whole school of opinion to
which he belonged, from its extremest right wing to its
extremest left wing. They must of course know just
what men need to render them happy and they must be
fearless in doing violence, that is, in trampling on liberty
and causing misery, in order to enforce happiness.

If now we look to see who are to be the victims of the
proposed re-adjustment of society, it is plain that they
are men who, at this moment, hold the world of trade, industry, finance, transportation, law, and politics in their
hands; and they hold it, not because they inherited it
or because they belong to any privileged class, but they
have obtained control of it by natural selection and because they have made it. Is it likely that they will be
intimidated? Are they men to be coerced by clamor, or
terrorism, or denunciation, or threats? So far there has
scarcely even been discussion except on one side, and the
disputants on that side are beginning already to count
the battle won. It takes a long time for men who are

absorbed in practical life to find out what the literary men are, for the time being, interested in, and still longer for them to make up their minds that talk is to come to anything; that point has not yet been reached, even by the educated community, in regard to the issue which I have described. When it is reached we shall see whether the people of the United States have lost their political sense or not.

It is impossible to look with any complacency on the probability that this issue is to be raised and fought out. No doubt the new power of mankind in these last two or three centuries to reflect on the phenomena and experiences of life has been and is rich in advantage for the race; it has taken the place of an instinctive living under the traditional and simple acquiescence in it, and has developed the reason and conscience of all; but it is at present a sort of disease. A society which brings all its inheritance of thought and faith into question at once, and before it has prepared an adequate apparatus for dealing with the questions and problems which it raises, may fall into chaos. And it is that issue in particular — one which shows that the people are not firm in their conception of liberty and are not ready and hard-headed in their judgment of social fads and whims — which brings with it the greatest jeopardy for the essential welfare of society.

Constitutional liberty, so far as we have been able to realize it, stands just now as a happy phase of civil institutions which we have been able to realize for a moment in the interval between the downfall of aristocracy and the rise of democracy; for there can be no doubt that the epidemic of socialism is only the turning of all social powers in obeisance and flattery toward the new and rising power. We are passing through a transition over to a new illustration of the fact that the thing which forever rules the world is not what is true or what is right, even relatively, but only what is strong. The main question which remains to be solved is whether the elements of strength in the new order are distributed as many now believe; whether democracy is a stable order at all or whether it will at once fall a prey to plutocracy. So surely as democracy yields to socialism, socialism will prove a middle stage toward plutocracy.

SPECULATIVE LEGISLATION

SPECULATIVE LEGISLATION

THE Germans have lately invented a new department of social interest — *Socialpolitik* — which is neither politics, political economy, nor social science; it is in fact a department of speculation as to legislative measures which might be adopted to alter existing social relations. Any legislation which does not proceed out of antecedents, but is invented in order to attain to ideals, is necessarily speculative; it deals with unverified and unverifiable propositions and lacks all guarantees of its practicability or of the nature of its results. It is, however, very easy and fascinating to plan such legislation; the enterprise is sure to be popular and remonstrances against it are sure to produce irritation. Such remonstrances imply that the speculators have undertaken too much or are too confident and self-assured.

Nothing can be more antagonistic to the spirit of Anglo-American law than speculative legislation. That law is marked by slow and careful growth, historic continuity, practical sense, and aversion to all dogmatism and abstractionism. While it is as broad in its general maxims and generalizations as the facts will warrant and bold enough to draw all the deductions which legitimately follow, it refuses to assimilate unverifiable elements.

Speculative legislation is really advocated by assertions which are predictions, and it is impossible to meet it by arguments which are other than contradictory predictions. But all men of sober thought and scholarly responsibility dislike to argue by predictions.

The most remarkable case of speculative legislation

in our history is the Inter-state Commerce Law: and, as it was not permitted to argue against it by predictions as to its effect, it is the more important to follow its workings closely.

Twenty-five years ago it would have been impossible to pass such a law. Part of the people would have said at once that it was unconstitutional, and these would have brought at once the sound instincts of their political sense to bear upon it. The real argument against it is now just what it always was and always will be: not that it produces one or another specific evil effect, but that it is opposed to the spirit of our institutions, wrong in principle, and sure to produce evil effects whether the specific evils could be predicted or not.

At present different interests are anxiously watching its workings to see whether they are to gain by it or not. They propose to take sides on it accordingly. But this means only that it will necessarily favor some interests at the expense of others, from which it follows that it must impair the prosperity and welfare of the commonwealth as a whole.

It is said of the law that it has come to stay, and that we shall never go back to the old state of things. It is to be feared that this is true; it is one of the worst facts in the case. When such a law has produced its effects, it has produced a distortion of the industrial system; but industry adjusts itself as soon as possible to new conditions of any kind. *When the distortion is effected the chance of observing it has gone by.* People get used to the new state of things; they suppose that it is the natural and only proper one. Reform or improvement is blocked by inertia, habit, and tradition; paper money and the tariff are already instances of this; this new law is making another.

It has been observed that the effect of the law is the same as that of the protective tariff on Ohio wool against California wool. It goes much further than this. If it bars California wool out of the European market, it is protective on other California industries which hitherto have not paid so well as wool. It will act as a protective tariff on all the separate local units or groups. It tends to divide the country up into separate economic units with a tariff around each.

Reasoning upon it in another way we reach the same result. There is no place in the world where railroads are as important as on this North American continent. It is a vast, solid piece of territory, cut by few water inlets when compared with Europe. Inside of it railroad communication is of commanding importance. So long as railroads are new, and their economic operation is as yet undeveloped, this continent must be the scene of many rude and abrupt changes, vicissitudes, and difficulties due to the development of transportation. The general effect, however, has been to open up the whole continent to superficial settlement, to unify the whole continent in industrial organization, to make local division of labor, to establish the widest and most healthful, because freest, industrial organization that ever has existed. In doing this railroads have often acted as if they laid one square mile over another or as if they drew a remoter place nearer than a nearer one. By giving greater mobility to capital and population they have distributed and redistributed them; have concentrated or dispersed them as the forces might act.

Now, to limit, counteract, and reverse the action of the roads, by the short-haul clause which really antagonizes the most peculiar and important fact in the economy of railroads, is to undo their action and to force (if the act could be carried out) the production of approximately that state of things which would have existed if there had been no invention of the locomotive, *viz.*, local economic units, each complete in itself, with low division of labor as between parts of the country and less interchange of products between them.

The fact that the industry of the country is producing food and raw materials only makes the mischief greater, for these products cannot be produced on a large scale unless they are transported. The act may put an end to passes and limit railroad wars, but its effect is to destroy the transportation business.

The act was one which nobody could construe. It was said that the Commission would construe it, but they now decline to do so; they say they must wait for cases, with real parties in interest. Plainly here are two systems of jurisprudence and administration mixed together. On the administrative-regulative system, *e. g.*, of Germany, the administrative body must establish ordinances and make known how it will act; it must solve the doubts of parties affected, give them directions, and relieve them of responsibility. It is the Anglo-American system to have no regulative-administrative officers, to leave administration to courts, and to let courts act only on cases. The Anglo-American system leaves the citizen to consult his legal adviser on the law, and to act on his own responsibility because it has left him free. If the law only defines terms and conditions of social and industrial life, it needs no regulative functionaries and has no place for them. Giving the citizen liberty, it holds him to responsibility. If our Commission does not interpret the law, what is it for? We have then only a blind enactment, and whatever course railroad officers take under it they may find after two or three years of litigation that they have made mistakes and incurred great liabilities. It is mischievous legislation to create any such situation.

The act is also producing a pooling system stricter than any which voluntary agreement could establish. Railroad authority of the highest rank has asserted that the effect of pooling in England has been to arrest railroad improvements there for the last fifteen years. Its effect must be to stereotype existing arrangements as to facilities and prices.

It is a characteristic of speculative legislation that it very generally produces the exact opposite of the result it was hoped to get from it. The reason is because the elements of any social problem which we do not know so far surpass in number and importance those which we do know that our solutions have far greater chance to be wrong than to be right. This act promises to be another conspicuous illustration—perhaps a stronger one than any previous instance, because in this case we did not know what we wanted to do, nor how we meant to do it, nor, when we got through, did we know what we had done.

Legislation among us is far too easy for us to endure speculative legislation. Among us the legislative machinery can be set in motion too readily and too frequently; it is too easy for the irresponsible hands of the ignorant to seize the machinery; a notion which happens to catch popular fancy for a moment can be too readily translated into legislation.

REPUBLICAN GOVERNMENT

REPUBLICAN GOVERNMENT [1]

[1877]

THE best definition of a republican form of government I know of is one given by Hamilton. It is government in which power is conferred by a temporary and defeasible tenure. Every state must have and exert authority; the state gathers together and enforces in concrete form the will of the governing body as to what ought to be done. I may leave aside here those cases in which the governing body is an autocrat or an oligarchy or an aristocracy, because these forms of the state are dead or dying, and take into account only the states in which the people rule and in which, therefore, the governing body is so wide as to embrace at least all who contribute to the active duties and burdens of the state. You observe that, even in the widest democracies, their body is not commensurate with the population. The "people," for political purposes, does not include women, or minors, or felons, or idiots, even though it may include tramps and paupers. The word "people," therefore, when we talk of the people ruling, must be understood to refer to such persons as the state

[1] William G. Sumner, professor of political economy in Yale College, delivered a lecture entitled "A Republican Form of Government," in the Sunday course, at McCormick hall, on yesterday afternoon. It was an effort of rather more grave and timely interest than experience would have led the average lecture patron to expect. The professor is still a young man; his appearance does not indicate a greater age than thirty-five. His clear and pleasant delivery added considerably to the power of his discourse in enabling his hearers to follow his line of argument, without any effort to concentrate attention upon each word. *Chicago Tribune*, Jan. 1, 1877.

itself has seen fit to endow with political privileges.
The true rule which every state which is to be sound and
enduring must set for itself in deciding to whom political functions may be entrusted, is that political rights
and political duties, political burdens and political
privileges, political power and political responsibility
must go together and, as far as may be, in equal measure.
The great danger of all wide democracies comes from the
violation of this rule. The chief doctrine of democracy
is equality, that is, equality of rights without respect
to duties, and its theory of power is that the majority
has the power without responsibility. If, then, it so happens that the rights and the powers fall to a numerical
majority, while the duties and burdens are borne by
a minority, we have an unstable political equilibrium,
and dishonesty must follow.

In a state, however, in which the limits of co-ordinate rights and duties are observed in determining who
shall be the people to rule, whether the limit includes
a greater or smaller number of the inhabitants, we see
the modern state which is capable of self-government
and realizes self-government. Those who pay taxes, do
jury duty, militia duty, police duty on the sheriff's
posse, or are otherwise liable to bear the burdens of
carrying out what the nation may attempt, are those
who may claim of right to have a voice in determining
what it shall attempt. They therefore make the national will, and out of the nation they form a state.
The nation is an organism like a man; the state is like
the man clothed and in armor, with tools and weapons in
his hand. When, therefore, the will of the state is
formed, the state must act with authority in the line
of its determination and must control absolutely the
powers at its disposal.

Right here, however, we pass over from the abstract to the concrete, from plain and easy reasoning on principles to practical contact with human nature. Power and authority in exercise must be in the hands of individuals. When wielded by boards and committees we find that they are divided and dispersed, and especially we find that, when divided, they escape responsibility. Thence arises irresponsible power, the worst abomination known to the modern constitutional or jural state. The most important practical questions are, therefore: Who shall be endowed with the authority of the state? How shall he be designated? How shall the authority be conferred? How shall the organs of authority be held to responsibility?

In constitutional monarchies these questions are answered by reducing the monarch to an emblem of stability, unity, and permanence, and surrounding him with ministers appointed by him, but under conditions which make them organs of the public will and which hold them to continual responsibility for all the acts of the state. The end is accomplished by indirect means which, nevertheless, secure the result with satisfactory certainty. In republics the organs of authority are designated by the express selection of the people; the people directly signify whom they choose to have as their organs or agents; they express their confidence distinctly either by word of mouth or by other convenient process; they show their will as to the policy of the state by choosing between advocates of different policies submitted to their selection. They do this either by the spoken word or the lifted hand, or by the ballot; they decide by majority vote or by such other combination as they may themselves think wisest; they confer authority for such time as they may determine; and they prescribe methods of responsibility such as they think adapted to the end. These general prescriptions and limitations they lay down beforehand in the organic law of the state.

It follows that elections are the central and essential institution of republics, and that the cardinal feature in a republican form of government is the elective system. We may therefore expand Hamilton's definition as follows: A republican government is a form of self-government in which the authority of the state is conferred for limited terms upon officers designated by election.

I beg leave here to emphasize the distinction between a democracy and a republic because the people of the United States, living in a democratic republic, almost universally confuse the two elements of their system. Each, however, must stand or fall by itself. Louis Napoleon gave the French democracy, under his own despotism; France is now called a republic although MacMahon was never voted for on a popular vote. If the principle of equality is what we aim at we can probably get it — we can all be equally slaves together. If we want majority rule, we can have it — the majority can pass a *plébiscite* conferring permanent power on a despot. A republic is quite another thing. It is a form of self-government, and its first aim is not equality but civil liberty. It keeps the people active in public functions and public duties; it requires their activity at stated periods when the power of the state has to be re-conferred on new agents. It breaks the continuity of power to guard against its abuse, and it abhors as much the irresponsible power of the many as of the one. It surrounds the individual with safeguards by its permanent constitutional provisions, and by no means leaves the individual or the state a prey to the determination of a numerical majority. In our system the guarantees to liberty and the practical machinery of self-government all come from the constitutional republic; the dangers chiefly from democracy. Democracy teaches dogmas of absolute and sweeping application, while, in truth, there are no absolute doctrines in politics. Its spirit is fierce, intolerant, and despotic. It frets and chafes at constitutional restraints which seem to balk the people of its will and it threatens all institutions, precedents, and traditions which, for the moment, stand in the way. When the future historian comes to critizise our time, he will probably say that it was marked by a great tendency toward democratic equality. He will perhaps have to mention more than one nation which, in chasing this chimaera, lost liberty.

If now a republican form of government be such as I have described it, we must observe first of all that it makes some very important assumptions. It assumes, or takes for granted, a high state of intelligence, political sense, and public virtue on the part of the nation which employs this form of self-government. It is impossible to exaggerate the necessity that these assumptions should be calmly observed and soberly taken to heart. Look at the facts. A people who live under a republican form of government take back into their own hands, from time to time, the whole power of the state; every election brings with it the chances of a peaceful revolution, but one which may involve a shock to the state itself in a sudden and violent change of policy. The citizen, in casting his vote, joins one phalanx which is coming into collision with another inside the state. The people divide themselves to struggle for the power of the state. The occasion is one which seems fitted to arouse the dead-

liest passions — those which are especially threatening
to civil order.

The opinion of the people is almost always informal
and indefinite. A small group, therefore, who know
what they want and how they propose to accomplish
it, are able by energetic action to lead the whole body.
Hence the danger which arises for us, in this country,
from incorporated or combined interests; it is and always
has been our greatest danger. An organized interest
forms a compact body, with strong wishes and motives,
ready to spend money, time, and labor; it has to deal
with a large mass, but it is a mass of people who are ill-
informed, unorganized, and more or less indifferent.
There is no wonder that victory remains with the interests. Government by interests produces no statesmen,
but only attorneys. Then again we see the value of
organization in a democratic republic. Organization
gives interest, motive, and purpose; hence the prelim-
inaries of all elections consist in public parades, meetings,
and excitement, which win few voters. They rather
consolidate party ranks, but they stimulate interest;
they awaken the whole mass to a participation which
will not otherwise be obtained. So far, then, it is evident that the republican system, especially in a democratic republic, demands on the part of the citizen extraordinary independence, power to resist false appeals
and fallacies, sound and original judgment, far-sighted
patriotism, and patient reflection.

We may, however, go farther than this. The assumption which underlies the republican system is that the
voter has his mind made up, or is capable of making up
his mind, as to all great questions of public policy; but
this is plainly impossible unless he is well informed as to
some great principles of political science, knows some-

thing of history and of experiments made elsewhere, and also understands the great principles of civil liberty. It is assumed that he will act independently of party if party clashes with patriotism. He is assumed to be looking at the public good with independent power to discern it and to act for it. Thus it follows, in general, that the citizen of a republic is animated by patriotism, that he is intelligent enough to see what patriotism demands, that he can throw off prejudice and passion and the mysterious influence of the public opinion of the social group to which he belongs, that he has education enough to form an opinion on questions of public policy, that he has courage enough to stand by his opinion in the face of contumely and misrepresentation and local or class unpopularity, that he will exercise his political power conscientiously and faithfully in spite of social and pecuniary allurements against his opinion, and that he is intelligent enough to guard himself against fraud. Finally it is assumed that the citizen will sacrifice time, interest, and attention, in no slight degree, to his public duty. In short, it comes to this: the franchise is a prerogative act; it is the act of a sovereign; it is performed without any responsibility whatever except responsibility to one's judgment and one's own conscience. And furthermore, although we are fond of boasting that every citizen is a sovereign, let us not forget that if every one is a sovereign every one is also a subject. The citizen must know how to obey before he is fit to command, and the only man who is fit to help govern the community is the man who can govern himself.

With these assumptions and requirements of republican self-government before us, you are ready to ask: "Where are there any men who fulfill the requirements?"

If we apply the standards vigorously no men satisfy them; it is only a question of less or more, for the assumptions of republican self-government are superhuman. They demand more of human nature than it can yet give, even in the purest and most enlightened communities which yet exist. Hence republican self-government does not produce anything like its pure, theoretical results. The requirements, however, must be satisfied up to a reasonable limit or republican self-government is impossible. No statesman would propose to apply the republican system to Russia or Turkey to-day; our American Indians could not be turned into civilized states under republican forms; the South American republics present us standing examples of states in which the conditions of republican government are not sufficiently well fulfilled for the system to be practicable. In our own experience faults and imperfections present themselves which continually arouse our fears, and the present condition of some of our southern states raises the inquiry, with terrible force and pertinency, whether the assumptions of republican self-government are sufficiently realized there for the system to succeed. I may add, in passing, that the current discussion of questions pending in those states is marked by a constant confusion between democracy and the republican form of government.

I go on, however, to discuss the theory of elections, since this is the essential feature of the republic. Recent events have forced us to re-examine the whole plan and idea of elections, although the institution is one in familiarity with which we have all grown up. When an election is held in a town meeting by *viva voce* vote, or by a show of hands, the process is simple and direct. When the town grows to such a size that the body of voters cannot be brought within the sound of one voice, the physical difficulties become so great that this method is no longer available. It becomes necessary to adopt some system or method, aside from those previously employed, by which the question can be put and the vote taken. We are so familiar with the ballot as hardly to appreciate the fact that it is a distinct invention to accomplish a purpose and meet a new necessity. Right here, however, lies the birth of the political "machine"; for in the next step it is found that organization and previous concert are necessary. With this comes the necessity for nomination, and it is then found that the center of gravity of the system lies rather in the nomination than in the election. The nomination takes the form of a previous and informal election; it offers an opportunity for the majority to exert controlling power. The machinery is multiplied at every step, and with every increase of machinery comes new opportunity for manipulation and new demand for work. The election is to be popular throughout the state, but, for the purpose of nominating, the constituency is broken up into districts which send nominating delegates. Thus this subdivision enables labor to be concentrated upon small bodies in which chicanery, bargaining, and improper influence can be brought to bear. By ward-primaries, caucuses, nominating committees, pledged delegations, and so on, the ultimate power is concentrated in the hands of a few who, by concerted action, are able to control the result. At the same time the body of voters, finding political labor increased and political duty made more burdensome, abandon this entire department of political effort, while the few who persist in it have the continual consciousness of being duped. Upon the larger constituency of voters it is impossible to act, save by public methods, by public writing and speaking, which, although they often deal with base and unworthy motives, are nevertheless generally bound in decency to handle proper arguments. With every increase of machinery come new technicalities, new and arbitrary notions of regularity, fresh means of coercing the better judgment of delegates, and new opportunities for private and unworthy influences to operate. I do not hesitate to say that the path of political reform lies directly in the line of more independent and simple methods of nomination.

To return, however, to the election proper, the theory is that the body of voters shall cast ballots with the name of one or the other candidate. The votes are to be secret in the interest of independence; they are to be impersonal or anonymous, no man's vote being distinguishable from that of any other man after it is cast; they are to be equal, that is, every voter is to cast but one. The law can provide guarantees for all these limitations. Can the law go any further? Having endowed certain persons with certain qualifications to cast ballots, under the assumption that they are fit and qualified to discharge the duty, can it go any further? I think not. I do not see how the law can even confer upon the voter a power to do his duty, if he does not possess that power. If the people think that a man who cannot read his ballot is not fit to cast it, they can by the law of the state exclude all persons who cannot read from the franchise; but if they do not judge that such a qualification is essential, while in fact it is, they cannot possibly eliminate from the ballot-boxes the error or mischief which has come into them by the votes of illiterate or incompetent persons. They can provide for universal education and in time they can thus eliminate this element of harm, but that cannot operate for the time being. Again, if the state by its laws has given a share in political power to men who cannot form an opinion, or can be cheated, or can be frightened out of an opinion, or can be induced to use their power, not as they think best, but as others wish, then the ballot-boxes will not contain a true expression of the will of the voters, or it will be a corrupt and so, probably, a mischievous and ruinous will; but I do not see how a law can possibly be framed to correct that wrong, and make foolish men give a wise judgment or corrupt men give an honest judgment which shall redound to the public welfare. There is no alchemy in the ballot-box. It transmutes no base metal into gold. It gives out just what was put in, and all the impersonality and other safeguards may obscure but they never alter this fact. If the things which the elective system assumes to be true are not true, then the results which are expected will not follow; you will not get any more honor, honesty, intelligence, wisdom, or patriotism out of the ballot-box than the body of voters possess, and there may not be enough for self-government. You have to understand that you will certainly meet with fraud, corruption, ignorance, selfishness, and all the other vices of human nature, here as well as elsewhere. These vices will work toward their own ends and against the ends of honest citizens; they will have to be fought against and it will take the earnest endeavor of honest citizens to overcome them. The man who will never give time and attention to public duty, who always votes with his party, who wants to find a ballot already printed for him, so that he can cast it in a moment or two on his way to business on election day, has no right to complain of bad government. The greatest test of the republican form of government is the kind of men whom it puts in office as a matter of fact, and in any republic the indolence of the public and its disposition to trust to machinery will steadily detract from so much virtue, honesty, wisdom, and patriotism as there may be in the community.

Here I say again, I do not see how the law can help in the matter. All the machinery of nominating conventions and primaries lies outside of the law. It is supported only by public acquiescence and it is the strongest tyranny among us. The fact is that everything connected with an election is political, not legal; that is to say, it is the domain of discretion, judgment, sovereign action. It is a participation in government; it presupposes the power and the will to act rightly and wisely for the ends of government. Where that power and will exist the ends of government will be served; where they do not exist those ends will not be served,— and it is plain that no one can create them. Law prescribes only methods of action; action itself comes from human thought, feeling, and will, and government is action. The autocrat of Russia governs Russia; suppose that he were corrupt or perverse, or ignorant, or otherwise incompetent, and it must follow that the purposes of government would be lost in Russia — no law could give the autocrat of Russia a better mind or heart for his duties. Just so if the sovereign people in any state taken as a whole have not the mind or heart to govern themselves, no law can give them these. We can never surround an incompetent voter by any legal restraint, or protection, or stimulus, or guarantee, which shall enable him to exercise his prerogative, if he is not able to do so as an antecedent matter of fact. His motives lie in his own mind, beyond the reach of all human laws and institutions; the conflicting arguments, prejudices, passions, fears, and hopes which move him meet in an arena where we cannot follow them. If a body of voters in the commonwealth, so large as to control it, are below the grade of intelligence and independence which are necessary to make the election process practicable, then you cannot apply the republican form of government there; it is a hopeless task to take any such community, and by any ingenious device of legal machinery try to make the republican form of government work there so as to produce good government.

It follows, then, that the law can only mark out the precautions necessary to be observed to secure the true expression of the people's will, provided there be a people present who are capable of forming a will and expressing it by this method. The domain of these precautions is in the period anterior to the election — the law must define beforehand who are people fit, on general principles, to share in the government of the state. It will necessarily define these persons by classes and will leave out some who are fit if examined rationally and individually, and it will include many others who are unfit if examined in the same way. It must aim at a practical working system; it must then provide by registration or other appropriate means for finding out who among the population come within the defined qualifications; it must then surround the actual act of voting with such safeguards as seem necessary to secure to each voter a single impersonal vote. When the votes are cast, however, and the polls are closed, the public will is expressed as well as it is possible to have it expressed by an election in that community at that time. It might have been possible to get an expression of the will of that community in some other way, and perhaps in some better way, but that would not have been a republican form of government. The republican way to find out what the people want is to hold an election. If anybody proposes an improved method it may be worth while to consider it as a matter of political speculation, for every one knows by ample observation and experience that the process of elections is open to serious imperfections; it is liable to many abuses, and scarcely ever does an election take place anywhere in which there is not more or less abuse practiced. We know that it is really an imperfect makeshift and practical expedient for accomplishing the end in view. It only accomplishes it better than any other plan yet devised, but if any one can propose a better plan we are ready to give it attention. One thing, however, we never can allow to be consistent with a republican form of government, and that is, that we should hold an election and then correct the result as thus reached by some other result, reached in some other way by guess, estimate, magic, census, clairvoyance, or revelation.

If we pursue the republican system, we must accept the fact that we have in the boxes an arithmetical product which represents the will of the people, expressed as accurately as our precautions have been able to secure. If there was a qualified voter who had no opinion, or was afraid to express it, we have not got his will there, but we have got all that the republican system could get. To secure the truth, now, as to what the will of the people is, we have before us a simple process of counting the ballots. The truth will be presented as an arithmetical fact; it will not be open to any doubt or guess, but will be as positive as anything on earth. Simple as this matter of counting mere units may appear, we all know that the greatest dangers of the election system lie in this very process. The question of who shall count has become quite as important as who shall vote. The whole republican plan or system runs its greatest risk in the manipulation of the ballots after they are cast, and the question of its practicability comes down to this: Can we secure simple fidelity to the arithmetical facts in the count? This we certainly cannot do unless it is understood that absolute fidelity to the facts is the highest and only function of all officers and persons who are allowed to handle the ballots after they are cast. Every man who has grown up in familiarity with the election process knows that when we abandon the count of the votes as cast we go off into arbitrary manipulations and decisions for which we have no guarantee whatever, and that the political power of the state, if we allow any such manipulation, is transferred from those who vote to those who manipulate. If it is charged that frauds have been perpetrated in the election, that is to say that any of the laws which limit and define the exercise of the elective franchise have been broken, such charges raise questions of fact. If the charges are proved true, each charge affects the result by a given arithmetical quantity, and these effects can be added or subtracted as the case may be. Here we are dealing with facts, not opinions; we have solid ground under our feet. We do not work backward from the results, we work forward from the evidence; and so long as we use tribunals which seek only facts and remain steadfast to the truth as proved, the republican system suffers no shock. If, however, legislative committees or any other tribunals decide, in cases of contested elections, not by the truth but by party interest, we are face to face with the greatest treason against republican institutions which can possibly exist.

I believe that the American people love republican institutions. I have no doubt whatever that if we keep our records clean in regard to what republican institutions are, so that we recognize and repel the first inroads upon them, we can adapt our institutions to any exigencies that may arise. I think that the country has, to a certain extent, outgrown some of its institutions in their present form. I believe it has given its faith to some false and pernicious doctrines about equality and the rights of man. I believe that the astonishing social and economic developments of the last few years, together with some of the heavy problems which are legacies of the war, have thrown upon us difficulties whose magnitude we hardly yet appreciate and which we cannot cope with unless we set to work at them with greater energy and sobriety than we have yet employed. Some of these things involve or threaten the republic in its essence. We can deal with them all under its forms and methods if we have the political sense which the system requires. Here, however, lies the difficulty. Political institutions do not admit of sharp definition or rigid application; they need broad comprehension, gentle and conciliatory application; they require the highest statesmanship in public men. Self-government could not be established by all the political machinery which the wit of man could invent; on the contrary, the more machinery we have the greater is the danger to self-government. Civil liberty could not be defined by constitutions and treatises which might fill libraries; civil liberty cannot even be guaranteed by constitutions — I doubt if it can be stated in propositions at all. Yet civil liberty is the great end for which modern states exist. It is the careful adjustment by which the rights of individuals and the state are reconciled with one another to allow the greatest possible development of all and of each in harmony and peace. It is the triumph of the effort to substitute right for might, and the repression of law for the wild struggles of barbarism. Civil liberty, as now known, is not a logical or rational deduction at all; it is the result of centuries of experience which have cost the human race an untold expenditure of blood and labor. As the result we have a series of institutions, traditions, and positive restraints upon the governing power. These things, however, would not in themselves suffice. We have also large communities which have inherited the love of civil liberty and the experience of it—communities which have imperceptibly imbibed the conception of civil liberty from family life and from the whole social and political life of the nation. Civil liberty has thus become a popular instinct. Let us guard well these prejudices and these instincts, for we may be well assured that in them lies the only real guarantee of civil liberty. Whenever they become so blunted that an infringement of one of the old traditions of civil liberty is viewed with neglect and indifference then we must take the alarm for civil liberty. It seems to me a physical impossibility that we should have a Caesar here until after we have run through a long course of degeneration. That is not our danger, and while we look for it in that direction we overlook it on the side from which it may come. There are numberless ways beside the usurpation of a dictator in which civil liberty may be lost; there are numberless forms of degeneration for a constitutional republic besides monarchy and despotism. We can keep the names and forms of republican self-government long after their power to secure civil liberty is lost. The degeneration may go on so slowly that only after a generation or two will the people realize that the old tradition is lost and that the fresh, spontaneous power of the people, which we call political sense, is dead. Such is the danger which continually menaces the republic, and the only safe-guard against it is the jealous instinct of the people, which is quick to take the alarm and which will not, at any time or under any excuse, allow even a slight or temporary infringement upon civil liberty. Such in-fringements when made are always made under specious pretexts. Kings who set aside civil liberty always do it for "higher reasons of state"; in a republic likewise you will find, especially at great public crises, that men and parties are promptly ready to take the same course and assume the rôle of "saviors of society," for the sake of something which they easily persuade themselves to be a transcendent public interest. The constitutional republic, however, does not call upon men to play the hero; it only calls upon them to do their duty under the laws and the constitution, in any position in which they may be placed, and no more.

DEMOCRACY AND RESPONSIBLE GOVERNMENT

DEMOCRACY AND RESPONSIBLE GOVERNMENT[1]

[1877]

THE notion seems to be widely and more or less definitely held that in civil government men may invent any institutions they please, unchecked by any such restraints as govern mechanical inventions. It seems to be believed, also, that the aim of political science is to invent some scheme of government which, when once found, will put an end to all troubles in the art of government and, being universally introduced, will make all men happy forever after. The notion seems to be more widely held that it is possible for us to make changes in political institutions, so as to hold fast all the advantages we have gained, and by successive amendments to advance toward perfection. It seems to be believed, furthermore, that any man may easily invent new political institutions or devise improvements on old ones, without any particular trouble.

I must preface what I have now to say about Democracy and Responsible Government by denying the truth of every one of these notions, because they will be apt, whenever they exist, to prevent a correct understanding of what I have to say.

ERRORS OF POLITICAL JUDGMENT. It is in utopias only that men have ever invented new political institutions. They have never put their utopian institutions to the experiment for the simple reason that every utopia begins with the postulate that the world must be made over again, from what it is into that

[1] From the *Providence Evening Press*, June 21, 1877.

kind of a world which the utopia needs in order to
be practicable. The *a priori* philosophers, who began
with a state of nature, and assumed such a state and
such men in it as suited their notions, got so far as to
try, in the French Revolution, for instance, to put some
of their plans into practice. Those plans failed, however, and their failure involved disaster. Many people
believe that American institutions were invented by
the fathers, and I presume that this is one reason why
the belief is so strong that men can invent institutions
of civil government. The truth is that the fathers
devised some expedients in governmental machinery,
all of which have failed of the objects they aimed at
or have been distorted to others; but American institutions are striking illustrations of the doctrine that
political institutions which endure and thrive always
are the product of development and growth, that they
grow out of the national character and the national
circumstances, and that the efforts of men to control
or limit them are restricted within very narrow limits
and even at that require an immense exertion of force
for the results attained. This fact with regard to American institutions will demand our attention further on.

ERRORS OF POLITICAL PHILOSOPHY. We must also
abandon all hopes of finding an absolutely "best"
system of government or one which will alter any of the
conditions of human life, except by undoing the mischief
which mistaken effort may have done. If we study
human nature and human history, we find that civil
institutions are only "better" and "best" relatively to
the people for whom they exist, and that they can be
so called only as they are more closely adjusted to the
circumstances of the nation in question. The *a priori*
philosophers have led men astray by their assumptions

and speculations, teaching them to look into the clouds for dreams and impossibilities instead of studying the world and life as they are, so as to learn how to make the best of them. We shall discover or invent no system of government which we can carry from nation to nation, counting upon uniform action and results everywhere, as we do, for instance, with a steam engine or a telescope.

Furthermore, experience shows that the hope of steady improvement by change is a delusion. All human arrangements involve their measure of evil; we are forever striking balances of advantage and disadvantage in our social and political arrangements. If by a change we gain more advantage on one side, we lose some on another; if we get rid of one evil we incur another. The true gains are won by slow and difficult steps; they consist only in better adjustments of man to his circumstances. They are never permanent because changes in men and in their circumstances are continually taking place; the adjustments must be continually re-established and the task is continually renewed.

GREAT PRINCIPLES FALSELY SO CALLED. In this view the worst vice in political discussions is that dogmatism which takes its stand on "great principles" or assumptions, instead of standing on an exact examination of things as they are and human nature as it is. The commonest form of this error is that which arises from discontent with things as they are. An ideal is formed of some "higher" or "better" state of things than now exists, and almost unconsciously the ideal is assumed as already existing and made the basis of speculations which have no root. At other times a doctrine which is true in a measure, as true as its author intended it, is con-

verted into a popular dogma and made the subject of
mischievous inferences. Thus I have heard a man who
did not know what a syllogism was, reason that a city
ought to give work to unemployed laborers, as follows:
"Isn't government for the greatest good of the greatest
number? We are the greatest number, and therefore,
it is for us." Other examples of dogmatism based on
"great principles" which are either fallacies or mischievous half-truths or empty phrases which people
want to force to vigorous realization, are common in
French history and in our own. I shall have to refer
to our experience of them again. I wish to say, at this
point, only that the social sciences are, as yet, the
stronghold of all this pernicious dogmatism; and nowhere
does it do more harm than in politics. The whole
method of abstract speculation on political topics is
vicious. It is popular because it is easy; it is easier
to imagine a new world than to learn to know this one;
it is easier to embark on speculations based on a few
broad assumptions than it is to study the history of
states and institutions; it is easier to catch up a popular
dogma than it is to analyze it to see whether it is true
or not. All this leads to confusion, to the admission
of phrases and platitudes, to much disputing but little
gain in the prosperity of nations.

FUNDAMENTAL DEFINITIONS. The science of politics
consists in such study of history as shall discern the
nature and laws of civil society and the general principles for obtaining its ends. The art of politics consists
in finding means for the ends of civil society as the
needs arise, under the general rules which the science
has derived from the study of a long and wide experience;
it is practical business in which special training, tact,
skill, sagacity, and acumen are valuable, just as they

are in the other practical affairs of life. Poetry, romance, tradition, feeling, and emotion have much weight in national life and in the development of political institutions, but pathos, rodomontade, vituperative declamation, and glittering generalities are only vicious.

It must also be observed that the only thing which we can ever accomplish by labor and forethought in the way of altering institutions to fit new needs is to follow the course of events, perceive the natural tendencies of the institutions themselves, and alter the arbitrary and artificial portions of our institutions at the proper moment and in the proper way to meet the requirement. Even this comparatively modest task requires the very highest statesmanship; to invent a new adjustment of civil institutions is not easier than to invent a new machine, but far more difficult.

RADICALISM REPUDIATED. I do not, therefore, now propose anything so ambitious as an invention for the readjustment of our political institutions; what I do propose may be set forth by pursuing one step further the analogy of mechanical inventions. It often happens that some art is checked in its development by the want of a machine to perform one simple, specific task. Before the steam-hammer was invented, it was possible to build steamships of any size, except for the difficulty that a mass of iron could not be forged for the shaft of an engine exceeding a certain size. The exact need was thus specified and the invention speedily followed. I desire to define and specify where we stand with our political institutions, and what we need in order that we may gain some advantage of position for the ultimate solution of the problem; and I desire to remember all the time that the duty of the good citizen is to support the existing institutions of his country as long as he can and to try to make them succeed, and that it is not his duty to find fault with them and to try to see what changes he can make in them.

THE POLITICAL GROWTH OF AMERICA. There is one observation with regard to the position of this country as compared with older countries which is not often made but which seems to me very important for our present purpose. As a young nation, springing up on a new continent, our history consists of a growth from the most rudimentary form of society to the stature of a great civilized nation. The first settlers brought here the traditions of English social and political order as they existed at the time of the migration; these traditions were the most favorable to liberty then existing. The colonists were able to leave what they did not want, and to bring what suited their purpose; we have had no old abuses to contend against, no vested interests to destroy, no old privileges to break down in the interest of liberty. In the old countries whose history we study the struggle has been away from excessive regulation towards liberty; whereas we began with the extreme of liberty and have gone on towards more and more regulation, as the growth of population, and the development of society have made it necessary. The two courses of development are, therefore, opposite to one another, and the fears and hopes, warnings and encouragements derived from European history, have often found an inverted application here. It is especially in regard to the development of institutions that this observation is important: a new country moving forward to greater complexity of social and civil organization will be forced to modify its institutions in the way of development, because they will be found inadequate, while an old country has to modify its institutions in the way of simplification and flexibility, because they tend to become stiff and restrictive. The two situations are distinct and require each its appropriate methods.

THE EARLIEST STATE OF OUR NATION. The first colonists of the United States found themselves on a substantial equality as regards property, education, and social antecedents. There was no opportunity for any to secure the position of landlords; there was no need for any to be peasant laborers. The inherited traditions of liberty found easy application here, for the need for political regulation was as slight as it ever can be in a civilized community. All were alike proprietary farmers. The republican method of electing public officers offered itself as the only suitable method of obtaining such officers. There were few old traditions, or venerable prejudices, or vested interests, or inherited abuses, to block the way to the freest possible organization of society. The political institutions of the colonies were therefore democratic in their character, republican in their form. They could not be anything else; there was no place for any monarchical institutions here; an aristocracy of title and descent would have been absurd under the circumstances. If it had not been for the intrinsic impossibility of the thing, the English government would have created a colonial aristocracy as a bond to hold the colonies to their allegiance. The colonists made no express choice of democratic institutions; they could not, in their circumstances, adopt any other. All were equal before the law, according to English law; all men were as nearly equal in their circumstances as men ever can be in this world, unless they belonged to the inferior races, Indians or negroes. Hence the great doctrine of political equality, to men in whose circumstances and experience it was true, seemed to be true universally. The struggle for existence took on none of its dark colors in a country where land was so plentiful and population so scanty that there was no social friction, while, on the other hand, the higher developments which come from intense social competition were wanting. The division of labor was very imperfect; the professions were only partially differentiated. The external dangers which generally promote the integration of states were here slight, although we find that wars with Indians and wars with the French had the same effect here which foreign wars have had elsewhere. When the danger passed, disintegration again prevailed.

SLAVERY. The doctrine of equality for white men was held without any apparent feeling of inconsistency with the notion that colored men were not the equals of whites. It has often been thought that these two notions involved an inconsistency so glaring that it must have been present to the minds of all men, and that the Southern slave owners were strangely classed as the strongest democrats of all. There does not seem to have been anywhere any feeling of inconsistency in the matter in the colonial times. If we look at the feelings now entertained by a great number amongst us in regard to Indians and Chinese I think that this inconsistency can be more easily understood. Indeed I am not sure but that a still closer explanation of it is furnished by the laboring man who declaimed against the emancipation of the negroes, asking angrily, "Who then will be under us?"

THE UNION AND THE CONSTITUTION. The union of the colonies was also the product of social forces which made it necessary. Whenever the wars with the French or Indians involved great danger and large effort, united action became necessary, and proposals for a permanent union were made; and the exigency of the struggle with the mother-country finally brought about such a union, under difficulties and in spite of great reluctance. The union was formed on the model of the United Netherlands and was not a completely new device. It took experience of the faults of the confederation to force the new constitution of 1787, not because anybody had proved that it would be speculatively better but because the old system had become intolerable. The constitution of the United States is as much an historical growth as any political institution in existence. Its framers did not invent it at all; they took what lay before them. The Union was a fact and a necessity — no one dared to break it up and leave the thirteen colonies to get on, as best they could, as independent members of the family of nations. The republican character of the government was given in the habits and the existing institutions of the colonies. The new union was chiefly distinguished from the old by greater integration of the central power. The need of power to levy taxes had been distinctly felt; the need of a federal supreme court had been experienced and experience had even indicated the character which the tribunal must have. The federal executive offered greater difficulty, and for this the constitution-makers went back to the English constitution as they understood it, that is, to the conception of the English Whigs of the first half of the last century. The student of the English constitution finds the germs of the peculiar features of the present English constitution in the reigns of William and Anne, but it is not strange that American statesmen of the time of George III did not recognize the force and tendency of English constitutional arrangements which never reached their full operation until the nineteenth century.

GOOD AND BAD LAW-MAKING. So far, therefore, our constitution-makers were guided by history and experience. Their contests, as is well known, took place over the adjustment of local interests and not over theories of government — there is no ground in history for the notion that they evolved out of their own wisdom the form of government under which we live. They really showed their wisdom by throwing aside all political dogmatism and making a plain, practical plan for attaining the necessary ends of civil government for the nation. They put in no definitions, no dogmas, no phrases, no generalities. We have not indeed been free from political dogmatism; we have had a great deal of it, but its source is not in the constitution. It is in the Declaration of Independence, where broad propositions containing no meaning, or any meaning each man chooses, stand in singular incongruity by the side of plain and business-like specifications of the grounds for declaring independence. It is not without reason that some have talked about bringing the constitution into accord with the Declaration of Independence; they did not find in the former document the dogmatic assumptions which they wanted. They had to seek them in the latter document, where they are as much to the purpose as the resolutions of a reform club about things in general would be, if appended to a statute.

Take, for instance, the latest case of political dogmatism. The mismanagement of cities has become intolerable and it has been proposed in order to check the abuse to give property especial power in municipal affairs. This is opposed on the ground that it would limit the suffrage. The dogmatic assumption here is that the privilege of all men to vote on all subjects is of sacred and inviolable and absolute right, which the state may not infringe upon on any grounds of expediency. In truth there are no such absolute rights at all in the individual. The community has a right to good government; this is the fixed and paramount consideration in politics and the question as to who may share, or how, in the public affairs, depends on what arrangement will best conduce to good government. A wide suffrage is based on the experience that it conduces more to good government than a narrow one. Those who hold any other doctrine must justify, as they can, the exclusion of women, children, idiots, felons, paupers, and those who cannot read, those who pay no poll-tax, or other exclusions which the laws of various states provide for.

ANTICIPATORY LAWS. The proposition I have laid down, that institutions and political arrangements cannot be arbitrarily created, finds its proof also in the attempt which the constitution-makers did make to foresee political exigencies and to provide for them by special devices. Most of these were devices against democracy, and every one of them has been brought to naught. The fathers never intended to have the President elected by a grand democratic *plébiscite*, for they were under impressions which were hostile to democracy, would have held any such project dangerous, if practicable, and would not have judged it likely to produce a good selection. They adopted the device of the electoral college to prevent this. At the fourth election, the first one at which there was a real contest, their plan broke down. It was amended in detail, but in its subsequent working a mass of tradition and unwritten law ha?

grown up upon it which has made it accomplish, only under state limitations, just what they meant to prevent. Thus impossible is it for law-makers to foresee the operation of arbitrary constitutional provisions, or to set any fetters to the development of the natural forces which lie in the genius or the circumstances of the nation.

In regard to patronage, again, the constitution-makers held utopian ideas in regard to the zeal and purity in the public service which might be expected in the republic. They had inherited the traditional European dread of the executive, a dread which never had any true foundation here, and so they gave the Senate power to confirm the appointments of the President, an arrangement which has been widely copied in our state constitutions and city charters. The idea was to restrain executive patronage, but the arrangement has been the source of great abuses of patronage, and has developed special abuses of its own, not known in foreign experience. Technical usages and unwritten laws here also have defeated the original intention.

On the other hand, many of the provisions which were fought for with the greatest zeal, such as the provision about direct taxes, have proved powerless against advancing opinion. In other respects arrangements which some of the fathers thought essential to the prosperity of the union, such as securing the adherence of the wealthy or attracting the ambitious by titles and orders, have proved of no importance. Still again, they failed to provide for the growth of the confederation in territory by purchase or treaty, so that the old Federalists were always able to denounce the admission of new frontier states as a violation of the original intention. Thus it has been proved, on all sides, that the organic law must move with the life of the nation. Either words change their contents, or interpretations vary, or roundabout methods are invented — in one way or another the nation fits its institutions in spite of all enactments or any pedantic rules of interpretation to its faiths, its tastes, and its needs.

A Senator, in a recent publication, has expressed the opinion that the constitution-makers, in these anti-democratic devices, failed to trust the people, and that this is why their devices failed; he also says that it is not the people who have wanted changes, but the philosophers. There seems to me to be here a great deal of that confusion which has been so mischievous in our own political discussions. The philosophers have philosophized after their manner and the world has paid just as much heed to them as it thought they deserved. Many of their suggestions have fallen dead and harmless, others have stimulated thought, and some have influenced the insensible growth of institutions and the accomplishment of great reforms. As for trusting the people, if we have any infallible oracle, whether it be the people, or the Pope, or a priest of Apollo, or Brigham Young, we make a fatal mistake not to trust it. In fact we have no oracle to solve our problems for us. The people is not such an oracle, because it has no organ even if it had the knowledge; the people is ourselves — you and I. The very root of the trouble is that I do not trust myself to solve the hard questions. When any number of us are added together, our folly and ignorance are added as well as our wisdom and knowledge; the people is no mysterious entity and numbers have no force where ideas are concerned. We are thrown back upon the necessity of bringing reason and judgment to bear upon those tasks and problems which are not physical in their nature. This, however, is just where we started, and when we have asked the people for an answer, we have only asked ourselves, it may be in a very loud voice. The questions of politics are always questions as to what we shall do. It is we, the people, who must decide, we who must act, we who must bear the consequences; to talk about trusting ourselves, therefore, is to use a meaningless phrase. The constitution-makers did not distrust the people, and did not intend to make anything but a system of popular self-government; they did not believe in democracy, but they meant to make a republic with a wide basis and constitutional limitations. The existing circumstances of the country produced democracy in spite of them and their limitations have all been swept away or made of no effect.

Furthermore, the scores of amendments to the Constitution which have been proposed by members of Congress have not been the work of the philosophers; it has been the people who have forced those changes which I have described, on the spirit and actual operation of the Constitution.

PURE DEMOCRACY. The changes which time has brought about in the working of the Constitution of the United States have altered its character. Our government has been called a representative democracy and, although the term is open to criticism, it is substantially a correct description. De Tocqueville, who studied our institutions during Jackson's administration, saw the American government in the full flower of that stage of its development, and he sought the germ of American institutions, rightly enough, in the New England township. A town democracy has its peculiar features which well repay study, and it is easy to discern in our system the theories and practices which belong to the town democracy but have been transferred to the national system.

There is in the town democracy no government, properly speaking; there are no institutions, or the institutions are of a very rudimentary character. The officers are only administrative functionaries; their powers are closely defined and limited, they act under immediate direction, they exercise routine functions, have no initiative and little discretion. In the town meeting the initiative lies with the individual citizen; that body also retains in its own hands the whole formative process and acts by committees when it is necessary to form measures which the mass meeting cannot conveniently do. The execution of special undertakings is also entrusted to committees or commissions created for the purpose.

The notion of special fitness for public functions is here contracted to its narrowest scope, both because the functions are reduced to their lowest form and because the members of the town meeting are so nearly on a level of fitness that the selection for fitness would not be important.

PURE DEMOCRACY IN CITIES. This arrangement is well adapted for a small and simple community where public duties are light, where the occupations and interests are substantially the same and equal, where the population is homogeneous, and where responsibility to the public opinion of neighbors and friends is great because universal observation follows every public detail. As soon, however, as the town increases in mere physical size, difficulties arise which multiply rapidly as the increase goes on. A large town has a large town meeting. The division of labor and the introduction of diverse occupations break up the old simplicity and uniformity; the requirements increase so rapidly that public affairs become far more important; universal acquaintance no longer exists amongst all townsmen; supervision is not close or continuous and responsibility declines. As soon therefore as the town meeting reaches a certain size it becomes an arena for chicanery and faction. Busy citizens cannot attend so as to make the meeting full, and the opportunity for "packing" a meeting is offered; the town is therefore the prey of any energetic faction with a well defined purpose which it is determined to accomplish. Private and special interests find an arena of conflict in the town meeting and in their conflicts with each other the conception of public interest is lost. The notion that the people desire only to have the public good provided for is a delightful political dogma which it would be pleasant to believe but which is contradicted by the observation of town democracies. The people do not positively want what is for the public good; they want, in a positive and active sense, what is for their interest. The vague and benevolent preference for the public good which men feel when their own interests are not involved does not rise high enough to produce self-sacrifice, work, and conflict.

Hence the public interest needs guarantees in constitutions, institutions, popular prejudices, and in the character of public men whose reputation and professional success lie in the defence of the public interest. The town democracy is weak in all these things and is therefore at the mercy of private interests; it is open to the instability which comes from impulse and passion and short-sighted motives. In the best case it has to limit itself by arbitrary rules which, if they prevent abuses on one side, restrain also the freedom of action which is necessary on another. If the town is a part of a larger civil body, the town meeting becomes the arena of the agitator, the wire-puller, and the petty demagogue. Party spirit reaches its worst forms in the rancorous strifes of a small neighborhood with no wide interests, and this is what furnishes the opportunity of all the political parasites.

THE EVILS OF OVERGROWN TOWNS. In such a political system, skill in party warfare becomes the most highly prized political ability; the talents which are the most valuable are knowledge of men and shrewdness in managing them. The struggle for majority becomes a conflict in which there is nothing to temper the arbitrary will of the victors and in which no rights of the vanquished are recognized. No leaders are openly recognized, much as the results may be governed by a few, and there is no room for the idea of a statesman. In fact the first requisite in a leader is that he shall deprecate leadership; he must at least feign modesty. To say that he wants office is to condemn the candidate; no one may offer himself to the suffrages of his fellow-citizens simply because he thinks that he can serve them and is willing to abide by their decision as to whether they think so too or not. Such action, which is open, honest, and honorable, seems egotistic, and the candidate is driven to secret manoeuvres and to hypocritical professions. This comes from the conception of offices as honors or privileges granted by the state, when, in truth, offices are duties and trusts, that is, burdens. In like manner a man who shows independent zeal in public affairs is thought to put himself forward; he is watched with keen jealousy lest he be presuming in wealth or education or position. Finally, it may be added that town democracies always develop a fondness for technicalities and a great zest for tactics in the conduct of public or political conflicts.

These are the faults and imperfections of town-democracies when communities outgrow them. They have been declining here for thirty or forty years, and have been supplanted by incorporated cities or absorbed in a higher organization of the state. Where they still remain, in conjunction with city organizations, they are purely mischievous.

THE TOWN SUPERSEDED. The first step in advance, therefore, consists in the adoption of representative government, not in its fullness as a separate political organization but as a makeshift to avoid the difficulties which come from physical size. This is the representative democracy. The representative of a democracy, however, is only a delegate; a representative is properly a man selected because he represents, and is endowed with independence and responsibility. The delegate of a democracy is an agent to perform a specific duty, for the democracy does not part with its sovereignty to the delegates nor leave them to use its sovereignty for it. It binds them by pledges and it claims to control them by instructions. The delegates are agents of local and other interests who are sent into an arena where interests are lost or won, to fight for particular ones. They do not, therefore, form a great council of the nation, but a body of struggling and scrambling attorneys. The public interest is a vague and indefinable notion which finds little expression amongst them and has little chance of prevailing, except so far as the local and private interests may neutralize each other. A man who went not long ago to a state capital to try to get something done, came back very much dissatisfied with the representative from his district, who had refused to help him; he said that the representative "was utterly unpractical"— that he kept referring to something which he called the "public interest," which was hostile to what he was asked to do.

DEMOCRATIC FEARS. The public interest, however, is the thing for which government exists. It is not the sum of private interests, nor a compromise between them, but a distinct conception by itself; and it is the true object of the statesman. It is neutral and impartial as to all private interests; it simply creates equal conditions under which private interests may develop.

In its relations with the executive the democratic legislature jealously guards its independence. Open and honest relations, which would therefore necessarily be proper, it will not allow. It preserves the initiative and restrains the executive to empty recommendations; it breaks up into committees as its only practical means of investigating facts and performing the drudgery of preparing business. The great guarantee of publicity suffers from this withdrawal of the public business into the committee room, while the same plan also offers facilities for private relations and doubtful influence on the part of the executive.

The democracy, in its dread of executive power, knows no better means of weakening it than to divide it amongst independent officers. It fears above all a "one man power" and sacrifices to this fear the efficiency of the administration. It insists also on electing all officers, or as many as possible, by popular vote, although it is impossible that the mass of voters can ever form any judgment as to the qualifications of candidates for purely administrative offices. The "ring" is a distinct outgrowth of this arrangement of executive power; an officer who is responsible for his subordinates never makes a ring with them; a ring is only possible between independent and co-ordinate officers.

As for the executive officers, under this system they are scarcely more than clerks or administrative officers. Their powers and functions are limited far below the point of efficiency. Official discretion is jealously forbidden, although, as a nation grows and its interests become diversified and complex, it must be that occasion will often arise for action on the part of executive officers which may be most timely and beneficial, although it has been ordained by no act of the legislature; and such action ought to be taken under responsibility to the representatives of the people. This, indeed, is what government means; it does not mean the mere mechanical execution of routine functions. It is the more urgently necessary because the present system affords opportunity for irresponsible action within the limits of routine duty which may not be sanctioned by the nation. A striking instance of this was furnished by the admission of Texas to the Union.

LINGERING EVILS OF POPULAR DEMOCRACY. The extension of the notions of the town-democracy to the administrative service of the nation excludes therefrom the conception of greater or less fitness. The traditional notion of public functions, as within the powers of any citizen, remains. The doctrine of equality, which no one believes in anywhere else, is supposed to be the great principle of politics. I presume that the great popular indifference to or dislike of civil service reform arises from the fact that the notion of comparative fitness or unfitness for office sins against the doctrine of equality, and the sincere inability of many to comprehend what is meant when it is said that civil appointments ought

to be made on business principles comes from the long
tradition that politics belong to another sphere from
business and ought to be controlled by other principles.
As the people have not yet learned to apply the test of
fitness to elected officers, they can hardly complain that
it is not yet applied to appointed ones. The right to be
chosen to office, or the passive electoral right, is valued
by every citizen, and if rightly understood it ought to
be valued. A moment's reflection will show, however,
that there is no absolute right of the kind. The only
right which exists is that of every man, without regard
to birth, wealth, or other conditions of life, to qualify
himself for public honor and trust, and to be privileged
of election or appointment if he be qualified. If the
absolute right be affirmed without the condition, the
state must continually suffer from bad service simply
to gratify the vanity and ambition of certain men. It
is only natural, however, that men should forget or
ignore the troublesome condition, and when they do
the dogmas of rotation in office and of frequent elections naturally follow. Those men, therefore, who said
there were a thousand men in a certain county who were
as good as the incumbent of a certain office, and that
he ought to be turned out on that account, spoke with
perfect good faith; the same notion has prevailed in all
democracies and it has always led inevitably to the
distribution of offices by lot.

SOVEREIGNTY OF THE MAJORITY. The sovereignty,
in the meantime, remains with the popular majority.
In any true conception of the nation the sovereignty of
the majority is a different thing from the sovereignty
of the people. The sovereignty of the people is an
expression for the assent of the nation to the course of
national affairs, for the power of the people to give direc-

tion to those affairs or, if it chooses, to arrest them.
The people, in this expression, is the nation as a great
community of men, women, and children, knit together
by a thousand bonds, having diverse interests, various
abilities, manifold diversities of circumstance, but yet
held to one common movement by the great laws which
govern human life.   In this sense the nation, as a whole,
has wishes, power, will, passions, motives, and purposes,
just like a man.   But the sovereignty of the majority
is not the equivalent for the sovereignty of the people,
nor yet an expression of it; it is only the assumption by
a part of the prerogatives which belong to the whole.
Majority rule is based on no rational principle; it is
not a permanent form of self-government; it is only
a very imperfect practical expedient, for want of some
better method of turning public opinion into a practical
determination as to what shall be done.   It is quite
probable that some better device for the same end may
yet be invented.   No fallacies in politics are more
pernicious than those which transfer to a popular majority all the old claims of the king by divine right, and
lead people to believe that the notions of arbitrary and
irresponsible power are not wrong, but only that they
were wrong when applied to kings or aristocracies and
not when applied to popular majorities.

This fallacy of course inheres in democracy by its
definition.   The majority profits by the subtlety of the
conception of the sovereignty of the people and enjoys
power without the responsibility which always follows
any king, however absolute he may be.   The majority
cannot be called to account, not because, like a constitutional king, it has no power, but, first, because it
cannot be found or seized, and second, because, like an
autocrat, it will submit to no accountability.   It has

often been remarked that the sovereign people has clothed itself with all the old prerogatives and is as tenacious of them as any other depository of political sovereignty ever was. The sovereign majority will not submit to criticism; it punishes criticism more harshly than by any press laws; it is as eager for flattery as any monarch and as inaccessible to harsh truths; it will not be sued for its debts; it claims the prerogative of deciding on its own obligations and sometimes shows an obliquity of conscience in this regard as great as that of some of the absolute monarchs of history. It is as tenacious of its honor, in the sense of demanding all due respect, as any other form of the state, but it is not always careful of its honor, in the sense of responsibility to itself, to do and to give all which may fairly be demanded of it — it is not always sensitive to its international reputation.

POPULAR DISLIKE OF ALL ARISTOCRACY. We are here engaged, however, more particularly with the behavior of democracy under representative institutions. Here it is marked by a jealous desire to hold in reserve as much power as possible and to delegate only what it cannot keep; one of its maxims, accordingly, is "measures, not men," expressing its desire to pass upon measures at the polls, when the mass meeting is no longer possible. In its jealousy of aristocracy it condemns, under that name, any prestige of wealth or education; it prefers to rob itself of useful forces rather than to recognize in those forces any contradiction to the notion of equality. The forces nevertheless exist and work out their results. Wealth is power, and knowledge is power; if it were not so we men would never work as we do to secure wealth and knowledge. When, therefore, wealth is denied any public recognition as a real and honorable force, which, like other forces, needs only to be regulated to be properly and honorably useful, it avenges itself by recourse to secret methods, to dishonorable uses, and exercises corrupt influence.   Knowledge has no more honorable application than to the service of the state; its power, in open and public use, brings the highest gratification to its possessor, while it is ennobled by such application.   If, however, we regard the superiority of knowledge in public affairs with suspicion and distrust, we rob ourselves of its service while it remains honorable, or we drive it, when employed in political life, into hypocritical humility and petty devices of cunning.

When it comes to actual political activity, the great practical need of a democracy is organization.   As we saw, the town-democracy is made up of an unorganized body with good intentions but few positive convictions and well formed wishes; hence it is a prey to a united and determined minority.   The union of all the good, a union long talked about and long looked for, would no doubt defeat all selfish factions; but the union of all the good lacks cohesive force and dissipates its energies in fruitless discussions.   Now when the democracy is large, and no longer local, organization takes the place of acquaintance, sympathy, and personal influence; parties rise into the highest importance.   To be in the minority is to be nothing; to be in the majority is to enjoy power and dignity and honor.   Party success depends upon organization; every exertion to secure unity and singleness of determination is demanded in a close division, and party loyalty and party effort are prized as the highest political virtues.   The severe party discipline and party warfare which belong to a legislature are here transferred to the mass of electors, who ought to be critics and judges — or rather, perhaps, jurors — and they are engaged beforehand as advocates to support or attack the majority or the opposition in its course.

OFFICIOUS MANAGERS. The need of organization and the value of organization rise as the constituencies become more and more heterogeneous and contain more and more uneducated classes. They reach a maximum where the population consists of two classes or, worse still, of two races, of very unequal culture. Where organization is called for the organizer will not long be wanting. He comes with his inventions, the primary, the caucus, the convention, and the party committee — machinery which does not belong to the town-democracy or to any other form of government but which is the peculiar product of the representative democracy and is essential to the operation of that system.

The combination of the organizer with the civil officer comes next in order of development. We are gravely told that the government cannot be carried on unless there are men to arrange the machinery, do the drudgery, and work up the interest; that the civil offices ought to be given to men who are capable of doing this work, and that their services ought to be secured in that way. It must be conceded that such a class is essential to the working of a representative democracy, but if we are to go on in this way it would be wise and economical to recognize such functionaries as a part of the political system, to have them regularly appointed and regularly paid, on the principle that every open and recognized activity tends to come under proper restraints while every subterfuge tends to abuse. If, however, any one means to say that the excitement and agitation of last year, which we now recognize as largely the work of the political janissaries, tended to any good, or that the government could not be carried on and our needs in the way of political action could not be met without going through what we went through last year to reach the point at which we stand to-day, he will find it very difficult to prove it. It is not self-government to have Congressmen appoint local civil officers and civil officers secure the election of Congressmen in perpetual reiteration. I call it a self-perpetuating oligarchy. It is not civil liberty to walk in processions and cast ballots once in a while under such a system. When we are told that we cannot govern ourselves except by this machinery, it seems a worse insult than to say that we cannot govern ourselves without a king, or a privileged class, or titles and ribbons, or pensions and parliamentary corruption. The people who make such assertions pique themselves on being "practical" when they are only base and vulgar; but it remains to be proved that the people need to be debauched with their own money and by their own servants, in order to carry on a government whose boast it is that it has thrown away all the old instruments of political debauchery. If it is true, then let us try to govern ourselves awhile or do without government until we have better. We may, at any rate, hazard the experiment.

THE SPOILS SYSTEM. The spoils doctrine arises from the corrupt conception of the civil service joined with the notion of party politics at war. The parties in a democracy carry on their contests as if there were no limits to the privileges of the victory — hardly those which humanity imposes in war; the current phraseology of parties is a series of war-metaphors. Autocrats and democratic majorities strike down opposition as criminal; they allow little room for the conception of consti-

tutional opposition. It is thought that to be heroic is
to be radical, and that when victory is won in a political battle nothing, least of all the protests of the minority, ought to arrest the self-will of the victors. There is
a vigor and ruthlessness which is totally out of place in
politics. When it has been established that the power
or the legal right to do a thing exists, it is considered
pusillanimous to have scruples about exercising the
power. Such notions are hostile to any true conceptions of party or party rule, and they lead to those
victories to win which parties destroy institutions.

Now when parties have definite principles, this conception leads to sweeping and tyrannical attempts to
realize their theories in fact. When they have few or
no principles, their contests degenerate into struggles
for power and place, and victory means that we or you
shall take the offices. Wm. L. Marcy was by no means
one of the bad men who have been prominent in American politics, and the education which could make such
a man enunciate the bold doctrine that "to the victors
belong the spoils" in the unblushing way in which he
uttered it is worth studying. Men of decent character
and good education do not invent such doctrines and
spring them on sedate deliberative bodies on the spur
of the moment, and the notion that Marcy invented
the spoils doctrine or that Jackson, out of his own evil
determination, set out to demoralize the civil service,
is both historically false and philosophically absurd.
These twin abuses were the culmination of a long history.
When Marcy said, "To the victors belong the spoils,"
he only gave new, distinct, and dogmatic expression to
the theories in which he had been educated, and the
context of his speech shows that he was not conscious
of uttering anything which ought to shock any one of

those who heard him. He thought that the victors ought to undertake the administration of the government, which is not disputed by any one; he had grown up, however, in conflicts which hinged on no principles of administration or policy, but chiefly on questions of who were to have the offices. He had grown up in a young and loose society where there were few great interests or important questions at stake; the people of New York in his day had no wearing political anxieties, no hard problems of internal or external policy, no heavy taxation, no old abuses, no stubborn vested interests. It was possible to gratify any man's ambition or vanity by giving him public office, with its light and meager duties; it would involve no heavy risks and he could do, at most, but little harm. Of a consequence parties formed around leaders and more as alliances to secure certain objects of interest and ambition; and to win the political battle was, of course, to win these objects. It is idle, therefore, to indulge in denunciation of the spoils doctrine; it is a phenomenon, with its own development and history; it demands our study for its causes and its meaning. The causes lie in the nature of parties amongst us, in the social and political circumstances of our communities, in the prevailing conception of party warfare, and in the importance of organization under our political system.

THE IMBECILITY OF OUR PRESENT ORGANIZATION. The greatest fault of this representative democracy, aside from its inadequateness for the needs of a great nation, is its weakness in the face of local demands and interested cliques. A system which is a representative of interests looks upon the effort to get what one wants as natural and in the order of things, to be resisted by those only whose interests may be threatened. The conflict of politics therefore degenerates into a struggle of will-force measured by votes; arguments are thrown away in all battles — when two bodies of men with opposing determinations meet, then force of the kind suited to the arena must decide. Hence the weakness of the representative democracy, in its inability to give support to the public interest, or the national welfare, or a permanent policy, or a far-sighted benefit, in the face of a sectional demand, or a temporary and short-sighted desire of a large number, or the selfish purpose of a strong clique. This weakness is especially apparent in face of the effort of a powerful corporation which can influence a large number of votes and has an interest strong enough to make it use money freely. The deepest disgrace which has ever come upon us as a nation has come from this source, and we are threatened with more. It does not seem possible that our previous experience, which so fully occupied the public mind only a few years ago, can have failed to make its due impression upon us.

GENERAL IRRESPONSIBILITY. The last observation I have to make on the representative democracy is that it nowhere involves political responsibility. The constitutional struggles of English history have consisted in the effort to bring the crown under responsibility to the nation in the exercise of sovereign powers. With us the sovereign powers are in the hands of a popular majority—but is it possible to make the majority responsible to the whole? Some think that the majority need not be made responsible, in other words, that the power and rights of the majority are in the nature of prerogative. Others think that the only responsibility which is necessary is that of a party. A party, however, is an abstraction; it cannot be held responsible or punished; if it is deprived of power it fades into thin air and the men who composed it, especially those who did the mischief and needed discipline, quickly reappear in the new majority. The responsibility of a party is only the responsibility of the nation to itself, or of an old majority to a new one, and it has no other form than a new election, for which it is only another expression.

PARTIES ARE IRRESPONSIBLE. Party responsibility is not, however, any guarantee of civil liberty nor any bond for the organization of governmental organs. It could not be very serviceable to good government unless parties were very free in their formation and dissolution and the public criticism of party politics very active. It is in this connection that the fast organization of parties, which seem, as we have seen, essential to democracy, is most mischievous, for it neutralizes the only form of responsibility which exists in a democracy. In our experience it has been proved that the Presidential election rallies and confirms party organizations every four years and that in the interval they decline and tend to freer combinations. The legislature, elected partly at these intervals and elected by detached constituencies in which the varieties and minor fluctuations of public opinion find expression as they do not in the great mass vote for President, constitutes a far more satisfactory exponent of national feeling and will than the executive. I do not hesitate to express the opinion that the government would to-day stand on a much higher plane of purity, energy, and efficiency than it now does, if it had followed the lines indicated in Congressional elections, without the periodical shocks of the Presidential elections. We define the functions of our public offices, and elect men to perform those functions for limited times. If we do not elect good ones we have no one to blame but ourselves. This is the only conception of responsibility which the system seems to admit, and the consequence of the political education which it gives is that people scarcely seem to understand what the notion of responsibility in government is.

THE DEMOCRACY NEEDED. I have not made this analysis and exposition of democracy with the idea that any amount of criticism could overthrow democracy or lead to the abandonment of it; on the contrary, when I see that institutions are rooted in the character of the people and in the circumstances of the country, I take them as they are. There is no fighting against them, if any one wanted to do it. Democracy has grown here, as I have especially attempted to show, because every condition favored it; we never could have had anything else; we cannot have, for a long time to come, any government in which the democratic element does not preponderate. Neither can I see that any other form of institutions, in spite of all the faults of democracy, would be, on the whole, so well adapted for us in our present circumstances. We are forty millions of people who, a little while ago, had nothing; and in the countries from which we came we had little chance of ever getting anything. They tell us that we have only a material civilization and that we appreciate nothing but the dollar. In the main the charge is true, but we are yet busy in accumulating the material capital which is the first condition of civilization and material greatness — we are laying the foundations of a great nation, and if we are laying them in the mud, that is where all foundations have to rest. Those who have accumulated capital complain, with great justice, that the democratic system throws on them exceptional burdens while it practically excludes them from the higher political privileges; those who want to pursue science, literature, and art complain of the unfavorable atmosphere for their work, and their complaint is just. These points of view only bring out the various aspects of our position — its advantages and disadvantages. We must take them both together and make the best of them.

DEMOCRACY AND WEALTH. Democratic institutions have had no positive effect in assisting this material development; it has rested on economic causes; but democratic institutions, by their looseness and simplicity, have left social competition free to act. That is the way they have involved a large measure of liberty, set against the conventional barriers of birth, rank, and social position. Under this régime merit has been able to find its level everywhere but in politics; in other words, liberty has tended to destroy equality in other spheres, and since the doctrine of equality prevailed in politics, the contradictions between political and social development are readily explained. That merit should prevail under free competition, where it relies only on itself, more easily than under an electoral system, where it relies on the recognition of men, is not strange.

The belief that democratic institutions have had positive efficacy in connection with material prosperity, and that it is due to them that conventional barriers have had so little standing here, has had much to do with the affection of the people, in times past, for those institutions. I have had in view, however, in my present undertaking, the discontents which mark the rise of a political skepticism which was unknown here twenty years ago. Doubts about American institutions have arisen in quarters where there was the fullest faith; lamentations over degeneracy and corruption have be-

come common — they will be renewed at the end of the
first year of the new Presidential term, which is always
our golden age.   In my contact with young men I am
continually and painfully struck by the fact that, although they have a great deal of feeling and enthusiasm
for parties and men, they do not respect the institutions
of their country and deem it no shame to express contempt for Congress or for state legislatures.   When I
turn to the newspapers it seems to me that a stranger
who read them would think that, throwing aside all
incidental and unimportant matters, the three essential
organs of the American government are the President,
the politicians, and the people, and that the practical
question of our politics is: Which two of these will combine against the other?   I have, therefore, attempted
to set forth both the strength and the limitations of the
American representative democracy.   I regard it as a
necessary stage in the political development of the
country; I regard it as inadequate for the needs of the
nation which is growing up; I regard the inferences
which have been drawn from it in regard to the abstract
goodness of democracy as entirely fallacious; I do not
see how democracy, in an old country, can ever be
anything but a short road to Cæsarism.

THE FUTURE. With regard to the future development of our system, we may be sure that it will take
place steadily and necessarily.   We shall not make any
great reforms or sweeping changes.   All that comes
about will have to proceed out of our past history, be
built upon it, and be consistent with it.   No constitutional or other changes can be brought about by congresses of learned men or by voluntary organizations
which are not in accord with the genius of the election
and its circumstances.   The revisions which have been

made in state constitutions during the last twenty-five
years have shown a distinct tendency to introduce
conservatism, higher organization (especially of the executive departments), longer terms of office, and so on.
The democratic tendency has passed its culmination,
and experience has shown the limitations of certain of
its dogmas and the error of others.   Many of the provisions of these later constitutions show that the people
do not trust themselves; they put away from themselves
certain powers which they have abused.   These provisions are like total abstinence pledges, needful as a prop
to self-control when it is weak, but, when made by states,
destructive of a liberty which it may, upon occasion,
be very necessary to exercise.

It is a popular opinion that popular institutions are
the only good ones and the only ones necessary.   This
is an error; civil liberty cannot exist without the institutions of power and authority as well as the institutions
which secure popular rights.   Civil liberty is a form of
national life which can be secured in its true equilibrium
only by a great body of institutions, which are good only
when all together and all in their due proportion.   Without their due proportion, nations fluctuate between the
liberty of the guillotine and the order of Cæsarism, but
never find the steady path of civil liberty; with the due
proportion of these institutions nations may enjoy civil
liberty according to the traditions and tastes of each,
under monarchical or aristocratic or democratic institutions.   We have hitherto had popular institutions in
abundance, and our popular institutions are strong,
but our institutions of order, authority, organization,
and responsibility have been weak.   Our circumstances,
both internal and external, have been such that we have
not felt the need; but those foreigners who infer from

our experience that an old country can dispense with its institutions of order and authority and get on without them as well as we, manifest a very shallow philosophy.

NECESSARY MODIFICATIONS. It is safe to say now that our future development will be in the way of extending and modifying our institutions so as to fit the needs of a great nation. The Civil War has had a great effect in hastening on this necessity and hastening the maturity of the nation, for it has overloaded our institutions with new and startling difficulties. To carry on a great civil war, to finish it and return to peace and order, seemed a great triumph for democracy; it now appears that that achievement was a comparatively slight one. No political system which has ever existed is so powerful or can develop so much physical force as a democracy when it is composed of a large, eager, and compact majority, animated by a spontaneous resolve for a single purpose. Its power is so great that it would be unendurable if it were possible to form any such majority by artificial organization.

THE WAR. The War, however, carried us on to another stage of civil life; it left us a large number of abuses such as are inseparable from war; it afforded an opportunity for great interests to become vested; it opened a new and wider arena to the demagogue, and in fact produced a differentiation in demagogues. The questions at issue in politics had their moral, religious, ethnological, emotional, and economical, as well as their political phases, and groups of persons were formed who seized upon such of these phases as came easiest to them, and obscured the questions while they befogged the public mind by superficial comments. The limits of political discussion were naturally obliterated and the correct conception of what are properly political considerations

was lost.   So far has this gone that some people seem
to think it low and degrading to discuss political questions by political arguments, but make a merit of mixing
up benevolence and business, patriotism and engineering
enterprise, charity and civil government, emotion and
legislation, sentiment and the administration of justice,
the rights of man and police control, education and punishment, moral training and criminal law, equality and
the supervision of industry, religion and sanitary regulation, humanity and the repression of vice.

This confusion has been anything but helpful in the
solution of the great problems which the altered state
of things has brought with it.   In the old ante-war times
this confusion would have made little difference, because
there was little occasion to put any theories into practice
on such a scale as to do great harm; but with a large
debt, a depreciated currency, heavy taxation, a new order of things to create in the South, and wasted capital
to replace, this confusion in political methods and in
the sphere of the various institutions amongst which
social work is divided has been most mischievous.

We have also reached, since the War, that stage in
many of our industries at which the organizing activity
of government becomes important to recognize and give
legal sanction to usages, to collect information, and to
furnish general public facilities.   It is evident that the
possible advantages from the Bureaus of Agriculture,
Education, Statistics, the Census, and the Signal Service, from explorations of the new territories and from
scientific expeditions, increase every year with the development of the nation, and that the loss is greater
every year if the management is not enlightened.

If we look at another department of public life we find
the same thing true.   Our notion of what a modern city

ought to be has expanded very much within twenty years, and to satisfy this notion there is a demand for great technical knowledge and skill, a permanent policy steadily pursued, and a large expenditure of money. The notion that any man can do anything, that any man is good enough to serve the public, does more mischief here, perhaps, than anywhere else.

REFORM. The effect of all these observations, as they force themselves one after another upon the attention of the people, must be to establish the conviction that our institutions are, in some respects, inadequate to the needs of to-day, and especially that the public tasks cannot be adequately performed save by competent men. The agitation for the reform of the civil service, little as it has as yet accomplished, bears witness that the public mind is already moving and that it has found its true point of attack. The most fatal breach in all existing abuses would be the separation of the office-holders from the work of organizing parties and managing elections, and any civil service reform which does not make that its aim is a delusion. With this reform accomplished, a chance will be opened for a better public opinion to act upon the elections and to make itself felt in the choice of legislators. Here, however, is where public opinion itself needs further development; in view of the great tasks which weigh upon us in public affairs, we shall have to abandon the notion that we can all solve those problems as easy incidents to our ordinary occupations. We shall have to do as we do elsewhere, adopt a new division of labor and a higher organization; we shall have to select men, who, if they are not already specially trained, enjoy our confidence in regard to their ability to investigate and decide, if they undertake this as a special duty. Such men will no longer be democratic delegates but true "representatives"; a body of such men selected from various constituencies would "represent" the nation or the state as no popular majority ever does. They would present the state in miniature; and any one who wanted to deal with the state would have to deal with them. For all practical purposes, they would be the state, would embody its wisdom and its will, and would decide on its action. They would constitute the great council of the nation; they would have to act on their judgment and at their discretion and would therefore necessarily be independent. They would be under the observation of the people, who would judge by the result who were wise and who were foolish, who were worthy of confidence and who were not, who were capable of filling the trust laid upon them and who were not. Such representatives would find their reputation and their professional advancement dependent on their success in promoting the permanent welfare of the state; the public interest would be their chief charge as against all private interests.

RESPONSIBLE GOVERNMENT. All associations of men form their own code, their rules of etiquette, and their *esprit du corps*. They are guided in this by a common interest which leads them to form such rules as will assist each member in what is necessary to success and protect each member against the most probable dangers. The code of any legislative body in the country, under existing circumstances, will serve to illustrate this. In such a body as I have described the code would adjust itself to the circumstances. The members would sustain each other against assaults which threatened the reputation of the body or the independence of members. The great desire of all public servants is for approval; re-election is desired oftener for this than for any other reason, and the fear of disapproval, or what we call political responsibility, offers a check upon such a body in favor of the true control of the people, which is perfect in its action and complete for the purpose. Such a system would indeed be a barrier to empty vanity and petty ambition, but it would give better government; and it will come when we learn, perhaps by bitter experience, that we cannot do without it. It would call the leisure class into the service of the state, for it is they who owe the state public service. The wealthy class, in this country at any rate, show by the acquisition of capital that they possess talent and force; they moreover possess independence, without which no man is a politician. Their employment in the public service would help to bring about the balance of burdens and privileges, rights and duties, power and responsibility, without which a highly developed state cannot enjoy permanent civil order. The decay of the old doctrine of "instructions" seems to me to mark some progress, if only slight, towards an independent and responsible legislature.

STATESMEN. It is, furthermore, in a body of independent and responsible legislators that statesmen are developed — I mean by a statesman a man who plans practical measures for rendering well-tested principles actually active for the welfare of a state. He always needs, also, to be able to defend his measures and to recommend them to people who are not yet convinced of their excellence. It is not possible that parliamentary eloquence which, in spite of all the sneers at it, is the grand educator of the nation under free institutions, should flourish under a system of committee legislation. That is a system which calls for intrigue and personal influence, leaves full opportunity for the abuses which flourish when sheltered from publicity, and allows public speaking to degenerate into a perfunctory performance. Parliamentary debate, when properly conducted, consists of discussion — of the conflict of mind with mind in all the exercises which tend to develop correct thinking and to force examination of a subject in all its bearings, so that the measure adopted truly represents the best wisdom of the body which passed it. This debate develops an eloquence of its own, pure, clear, simple, and business-like — as free from bombastic rhetoric as from pedantry; a deliberative body which practices it is a school of statesmen. I notice no tendency which seems to me more to be regretted than the apparent loss to the public mind of the true notion of a free discussion.

The principle of responsibility has its bearing also upon the opposition. The opposition has a peculiar function, under constitutional government, to criticize, resist, and bring out opposing considerations; it enforces care and deliberation. Its great danger is lest it become factious and reckless; and the great safeguard against this is the requirement that the opposition, if successful, shall assume the administration and the responsibility and make its criticisms good. With this prospect before it, it is forced to moderation and reflection. It is sometimes said of a public man that he would be spoiled if he took administrative office, but it would be impossible to pass a more complete condemnation upon a person in such a career. It stamps him as a mere vulgar agitator.

THE EXECUTIVE. The executive must also be brought under the principle of responsibility. How this is to be accomplished under our system is not yet clear. That the executive must be brought into open and honorable relations to the legislature for the development of good government is certain; but how to engraft the English plan on our system I do not see. The man who should devise an expedient as well suited to our system as the English plan is to theirs would deserve to rank amongst the greatest public benefactors.

At present the President of the United States has both too much power and too little. He has more than any man ought to have without responsibility, and he has less than a competent head of the nation needs to have, if he is responsible for its exercise only by the continuance or loss of power. He needs to act often with a wide discretion on his judgment of the public interest. He also wants an organ for influencing public opinion to secure support or deprecate opposition. Formerly this need led him to have a newspaper under his control; now he has recourse to the unworthy and untrustworthy expedient of the interview or an irresponsible utterance to a correspondent. He needs also a means of communicating with Congress other than the tedious and lifeless message or the private interview with members.

The old writers thought that good government could be secured by a division of departments and by a system of checks and balances. But the division of departments — if it means that we need only make them sufficiently independent of one another and then that they will be sure to go right — is an empty dogma; and the system of checks and balances, if it were perfect, would bring equilibrium — that is, no movement at all. The more difficult task is to secure harmonious action, in due proportion, without friction — in other words, to give to political organs an organic instead of a mechanical activity. The principle of responsibility fulfills this purpose; it allows freedom with control. There is no fear whatever that there will be abuses of power, no matter how great, in law and theory, the power may be, if there is responsibility. Every public man dreads responsibility and it is the mark of a great statesman to step forward and assume it bravely when the occasion demands. The best critics of the English Constitution agree that its weakness is in the lack of independence in the executive. Ministers who have to face Parliament are only too anxious to do nothing which they can help, and to accomplish what they do accomplish, not as they think it ought to be done, but so as to hold their majority together. The principle of a strong executive, held to strict responsibility, may be set down as the great gain of the last century in the science of politics; it is essential to the good government of a great nation with complicated interests.

The initiative in legislative matters belongs to individual representatives, but it is best exercised by the executive. The executive as the permanent part of the government, charged with its administration, acquires familiarity with its workings, its excellencies, its faults, and its needs. This department, therefore, is in the best position to prepare and lay before the legislature measures which shall be well drafted and correctly adapted to what is needed. Where individual members introduce bills as their whims or their vanity dictates, instances of crude and incoherent legislation continually occur. An executive cannot be expected to give very efficient administration to laws which he disapproves or whose mischievous action he sees, and he cannot be held responsible for legislation about which he was never consulted or which he has resisted. All this has especial reference to the financial administration, which can never combine efficiency with economy unless the reputation of those who have the immediate control of it is

at stake to bring about that combination.   If your ships
of war go to the bottom the Secretary of the Navy tells
you that he spent all the money Congress would give
him, and that they did not give him what he wanted; if
extravagant sums are spent on the navy, you are told
that Congress appropriated and ordered it.   But if you
try to vent your disapproval on Congress, you find that
you are dealing with a body for whom responsibility has
no meaning.   Can you search for the votes?   Can you
find out who was to blame?   Can you go to committee-
room deliberations to search for the real parties in fault?
Can you reach any Congressman but your own representative?   Will changing your party satisfy your desire
to disapprove?   It is these difficulties which render
responsibility unknown to us.   It is only when you confer on a man power to do something that you can bring
reward or blame home to him when the thing is done
well or ill; and it is only when you bring blame home
to a man that you can inflict consequences which bear
upon the future.

Some critics of responsible government have said that
everybody was responsible to everybody else throughout
the whole system but that there was no starting point,
or point of reaction, for the whole.   This is, in fact, its
great merit.   There is no irresponsible authority or arbitrary power in it; it embodies the idea which the old
writers were trying to express in their theory of checks
and balances.   The true system of self-government for
a nation comes nearest to self-government in a man;
the man who governs himself must find the resources
for reform, resolution, and self-control in himself, and the
great system of responsible self-government in a nation
is, in like manner, only a part of the national life with
its springs, motives, and forces in the nation itself.   The

analogy with a machine is false; the true analogy is with organic life.

To sum up, then, the suggestions which I have endeavored to make: there is no absolutely "best" system of government; democracy is grounded in the circumstances of this country and has been so suited to the people and their needs that no other system has been possible; democracy is only available as a political system in the simple society of a new country — it is not adequate for a great nation; we have reached a point at which its faults and imperfections are mischievous, and, in the growth and advance of the nation, these evils must become continually more apparent; the remedy will lie in a greater division of labor and higher organization, produced by such modifications as are germane to our popular feelings and prejudices and consistent with our history; they will consist in conservative institutions, and the first of these will be a body of statesmen or public men trained to their work; and further development will consist in a well organized system of government, held within due limits and harmonious action by responsibility to the representatives of the people and to the people themselves.

ADVANCING SOCIAL AND POLITICAL
ORGANIZATION IN THE UNITED STATES

ADVANCING SOCIAL AND POLITICAL OR-
GANIZATION IN THE UNITED STATES

[1896 OR 1897]

Colonial society; embryonic society. — American history disproves the notion
of the "Boon of Nature, etc." — Movement of American history away
from anarchistic liberty. — Colonial industrial organization the slightest
possible. — No employer and employee or other classes. — Social organization was characterized by equality and democracy. — But there were
modifications of democracy: 1. Aristocratic distinctions, so far as possible; 2. Distinctions by talent and industry; 3. Slavery. — Summary
of points about democracy and classes.— Colonial society furnishes a
test of the village community notion. — No society of free and
independent tillers only. — Analysis of democracy; definition of its
varieties. — Aristocracy of slavery. — Jacobinism and sansculottism.
— The Constitution-makers and democracy. — Sense of radical and
conservative in America. — Upper classes and political duty. — Significance of organization. — Advantages of a new country. — The escape
from tradition. — No manors. — Agriculture and land tenure in the
colonies. — The town and township. — Extension of loyalty from town
to province, then to Union. — The advancing civil organization. —
Disruptive forces. — Anarchistic liberty; it is limited in towns by unpopularity and gossip. — Character produced by anarchistic liberty. —
Character produced by great chances of wealth. — Liberty due to freedom
from powerful neighbors. — Merits of the quarrel with England, 1763–
1775. — Effects of disorganization in the Revolution. — Effects of disorganization under the Confederation. — Constitution unwelcome; why? —
Grand extension of discipline and reign of law. — How the federal government took the place of Great Britain. — It had to deal with the same
anarchistic elements. — Necessity that these should be overcome. — The
work of the Federal party. — The course of the Jeffersonians. — The
Supreme Court has helped the integration. — Police were needed in cities
to uphold the authority of law. — Survival of Revolutionary delusions in
the Civil War. — Latest phenomena of those delusions. — Combination
of the different stages of organization in the United States now. — Inevi-
tableness of struggle for mastery in the Union. — The future will see
condensation of the organization. — Advantage of rapidity of growth. —
Institutions in the Constitution. — War between democracy and institu-

THE fact which gives chief value to the study of the early history of the United States is that in it we can see a society begin from its earliest germ and can follow its growth. It is a case of an embryo society, not however of savages but of civilized men. They came armed with the best knowledge and ability which men, up to the time of their migration, had won. They began with the laws, customs, institutions, arts, and sciences of their mother-country at the time, and of course they tried to imitate the social organization in which they had been brought up. This they did not do, however, without some variations, for they had notions of their own about government, religion, and social order. The emigrants were, in many cases, the radicals of their time and in coming to America they seized the opportunity to try to realize some of their pet ideas.

Very soon also it became apparent that transplanted institutions and customs must undergo change. Under changed physical and social circumstances the social relations alter and the social organization is forced to adapt itself. That is what happened here; and it is the perception and appreciation of such changes, in their causes and nature, which is one of the chief objects to be sought in the study of our colonial history. It is often said that this colonial history is dull and insipid, and so it is if you look only at the magnitude and complication of the events or the grade of the passions at play and the interests at stake. It is from the point of view which I have just indicated and in the study of the facts which I have described that that history wins very high philosophical importance and presents elements to the student of society which he can find nowhere else; for later colonial enterprises have been undertaken with the help of steam and constant communication between the colony and the mother-country, and so under conditions of less complete isolation. Our colonies consisted of little groups, thrown on the coast of this continent and left to find out how to carry on the struggle for existence here, in ignorance of the geography, the climate, and other most essential facts, with very little capital, and with only the most imperfect connection with the mother-country from which they must expect help and reinforcements. It is, however, just this isolation, with the necessity of self-adjustment to the conditions, which gives interest and value to the story of the colonies as social experiments. It is a fact of more importance than the story of dynasties and wars that not a single permanent settlement could be made on the territory now occupied by the United States until more than a hundred years after Columbus discovered America; for it is a fact which at once proves the folly of the notion that there is such a thing as a "boon of nature," or that "land" is a free gift from nature of a thing useful to man. Why did a hundred men perish miserably when trying, in the sixteenth century, to found a settlement on territory where now seventy million live in prosperity? It was because nature offers, not a boon but a battle; not a gift but a task; and those men, with the means they possessed, were not competent for the task or able to win the battle. Although the settlements at Jamestown, Plymouth, and Massachusetts Bay did not perish, the story of their first years shows with what toil, pain, and risk a foothold could be won for beginning the struggle for existence here. It is anything but a picture of men quietly walking in to take their places at the "banquet of life," bounteously and gratuitously offered by nature.

But from the social germ planted by these colonists all that we have and are has grown up by expansion, adaptation, absorption of new elements, death or abolition of old ones — in short, by all the working and fighting, suffering and erring which go into the life of a big, ambitious, and vigorous society.

In following out this conception of American history we shall find that it presents a very remarkable contrast to the history of modern Europe. In the latter the movement which runs through the history is one of advancing organization, attended by an extension socially, industrially, and politically, of individual liberty; in the United States, however, while the social organization has advanced with gigantic strides, it has been attended by restrictions of individual liberty. Here I use the word "liberty" in its anarchistic sense of exemption from restraint, and not in its legal and institutional sense. While the progress of time has brought in Europe the abolition of minute and vexatious restrictions upon individual self-determination, in the United States it has increased the number of laws, customs, and usages which, extending over all departments of social activity except religion, interfere with the freedom of individual action. This is one of the penalties of high organization. If as a member of a great and strong organization you win advantages, you must pay for them by conformity and co-operation within the organization; but these will limit your individual liberty. If we bear in mind this contrast between American and

European history, it will help to explain many apparent contradictions in their philosophy which may perplex us when studying them side by side. All that I have yet to say will further expound and develop this contrast.

We shall also find another and most remarkable fact of American social history in this: that, while the lines of the social organization have been more strictly drawn and the social discipline has been steadily made more stringent, there have been new and other developments of individual activity which have far more than offset the loss of the earlier rude and, in truth, barbaric liberty.

A very amusing incident is mentioned in Winthrop's history of New England.[1] A land-owner hired a man to work for him, but, not being able to pay the stipulated wages, he gave the man a pair of oxen and discharged him. The laborer asked to go on with their relation. "How shall I pay you?" said the employer. "With more oxen," replied the man. "But when the oxen are all gone?" "Then you can work for me and earn them back again." There is in this story a whole volume of demonstration of the social relations of that time and that society. We can see that the relation of employer and employee was, under then-existing circumstances, impossible; when land was available in unlimited amount, how could one man be land-owner and another laborer? Why should not the latter go on a little further and become another land-owner? The two would then be alike and equal.[2] If, however, one of them worked for the other, what wages would he

---

[1] II, 220; compare Coxe's Carolina emigrants who became herdsmen because poor; their servants became rich.

[2] Franklin's Works, IV, 19, 24, 171; II, 475.

demand?   Evidently as much as he could gain by taking up land and working for himself.   But this would equal all that he could produce as a laborer for another or all that his employer's land could produce, so far as it occupied one man's labor.   Hence the laborer and the employer could only exchange places and impoverish each other alternately; and so no wages system was possible.   For the same reason no complete wages system exists yet.   Where increased human power was required in the colonies, it must be got by free co-operation, as in log-rolling and barn-raising.   But this means that there was no industrial organization.   All were farmers; ministers, teachers, merchants, mechanics, sailors carried on other occupations only incidentally; all owned land and drew their subsistence in a large proportion directly from land.   It was far down in the eighteenth century before mechanics, sailors, merchants, lawyers, and doctors were differentiated as distinct and independent classes of persons.   Thus in a century and a half or two centuries there has grown up here all this vast and complicated industrial organization which we now see, with its hundreds of occupations, its enormous plant and apparatus of all kinds, connected throughout by mutual relations of dependence, kept in order by punctuality and trustworthiness in the fulfillment of engagements, dependent upon assumptions that men will act in a certain way and want certain things, and, in spite of its intricacy and complication, working to supply our wants with such smoothness and harmony that most people are unaware of its existence.   They live in it as they do in the atmosphere.

I shall return to this point in a moment and try to show the commanding significance of this fact that we all earn our living in and as parts of a great industrial organization; and indeed the purpose of this entire essay will be to try to get some due appreciation of the whole social and political organization, especially in its advancing phases, and of its dominion over us and our interests. But we have not yet quite exhausted all the significance of the incident which I mentioned at the outset. We see from it that not even the simplest class distinctions, those of employer and employee, were possible here at that time. No man could gain anything by owning more land than he could till; the people who got grants of land made disagreeable experience of the truth of this. Because land was the best property a man could own in England, and ten thousand acres was a great estate there, they supposed that a man who got a grant of ten thousand acres in America got a great fortune, whereas in reality he got only a chance to sink a fortune without hope of return. As there could be no landlord, there could be no tenant; no man would hire another's land when he could get land of his own for the labor of reducing it to tillage. Now landlords, tenant-farmers, and laborers are the three groups which form the fundamental framework of a class-divided society; but if they are all merged in a class of peasant-proprietors or yeomen-farmers, there is absolutely no class organization. All are equal, by the facts of the case, as nearly as human beings can be equal.[1] A farmer tilling as much land as his own labor will suffice to cultivate never can accumulate a fortune in the midst of a society of others just like himself. Neither need any one of them lack subsistence for himself and family. His children are not a burden but a

[1] St. Jean de Crèvecœur, Lettres d'un Cultivateur Américain, Paris, 1787, I, 267.

help; they offer the only aid which he can hope for, since the relation of hire is impossible. If his sons, as they grow up, go off and take up land of their own, it is an advantage to him to have many sons, that the series may last as long as his own working years. If the minister and schoolmaster, as the only representatives of the professional classes, live amongst these farmers in the same way and on the same scale, and if the merchants of the commercial towns are few and their gains are slow and small,[1] there result just such commonwealths as existed in the northern colonies. The people of a town all club together to support a school for their children and a "common school system" is born unawares. It is plain that *equality* is the prevailing characteristic of this society; its members are equal in fortune, in education, in descent (at least after a generation or two), in mode of life, in social standing, in range of ideas, in political importance, and in everything else which is social, and *nobody made them so.* Such a society was what we call democratic, using the word in reference to the institutions, ideas, customs, and mores existing in it, and without reference to politics. It was made so, not by any resolutions or constitutions, but by the existing economic circumstances, of which the most important was the ratio of the population to the land. Nobody could have made the communities otherwise than democratic under the existing circumstances under which the struggle for existence was carried on.

The picture of colonial society which I have just

---

[1] The West India trade was a great source of wealth at Hartford. Three persons there, in 1775, were said to be worth about $80,000 each. Hinman, R. R., A Historical Collection . . . of the Part sustained by Conn. during the War of the Revolution, Hartford, 1842, p. 15.

drawn is the one which is generally presented and it may be familiar to the reader. In order to render it truthful, however, it is necessary at once to add some very important modifications.

In the first place, the English traditions and prejudices which had been inherited were distinctly aristocratic and the pet notions and doctrines of the colonists were not those of equality. If any man had anything to pride himself on as a distinction, he made the most of it, as nearly all men everywhere have done; and if the distinction was one of relationship to people of social importance in England, it was quite tenaciously nourished. Social distinction, however, if we may trust some reports, cost a man political ostracism. St. Jean de Crèvecœur [1] says that the richest man in Connecticut in 1770 was worth about $60,000; but he could not be elected to any office, and with difficulty obtained for his son a position as teacher in a Latin school in order to keep him in and of the people.

Then again, the innate and utterly inevitable inequality of men in industry, energy, enterprise, shrewdness, and so on, quickly differentiated these yeomen-farmers. Some families kept up the industrial virtues for generations; others manifested a lack of them. There were social failures then as there are always. Most of them "went West," choosing an avenue of escape whose immense importance in the whole social history of this country must not for a moment be lost sight of; but we hear also of shiftless, lawless, and vagabond people who lived on the mountains or on the outskirts of the town, given to drink, quarreling, and petty thieving. This phenomenon warns us that the pleasing picture of an Arcadian simplicity, equality,

[1] *L. c.*, I, 242.

and uniformity, such as has often been applied to our
colonial society, is unreal. It is impossible in human
nature. Put a group of men in equal circumstances,
under wide and easy conditions, and instead of getting
equal, uniform, and purely happy results, you will get
a differentiation in which some will sink to misery, vice,
and pauperism.

Yet again, when considering inequality, we must
remember the existence of slavery in this society; of
that I will speak presently in another connection.

We must, therefore, understand that the notion of our
colonies as pure and ideal democracies is unhistorical.
While broad features might seem to justify it, the
details, in which lie all the truth and reality, greatly
modify the picture.

But there is a wider aspect of this matter and one
which, so far as I know, has never been noticed at all.
I cannot find anywhere in history any case of a society
of free and equal men consisting exclusively of independent tillers of the soil.   We are forced to ask whether
such a thing is a social impossibility.   A notion has had
wide currency within the last thirty years that "village
communities" are a stage of primitive democratic
organization through which most modern civilized
societies have passed. That there have been villages
which were organized for industrial and social purposes
is as certain as that there have been states; but the
"village community" has been personified and elevated
to the rank, not of a social organization expedient for a
purpose, but of an independent organism, something
more than a society although less than an intelligent
being. Hence it has been made to appear that the
breaking up of village communities was not the abandon-

ing of an organization which was no longer useful, but was the killing of something of an exalted and ideal character. This is all mythology. It is impossible to find any village community which was ever anything more than a group of people who were trying to get their living out of the ground as well as they could under the circumstances in which they found themselves. That is just what we are doing now. The most peculiar features of the village community were dictated by envy and jealousy, lest one man should be better off than another, and the chief lesson the study of them enforces is that when laws and customs are made with a view to equality they crush out progress.

But the point to which I wish now to call attention especially is even stronger if we assume that village communities were once such ideal societies, with vigorous and healthy forces inside of them; if they ever consisted of free and equal men, standing sturdily together, working industriously, sharing fairly, maintaining rights and justice of which they had a clear and natural apprehension, making every man do his duty, letting no man encroach upon another, and resisting all oppression from without. For the question then is: If any territory ever was occupied by such units, why did they sink into serfdom? The things which are strong vindicate their strength by their resistance and their achievements; it will not do, therefore, to say that the village communities were overridden by force; what is claimed for them is that they contained the most powerful and persistent social forces which can be called into play. All western Europe was feudalized and its cultivators of the soil were reduced to serfdom. Scandinavia was only partially feudalized, but it illustrates the point even better, because we can follow the reduction of free peasants as far down as they went towards serfdom, and we know that it was not their own energy of resistance which kept them from going lower. Furthermore, all over Europe among the peasant-tillers of the soil, while they were free yeomen (if they ever were so), there were slaves. These were owned by the freeholders. But if the yeomen were themselves slaveholders, their society is excluded from my proposition, for the society does not then consist of free and equal tillers of the soil alone.

I wish to bring into connection with this another fact which may seem at first to lie far removed from it. In stages of half-civilization where tillage is just beginning we find that the tillers are ruled by warlike nomads. This relation has been found all over the globe; especially where the tillers occupy a fertile plain below steppes or mountain slopes, the latter are inhabited by wild and wandering tribes which periodically descend into the plains to rob and plunder or levy tribute. A large part of Africa has long presented this state of things. It is evident that the settled tillers unlearn the arts of war, for they want peace, order, regularity. They must spend great labor on permanent works of construction and irrigation which are, however, at the mercy of an invader. The nomads are warlike and have greater physical power; they either make periodical raids or they compromise for a regular tribute. Great states have grown in the course of time out of this latter relation, the ruling nomads becoming the nobles and the tillers the peasantry or serfs. The first of these stages shows us militarism and industrialism in conflict; the second shows us the two combined and adjusted in a great state. This antagonism of militarism and industrialism is the most important thread of philosophy which can be run through history.

Here, then, is a startling phenomenon and a problem for the sociologist to elucidate. Does the tiller of the soil gravitate to servitude by some inherent necessity? There are no peasant-proprietors now in Europe who are not maintained by arbitrary operation of law. Whole schools of social philosophy have taken up the notion that peasant-proprietors are fine things to have and that they must be got or produced at any price in the old countries. It is not my intention now to discuss the problem thus raised, but I hasten to bring what I have said to bear on the subject before us. We see why it is interesting and important to ask whether the American colonies do present an exceptional case of what we are looking for, *viz.*, a society consisting exclusively of free and equal tillers of the soil. To this the answer is that they do not. They used slaves; the great need of an organization of labor by which combined effort could be brought to bear was what caused the introduction of slavery. We have positive testimony from the colonial period that the practical reason for slavery was that without it laborers could not be induced to go and stay where the work was to be done, especially in remote districts. Slavery, of course, became developed and established more and more to the southward, as those districts were reached whose products — tobacco, rice, and indigo — could be cultivated only on a large scale by a great organization of labor, many laborers being combined under one overseer. In the northern states, when slavery was abolished, towns had grown up, professional classes had begun to be formed, artisans and merchants constituted distinct classes, and the whole social organization had become so complex that the simple society consisting exclusively of tillers of the soil was not to be sought there. It is true that our new states have, within a hundred years, come nearer to presenting us that phenomenon than any other communities ever have; but then again it is to be remembered that they are parts in a worldwide organization of industry and commerce and are not any longer distinct communities.

In the course of my remarks on the last point, I have touched upon the case of slavery in the South. It has often been said that slavery in the South was an aristocratic institution. Aristocratic and democratic are indeed currently used as distinctly antagonistic to each other, but whether they are so or not depends upon the sense in which each of them is taken, for they are words of very shifting and uncertain definition. It is aristocratic to measure men and scale off their social relations by birth; it is democratic to deny the validity of such distinctions and to weigh men by their merits and achievements without regard to other standards. In this sense, however, democracy will not have anything to do with equality, for if you measure men by what they are and do, you will find them anything but equal. This form of democracy, therefore, is equivalent to aristocracy in the next sense. For, second, aristocracy means inequality and the social and political superiority of some to others, while democracy means social and political equality in value and power. But no man ever yet asserted that "all men are equal," meaning what he said. Although he said, "all men," he had in mind some limitation of the group he was talking about. Thus, if you had asked Thomas Jefferson, when he was writing the first paragraph of the Declaration of Independence, whether in "all men" he meant to include negroes, he would have said that he was not talking about negroes. Ask anybody who says it now whether he means to include foreigners — Russian Jews, Hungarians, Italians — and he will draw his line somewhere. The law of the United States draws it at Chinamen. If you should meet with a man who should say, as I would, although I do not believe that all men are equal in any sense, that such laws are unjust and that all men ought to have an equal chance to do the best they can for themselves on earth, then you might ask him whether he thought that Bushmen, Hottentots, or Australians were equal to the best-educated and most cultivated white men. He would have to admit that he was not thinking of them at all. Now, if we draw any line at all, the dogma is ruined. If you say: "All men are equal except some who are not," you must admit tests and standards and you are like the aristocrats, only that they may have other standards than yours and may draw the line around a smaller group. Furthermore if you define a group and then say that all are equal within it, that is pure aristocracy; all peers are equal — that is what their name denotes. School-boys learn from their Greek books enthusiasm for Greek democracy, but in the height of Athenian glory there were four slaves for every Athenian freeman and "democracy" meant the equality of these latter in exploiting the emoluments of the Athenian state. This brings us to the case of our Southern slaveholders. It was not a paradox that the great Virginians were slaveholders and great democrats too; the paradox is in the use of the words, for we see that the terms dissolve into each other. Before you know which you are talking about, it is the other. The Southern democrats drew their line between white and black, but they

affirmed the equality of all whites, that is, of all who
were in the ring.   This made them great popular leaders
— of whites.   If we should repeal our naturalization
laws, admit no more immigrants to citizenship, restrict-
ing political power to those now here and letting them
and their descendants possess it by universal manhood
suffrage, we should create a democratic-aristocracy in
a generation or two.   Hence it is clear that a democratic-aristocracy is not a contradiction in terms.

So far then, we see, I think, that democracy in the
sense of political equality for the members of the ruling
race was produced in the colonies out of the necessities
and circumstances of the case.   No convention ever
decreed it or chose it.   It existed in the sense of social
equality long before it was recognized and employed as
a guiding principle in institutions and laws; its strength
in the latter is due to the fact that it is rooted and
grounded in economic facts.   The current popular
notion that we have democratic institutions because
the men of the eighteenth century were wise enough
to choose and create them is entirely erroneous.   We
have not made America; America has made us.   There
is, indeed, a constant reaction between the environment and the ideas of the people; the ideas turn into
dogmas and pet notions, which in their turn are applied
to the environment.   What effect they have, however,
except to produce confusion, error, mischief, and loss
is a very serious question.   The current of our age has
been entirely in favor of the notion that a convention
to amend the Constitution can make any kind of a
state or society which we may choose as an ideal.   That
is a great delusion, but it is one of the leading social
faiths of the present time.

I turned aside from the second sense of aristocracy

and democracy to show how the distinction applied to the case of our southern colonies. It will be an economy of time if I now return to that analysis before going further. Aristocracy means etymologically the rule of the best. Cicero [1] says: "*Certe in optimorum consiliis posita est civitatum salus.*" If there were any way of finding out who are the best and of keeping them such in spite of the temptations of power, we might accept this dictum. In practice aristocracy always means the rule of the few. Democracy means the rule of the many; in practice it always means the rule of a numerical majority. A dogma has been made out of this and it has been affirmed that the majority has a right to rule in a sense as absolute as that in which the divine right of kings was formerly laid down. It has been asserted that the majority had a right to misrule, to waste money, to perpetrate injustice, and so on, if such was its good pleasure. This doctrine is democratic absolutism and it is as slavish and false as any doctrine of royal absolutism. In the working of majority rule it always degenerates into oligarchy; a majority of a majority is endowed with power, in one sub-division after another, until at last a few control. On the other hand, many cases can be found in history where an aristocracy has applied majority rule inside of itself with a dogmatic absoluteness surpassing that of democracy itself.

The degenerate form of democracy, when it runs out into an oligarchy or when it is entirely unregulated by constitutional provisions, is often designated as jacobinism. It is the rule of a clique, arrogating to itself the name of the people or the right to act for the people. It is the inevitable outcome of any form of

[1] De Republica, I, 34.

democracy which is not restrained and regulated by institutions. A still more excessive degeneration of democracy is sansculottism. As a political form this is the rule of a street mob; as a philosophy it is hatred of all which is elegant, elevated, cultured, and refined. It stamps with rage and contempt on everything which is traditionally regarded as noble, praiseworthy, and admirable and it embraces with eagerness whatever is regarded by tradition as foul, base, and vulgar.

Returning now from this more philosophical analysis, which seemed necessary to a full understanding of terms, let us come back to the historical aspect of our subject. It does not appear that anybody paid any attention to the first paragraph of the Declaration of Independence when it was written or that anybody except Thomas Paine then held to the dogmas of democracy. The men of that generation were all afraid of what they always called unbridled democracy. The disturbances of public order between 1783 and 1787 greatly intensified this fear, so that the Constitution-makers were not in a mood for any pure democracy. A few of them held to the system of political maxims which simply expressed the satisfaction of the great mass of the people with the loose political and social organization which had existed up to that time; but these men had very little influence on the result. The Constitution of 1787 is also remarkable, considering the time at which it was framed, for containing no dogmatic utterances about liberty and equality and no enunciation of great principles. Indeed this was made a ground of complaint against it by the leaders of the popular party; they missed the dogmatic utterances to which they had become accustomed during the war and they forced the passage of the first ten amendments. Even then, however, the Constitution contained no declaration of rights, but was simply a working system of government which was constituted out of institutions and laws already operating and familiar. In the one or two points in which the Constitution-makers endeavored to devise something new and clever with which to avert an apprehended danger, as for instance in the case of the Electoral College, their wisdom has all been set at naught. It is noticeable that this was a safeguard against democracy. In another case, when they set no limit to the number of re-elections which a president might obtain, the democratic temper of the country has forced an unwritten law limiting the terms to two. Here I should like to point out a confirmation of one thing which I said at the outset, that the direction of political movement in this country and in Europe has been opposite. According to European usage, which has become current here also, we should want to call the Anti-federalists radicals, and we should call Hamilton, Madison, and the other advocates of the new Constitution conservatives. But if conservative means clinging to the old and if radical means favoring change and innovation, then the Anti-federalists were the conservatives and the Federalists were radicals.

There are people amongst us who are thrown into a flutter of indignation by the suggestion that there are any classes in our American society, yet from time to time we hear blame cast upon the educated and property classes for not taking a due share in politics. The existence of some class differentiation is then recognized. Democracy is in general and by its principles jealous of the interference of any who are distinguished from the mass by anything whatever; as soon as anybody is distinguished in any way he ceases to be one of the people. We hear the word "people" used in this way all the time and we know that it means, not the population but some part of the population which is hard to define but which, I think, means the mass with all the distinguished ones taken out. This is another recognition of class. Now it is part of the system of theoretical or dogmatic democracy to hold that wisdom is with the people in the sense just defined. They are said to know; they judge rightly; they perceive the truth; if we trust them, they will govern aright. Incidentally scorn is often cast on the sages and philosophers, the theorists and bookworms — and it is probably for the most part well-deserved; but the implication is that the mass of men have by nature and common sense the wisdom which the sages and philosophers lack. In any democratic system, therefore, the distinguished classes are kept aloof from the active control. There is nothing which the stump-orator, ambitious for influence and position, more energetically disclaims than the assumption that he is any better qualified to teach than any of his audience; he anxiously insists that he is only a common man and one of the people. This is the great reason why civil service reform has never won wide popular support — that it is considered undemocratic. It is so because it assumes that some men are more fit and capable for public office than other men are. Most of the time we give office to people whose vanity will be gratified by it, not to those who can serve us in the position. Those who have special ability, skill, capital, or knowledge are called upon in emergencies to help us out of difficulties, but they are watched with great jealousy lest they get a notion that they are essential and begin to assume that they must be retained and rewarded. They are therefore dismissed again as soon as possible and without reward. So far we have not got many of them to accept the rôle which is thus allotted to them, and although we scold them and tell them that they ought to carry the burdens, do the work, and take the blows while somebody else gets the glory and the pay, we do not seem to make much impression on them. As a class they turn to money-making as a far more pleasant and profitable occupation.

We began with an employer and an employee face to face with each other and we have been brought to notice the lack of industrial organization and the incongruity of class distinctions in the colonial days on account of industrial facts. Already, then, we begin to see that the conditions of the existing social organization are controlling facts for the welfare and interests of men. Let us try to realize the full significance of this observation. We can perhaps understand it better now, having begun with the interpretation of a concrete case. Every one of us is born into society, that is to say, into some form and kind of society — the one which is existing at the time and place; we must live our lives in that society under the conditions which its constitution and modes of action set for us. We can imagine the same human infant taken either to the United States, to Russia, to Turkey, to China, or to Central Africa, and it is plain that his career and existence would be determined in its direction, modes, and possibilities by the one of those societies which should become his social environment. It is equally true, although not so obvious because the contrast is less strong, that a man could not be and become in Massachusetts in the seventeenth or the eighteenth century what he can be and become there in the nineteenth. The social organization is produced by the reaction between the environment and the society, in the process of time. At any point of time the existing social organization determines the character of the great mass of the people; only the élite amongst them react against it and slowly mold it from generation to generation. The social organization existing at any time also determines the character, range, and vitality of political institutions; it determines what ideas can take root and grow and what ones fall unnoticed; and it determines the ethical doctrines which are accepted and acted upon. You need only compare mediaeval and modern society to see how profoundly true this is at every point.

The social organization of these colonies was that of a new country and a young society. Its first advantage was that it could throw off all the traditions of the old countries which it did not like and retain all the knowledge, arts, and sciences which it wanted. It is one of the commanding facts in the history of the globe that one part of it was hidden and unknown until a very late day. Men living on the part which they did know developed civilization, but their civilization was mixed up with all the errors and calamities of thousands of years. Then they found a new world to which they could go, carrying what they wanted out of all which they had inherited and rejecting what they did not want. They undoubtedly made mistakes in their selection, because human error is ever present and is as enduring as humanity; but some things which they brought and should have left at home died out here under the influence of the environment. The most remarkable case of this is the manor system. A European of the seventeenth century could not think of society outside of the manor system and we see manor ideas and institutions imported here in more or less definite form; but they all shriveled up and became obsolete because they were totally unfit for a society in which land was unlimited and civil authority adequate to maintain peace. The only element of manor-making which was at work here was the lack of laborers. Serfdom and villainage were in large measure due to the necessity of holding the laborer to the spot in order that tillage might be carried on. In this country, at least in the northern states, slavery was due to the necessity of holding the laborer to the spot in order that tillage might go on.[1] Slavery, therefore, must be regarded as a product of some of the same conditions which in Europe made serfdom. Plantations took the place of manors in the South and yeoman farms with a small amount of slavery took the place of them in the North. This difference in land tenure and agricultural system between America and the old countries, which was foreseen and devised by no man but was imposed upon the colonists by the facts they had to deal with, became, of course, the cause of the greatest differences through the whole social organization. The development here was new, fresh, and original. Slavery appears as an incongruous element at first; as the population increased and the organization became more developed, that institution was dropped in the northern states. There its incongruity with the whole social system and the ethical ideas of a body of yeomen tilling their own soil first became apparent. At a later time, by the progress of the arts, slavery became dispensable and it has disappeared entirely. With its cessation it seemed that every vestige of a manor system or analogy to it had vanished

[1] Franklin's Works, II, 314.

from the land, but among the tentative organizations
of labor in the southern states at the present time, out
of which some new and suitable system for the conditions of industry there existing will be developed, there
is a kind of manor system with labor rents.   The problem of land tenure and of the agricultural system upon
which a great free state can be built contains difficulties
and mysteries which have not yet even been defined;
but if one gets near enough to them to even guess at
their magnitude and difficulty, he sees in a very grotesque
light the propositions of the "single tax" and of state
assumption of land.   In our colonies, where these things
shaped themselves with the greatest freedom to suit
the welfare of the settlers themselves, all the principles
of the English common law were overridden, so that
this did not determine the result.   The land of a town
was originally divided equally between the settlers
because all shared equally in the risk and trouble of
settlement.   Small estates existed because, as we have
seen, there was no object in owning big ones.   Equal
division of estates in case of intestacy was introduced
because, if primogeniture had been retained, younger
sons would not have lived and worked on the father's
land.   Finally, land tenures gradually became allodial.[1]
But an allodial tenure is the utmost private property in
land conceivable; it makes of every freeholder a petty
sovereign on his domain.   We can plainly see that no
other tenure would attract and hold settlers on raw land.
The so-called unearned increment is the reward of the
first settler who meets the first and greatest hardships
incident to the peopling of new land.   Thus we see
that the land tenure and the agricultural system were

---

[1] Originally the tenures were in free and common soccage.   These are so
now in Pennsylvania.   In every other state they are allodial.

fully consonant with the loose industrial organization and the democratic social organization which we have already noticed.

The settlements were made in little groups or towns. No civilized people have ever had so little civil organization as the colonial towns early in their settlement; there was little division of labor, scarcely any civil organization at all, and very little common action. Each town was at the same time a land company and an ecclesiastical body, and its organization under each of these heads was more developed than in its civil or political aspect. The methods of managing the affairs of a land company or a congregation were those of the town as a civil body also and the different forms of organization were not kept distinct. The administration of justice shows the confusion most distinctly: all common interests were dealt with by the one common body without distinction or classification; and as committees for executing the decisions of the body were the most obvious and convenient device for executive and administrative purposes, we find that device repeated with only slight variations.

Attempts have been made to endow this primitive system with some peculiar dignity and value. People have talked of "townships" instead of towns. Whenever the abstract is thus put for the concrete, our suspicions of myth-making should always be aroused. A town was a number of people living in a neighborhood and co-operating for common interests as convenience required; a township could be endowed with life and functions and could be made, by myth, into a force or sort of ruling providence. This township has been connected with so-called village-communities which we have seen to be another case of myth. The utility of the study of the New England towns is, in part, in the critical light which is thrown on the whole notion of village-communities as it has become current in our literature. The New England towns certainly lacked the communal element; religious sympathy was the strongest associative principle there was in them, but otherwise the sentiment was strongly individualistic. They were also so utterly loose in their ties, and the internal cohesion was so slight, that they never exercised that educating and formative influence which peasant villages in Europe, having through centuries retained the same institutions and customs, undoubtedly did exercise. In the South, where the plantation system existed, not even these nuclei of social organization were formed. Thus the whole of this country, until the beginning of the eighteenth century, presented the picture of the loosest and most scattered human society which is consistent with civilization at all, and there were not lacking phenomena of a positive decline of civilization and gravitation towards the life of the Indians. Political organization scarcely existed and civil organization was but slight. Later generations have condemned and ridiculed the religious bigotry of the colonists with its attendant religious persecution and the political ostracism of all but the ruling sect; but if this strong religious sympathy had not existed, what associative principle would they have had to hold them together and build up a civil society?

I have said that the picture presented by the settlements in this country until the beginning of the eighteenth century was that of little groups of farmers scattered along the coast and rivers, forming towns under the loosest possible organization. Names such as Massachusetts, Connecticut, were used then to cover areas very great as compared with the amount of land under cultivation. Those names had very little meaning to the people of that time, for life and its interests were bounded by the town. Only in the eighteenth century can we see the horizon extend so that the province grows to be the real civil unit and grows into a real commonwealth; the process was slow, however, and for the most part unwilling. In the nineteenth century the conception of the national and civil unit has expanded so that our sense of nationality cleaves to the Union as a great confederated state. This advance in the feeling of the people as to what the country to which they belong is, and what that is which is the object of patriotism, is one of the interesting developments of our history. The merging of the town into the state and of the state into the United States has been brought about by the increase of population, the filling up of the country, the multiplication of interests reaching out all over it and grappling the people together. The bonds are those of kin, of industry and commerce, of religion through the various denominations and churches, of common pursuits in education, science, and art, and of associations for various purposes of culture or pleasure. This is what we mean by the advancing social organization. It unites us into a whole; it forms us into a society; it gives us sentiments of association and co-operation. Our states, instead of being separate bodies united only by neighborhood and alliance, are formed into one body with nerves running through it; and it is by virtue of these nerves, that is, of the lines of common feeling and interest which I have mentioned, that a touch at one point brings out a reaction from the whole.

There are other causes which are always at work in

the contrary direction. They are the forces of discord
and divergent interest. In a state of seventy million
people scattered over a continent the forces of disruption
are always at work. The great social organization all
the time tends to promote a great political organization; as the interests multiply and become complex,
there is a call for federal legislation in order to get
uniformity, *e.g.*, as to marriage, divorce, bankruptcy.
The laws also get extensions from use and new application, the effects of which in a few years amaze us by their
magnitude and importance, as, for example, the Inter-
state Commerce Law. Now all this extension, system-
atization, and uniformity-making produces symmetry,
order, and elegance, but it goes with the old terror of
our statesmen — consolidation. It is making of us a
great empire. Few people, even of those who have
lived through it, seem to notice the great change which
has come over our federal system since the Civil War.
The most important alteration is that in the feeling of
the people about what sort of a government there is at
Washington — what it is and what it can do. Young
people should understand that the indescribable sense
and feeling about that question, which we carry with
us now, is totally different from the sentiments of our
fathers between 1850 and 1860. Now there is a danger
in centralization. A big system never can fit exactly
at more than a few places, if at any; elsewhere it strains
a little in its adaptation and it may strain very much.
If it does, we shall hear an outcry of distress and it may
be of anger and revolt, for the movement to higher
organization means a movement away from liberty,
and is always attended by irritation until men become
habituated to the constraint of the organization and
realize its benefits. In the course of our history this

has been fully illustrated. Every step of the way up to the present system which, I think, we regard almost unanimously as an advance and a gain, as we look back upon it, has been contested. The advancing organization draws together and consolidates, provided its action is not so abrupt and harsh as to provoke rebellion and disruption. In every case it produces a more prompt civil reaction. By this we mean that there is a more prompt obedience to authority, greater punctuality in the performance of legal duties, and greater exactitude in the co-operation of institutions and persons who are called upon by the civil authority to perform civil functions for the good of the state. This means greater discipline and less liberty.

Here I use the word "liberty" in its primary sense: a status in which there are no restraints on the self-determination of the individual. That liberty is, of course, never more than relative, for there are restraints wherever there are any institutions, customs, or laws at all. Therefore this kind of liberty, if an attempt is made to realize it against laws and institutions, is anarchistic. I shall refer to it sometimes in speaking of the later history as anarchistic liberty.

No men on earth have ever been as free to do as they pleased as these American colonists were. Savage men are not free to do as they please and may be dismissed from comparison; civilized men in the Old World were born into a society already old; here, however, were civilized men who, after they had secured a footing, were limited by the very least restraint of any kind which can exist in human life. The fetters which they laid on themselves in accordance with their religious dogmas were no doubt a good thing, for otherwise there would have been no discipline at all, and for human welfare liberty and discipline need to be duly combined. In fact, the colonists, after two or three generations, threw off the puritanical restraints only too much.

Liberty had its cause and its enduring guarantee in the circumstances of the case. If a man lives alone in the middle of a farm of one hundred acres, what he does there will make little difference to his neighbors, each living in the same way. But if he and his family live in a tenement house, with a score of other families, separated only by thin partitions and floors, everything that he does or neglects will make a great difference to others. Therefore there are few laws made by the community as to how a man shall behave on a farm, whereas there are strict regulations by the state, the city, and the landlord as to how people shall behave in tenement houses. The latter regulations are no proof of meddlesomeness and officialism — they are a necessity of the case. On the other hand, the "liberty" of colonial farmers was no choice of theirs, no creation of law, no proof of clearer wisdom than that of Old-World statesmen — it was a necessity of the case.

In one respect, indeed, the townsmen of a colony lacked liberty — for in no case and in no sense can you find absolute liberty on this earth; that is an anarchistic dream. The public opinion of a town was an impervious mistress; Mrs. Grundy held powerful sway and Gossip was her prime minister. This accounts for the remarkable subserviency, in the early days of this country, of public men to popularity. Unpopularity in a town or petty neighborhood where everybody knows everybody else intimately is an extreme social penalty; it reaches a man through his wife and children and it affects him in all his important interests and relations. It was a powerful coercive force here and was, as far as it went, a restraint on liberty. It was not, however, an organizing force, and its influence does not contradict the observation that the organization was loose and slight.

The effect of this great liberty on both the virtues and the vices of colonial character was clearly marked. The people were very bold, enterprising, and self-reliant; they were even imprudent in their enterprises; they took great risks because the trouble and cost of precautions were great. They were not painstaking because there was so much to be done in subduing a continent that they could not stop to be careful; they had to be contented with expedients and to sacrifice the long future interest to the immediate one. It would have been unwise and wasteful to do otherwise. They were also very versatile; a man had to be a jack-of-all-trades because there was no elaborate industrial organization. They also took things very easily. They were not energetic; they could with ease get enough and they were not willing to work very hard to get a little more. They were optimistic; they went on, never fearing but what they could conquer any difficulties they might meet and borrowing very little trouble. Most of these traits, as we know, have become fixed in the national character. As a consequence, the colonists were divided into two well-marked types: one industrious and steady, the other shiftless and lazy. There were very few avenues to wealth and so there were few rewards for great exertion. The love of trading was due to the fact that it offered quicker and larger gains than could be got from tilling the ground. It is the opening of grand chances of exceptional success in the nineteenth century which has wrought a great transformation in the national character, for it has offered rewards for exceptional ability and exceptional achievement which have stimulated the whole population. Here is a fact — and it is one of the most salient and incontrovertible facts in our own history — which shows the shallowness and folly of a great deal of current lamentation or denunciation of the accumulation of wealth. If you will turn to European history, you will find that the moment when land would produce, not merely a subsistence for those who tilled it but also a profit, that is, the moment when it would bear rent, is the moment when the modern world began to spring into energetic life. Here land has never yet borne rent, but transportation rates have taken the place of rent and, together with manufacturing on a large scale and the application of capital to develop the continent, have opened far broader avenues of profit and have offered greater prizes than land-rent in the Old World. It is these chances which have filled the population with a fever of energy and enterprise and enthused them with hope, and in the might of such driving forces they have done marvellous things. It is true, as the French proverb says, that they have not made omelettes without smashing some eggs; and we have many social philosophers who are crying over the eggs.

What I have said thus far of liberty has referred to individual liberty. Political liberty inside of any country depends very largely upon its external relations. The great force for forging a society into a solid mass has always been war. So long as there were Indians to be fought, and so long as the Dutch were in New York or the French in Canada, the colonies had a foreign policy; they had enemies at the gates. Such a state of things forces some attention to military preparations. The state must make calls on its citizens for money and for military services and this state-pressure limits political liberty. After the French were driven out of Canada there was a great change in this respect: there was nothing more to fear, and all military exercises, being regarded as irksome, were almost entirely neglected. Internal liberty took a new expansion. In the prevailing dullness of colonial life one of the chief sports had been to bait the colonial governor; and the colonists now gave themselves up to this diversion with greater freedom than ever. Internal discord involved no risk of weakness in the presence of a neighboring enemy. Note well that those people are easily free who have no powerful neighbor to fear. Imagine, if you can, that the boundary of Russia had been at the Mississippi River and that she had been meddling with us in the eighteenth century as she did with Sweden and Poland — do you suppose that we could have got this liberty which our historians and orators talk about? If not, then you may be sure that no human shrewdness or wisdom entailed it on us as it is, but that it was born of a happy conjuncture of circumstances.

The absence of powerful neighbors has been an important fact in all our later history. It has freed us from the militarism which now weighs so heavily upon Europe and it has made it possible for us to develop to its highest limit a purely industrial social organization. It is true that the Civil War with its debt, taxation, bad currency, and pension burdens has made us acquainted with some of the burdens of militarism, but that is all our own fault; by virtue of the lack of strong neighbors we had a right to be free from it if we had been wise enough to profit by the advantages of our situation.

But an industrial society brings to bear upon its members an education widely different from that of a military civilization; the codes of citizenship, the conception of what is heroic, the standards of honor, the selection of things best worth working for, the types to which admiration is due, all differ in the two systems. Militarism is produced by a constant preoccupation with the chances of war and the necessity of being prepared for it, and this preoccupation bars the way when people want to think about the reform of institutions or the extension of popular education or any other useful social enterprise. From all that preoccupation the people of this country have been free; they have been able to give their attention without reserve to what would increase the happiness and welfare of the people.

Let us sum up what we have thus far gathered from our review of the colonial period. We have seen that the division of labor was slight; that there was scarcely any industrial organization; that, if slavery be left out of account, there was but little differentiation of classes; that the social ties, even before religious enthusiasm died out, were very few and narrow and strictly local; that, after that enthusiasm died out, such ties scarcely existed at all; that the horizon of life was the town and only at second stage the province. We have also seen that the most peculiar characteristics of the colonial society were the equality of its members and the large liberty of self-will enjoyed by individuals. We know that the separate provinces had very little sympathy or even acquaintance with each other; at one time and another, under the influence of a common danger from the Indians or the French, a feeble thrill of common interest ran through some of them, but it never proved strong enough to unite them. These social and political elements were the inheritance of the Union from the colonial period.

I by no means agree with the current histories about the facts and merits of the quarrel with England between 1763 and 1775. They are all tinctured with alleged patriotism and the serious facts of the case are sometimes passed over in silence. The behavior of the colonists was turbulent, lawless, and in many cases indefensible; and the grounds on which they based their case were often untenable in law and history and often inconsistent with each other. They sought these grounds as a lawyer seeks grounds on which to argue his case, choosing them, that is, on the basis of whether they will make more for him than against him, not whether they are true or not. The principles of 1774 were distinctly anarchical because they were put forward as a basis of continued relation to Great Britain but were inconsistent with that relation. Another cause of rebellion which was very strong in the South, although little stress is laid upon it in history, was the accumulated debt to British merchants which it was hoped would be cancelled by war. It is true that the English colonial policy of the eighteenth century did not rise above the eighteenth-century English level, which from our standpoint was base; but that it was not very shocking to eighteenth-century Americans is shown by the fact that they never fully, clearly, and in principle revolted against the Navigation Act, which was their greatest grievance. Even as to taxation the Americans never put their case on a clear and intelligible ground; they talked of various *abuses* of taxation, but they showed that they would not consent to any taxation. Adam Smith, taught no doubt by study of the case of

our colonies, said: "Plenty of good land and liberty
to manage their own affairs in their own way seem to
be the two great causes of the prosperity of all new
colonies." [1] The American colonies had the land but
not the liberty. If they wanted to do anything which
they thought expedient for their own interest they had
to send to England for permission. Even if the reply
was reasonably prompt, this cost a year; but inasmuch
as applications were bandied about, neglected, and
forgotten, in spite of the zeal of agents, there were fetters
laid upon colonial development. As soon, therefore, as
the colonists were able to be independent and dared be
independent, it was necessary that they should be so.
That is the cause and the justification of the Revolution. The rest is all the wrangling about rights, dogmas,
laws, and precedents which accompanies every revolution. I see no use at all in the study of history unless
the historian is absolutely faithful to the truth of the
matter; but when, in a moment, my reason for intro-
ducing these remarks here appears, the case will then
serve to prove, I think, how much more the truth is
worth than anything else is worth in history.

All the laxness of the social organization, all the mischief of what has been called church-steeple patriotism,
and all the weakness of anarchistic liberty appeared
most distinctly in the Revolutionary War. In Congress, in the army administration, in the finances, in
the medical department, the faults of lack of organization were conspicuous and their consequences were
humiliating. The effects of lack of organization may
be summed up in a word: such a lack makes it impossible to bring the power and resources of the community
to bear on the task in hand. That is what was proved

[1] Wealth of Nations, II, 152.

in the history of the War. In the meantime the bonds
of social order were relaxed on every side: the "committees" accustomed the people to arbitrary and tyrannical action; the cruel and wicked persecution of the
Tories demoralized the Whigs; the corruption of the
paper money produced bitter heart-burnings and discontent; the sudden enrichment of a few by privateering
and speculation presented an irritating phenomenon
which had not been seen before. The heated declamation about liberty had produced vague expectations and
hopes which were, of course, disappointed; and all this
culminated in the period of the Confederation, when
it seemed to some that the whole social and political
fabric was falling to pieces. There was, however, a great
deal of jacobinism, to use a later term, the adherents
of which were perfectly satisfied that things were going
in the right direction.

Now if we do not know these facts and give them
their due weight, how are we to appreciate the work of
the Constitution-makers? How can we understand
what their task was, what difficulties they had to overcome, what the grounds were of the opposition which
they had to meet? Everyone knows nowadays that
the people by no means leaped forward to grasp this
Constitution, which is now so much admired and loved,
as the blessing which they had been praying for. Why
did they not? To put it in the briefest compass, the
reason why not was this: that Constitution was an
immense advance in the political organization at a
single step. It made a real union; it reduced the
independent (I avoid the word "sovereign") states to
a status of some limitation; it created a competent
executive — one who could *govern*, not influence or
persuade; it created a treasury which could reach the

property of the citizen by taxes, not by begging; it created a power which could enforce treaties. Considering the anarchical condition of things and the waywardness and irritation of the public temper, it is amazing that such a step could have been accomplished.

Its opponents declared that the new Union was simply taking the place which Great Britain had occupied; that its dominion was as intolerable as hers had been; that they had only changed masters by the War. Here is the point at which we need to recall what has been said about the attitude and behavior of the colonists between 1763 and 1774. If this is done it will be seen that the allegation about the Union having come to occupy the position which Great Britain had occupied was true; it had to claim what she had claimed and to meet with the same insubordination which she had met with. One cause of quarrel with England had been the regulation of commerce; but the Constitution had given Congress the power to regulate commerce — and we are still quarrelling about what this power means and how to use it. Another cause of quarrel had been over the legal-tender paper money, which Great Britain had tried to forbid; but the Constitution forbade legal-tender paper money to the states and, as was then believed, to the Union too. It forbade the states to impair the obligation of contracts, which went farther and was more explicit than anything Great Britain had done. Where England had been very careful about coming into direct contact with the individual citizen in the colonies, the Constitution distinctly and avowedly brought the Union into contact with the individual through the judiciary and through indirect internal taxes. The necessity had been experienced during the War of frowning down any partial confederations be-

tween less than the whole number of states, but precisely by so doing was the disapproval of England
against the Stamp Act Congress and other congresses
justified. The state governments had already found it
necessary to use measures against smuggling like those
which had given so much offence when used by Great
Britain. In the treaty of peace, again, which the federal
government was now authorized to enforce, British
creditors were ensured the use of the courts to enforce
payment. Finally in the matter of taxation the Union
inherited all the embarrassments of Great Britain.
The states had shown that they would not freely consent
to any import duties in their ports for the federal treasury; but now the federal government had power to lay
and collect them by its own officers. It also proceeded
at once to use its power to lay excise taxes, and when
this produced a rebellion, it put down the rebellion by
armed force with a vigor and promptitude far surpassing anything which the English did, even during the
War. In the trials which ensued to punish the violators
of law, to which there is no parallel whatever in anything done by the English during the colonial period,
the doctrine was laid down that it was high treason to
go with arms to the house of an administrative officer
of the law with intent to injure his property or otherwise
intimidate him from the performance of his duty. But
according to that ruling very many of those who took
part in the Stamp Act riots were guilty of high treason.
Therefore, to sum it up, the doctrines of the radical
Whigs were now the doctrines of the radical Anti-
federalists. The latter claimed with truth that they
were consistent, that they had all the same reason to
oppose and dread the Union which they had had to oppose Great Britain, and that the Union had inherited

and was perpetuating the position of Great Britain. It became a current expression of discontent with the federal system, of which you hear occasional echoes even now, that it was an imitation of the English system invented and fastened on the country by Alexander Hamilton — and this was rather a distortion of the true facts than an utter falsehood.

What, then, shall we infer from all these facts? Plainly this: that the Revolutionary doctrines were anarchistic, and inconsistent with peace and civil order; that they were riotous and extravagant; and that there could be no success and prosperity here until a constitutional civil government existed which could put down the lawless and turbulent spirit and discipline the people to liberty under law. This is the position which was taken by the Federal party; this is why New England, although it had been intensely Whig, became intensely Federal. The people knew the difference between war measures and peace measures and they realized the necessity of tightening again the bonds of social order. This is also why the Federal party was so unpopular; it was doing a most useful and essential work, but it is never popular to insist upon self-control, discipline, and healthful regulation. On the other hand Jefferson and his friends always prophesied smooth things, assuring "the people" that it was showing the highest political wisdom when it was doing as it had a mind to. Their doctrine was that "the people," that is, all the population except the educated and property classes, knew everything without finding it out or being aware of it, and distilled from votes infallible wisdom for the solution of political problems, although the individuals that made up "the people" might have no wisdom in their individual heads. Of course this was popular; men are delighted to hear that they have all rights without trouble and expense, that they are wise without hard experience or study, and that they shall have power without being put to any trouble to win it. The Jeffersonians, therefore, preached relaxation, negligence, and ease, while the Federalists were working for security, order, constitutional guarantees, and institutions. However, when the Jeffersonians got into power, the conservatism of authority got possession of them and they, in their turn, increased the federal power and developed and intensified the political organization. Perhaps they did it more prudently, wisely, and successfully than the Federalists did, just because they advocated it in phrases borrowed from the old pet doctrines of relaxation and undiscipline.

I shall no more than mention the development of the power of the Supreme Court in the interpretation of the Constitution; this began after the second war with England and was a powerful influence in carrying on the development and integration of our political institutions. I might also mention the introduction of police into our large cities, a measure which, when it was done, was viewed with great disfavor by the friends of liberty, although our large cities had been disgraced by frequent riots, and the dangerous classes in them had become organized and were almost independent of the law.

In the Civil War the delusion of the Southerners was, in large part, a survival of the old anarchism of the Revolutionary period. All the jargon of Secession is perpetuated from the period before the Revolution; the genealogy of it, down through the resolutions of '98 and Nullification, is clear and indisputable. It is pitiful to see with what sublime good faith the Southerners repeated the old phrases and maxims; they thought that they were enunciating accepted and indisputable truths and evoking, on their own behalf, the memories of our heroic age. But the defeat of the South in the War has not meant the definitive extrusion of those maxims and notions from our political system. If we do not wish another generation to grow up with another set of delusions to be cured by bloodshed, it would be well to correct the stories in our popular histories about the Boston Massacre and the Boston Tea Party and the doctrine about "no taxation without representation," as well as those about natural rights and the equality of all men. It is by no means true that what our young people need is an uncritical patriotic inflation. The principles of '76 were: (1) revolution, because there was a revolution on hand — but this principle can have no utility or applicability until there is another revolution on hand; (2) rebellion against the crown of England and secession from the British empire — but this principle, as we have found by experience, was good for once only, when the causes were serious enough to justify it; (3) independence — but independence is not a general principle; if it were, it would require a series of revolts until every town stood by itself. The commonwealers of last summer built their whole platform on delusive constructions of the popular dogmas of liberty and on phrases of historical reference to the Revolution. In these great strike riots you hear echoes of all the Fourth of July sentiments and corollaries of all the great Revolutionary principles. They are all delusions as to what this world is, what human society is, what we can do here. The uneducated and half-educated men who utter them are not half to blame for them. They have been taught so; they have caught up catchwords and phrases; and now they are converting these into maxims of action. Such delusions are never cured without much pain and many tears.

When we gather together the observations we have made, showing the advance of the entire social organization from the colonial settlement up to the present time, in all its branches — the industrial system, the relations of classes, the land system, the civil organization, and the organization of political institutions and liberty — we see that it has been a life-process, a growth-process, which our society had to go through just as inevitably as an infant after birth must go on to the stages of growth and experience which belong to all human beings as such. This evolution in our case has not been homogeneous. The constant extension or settlement into the open territory to the west has kept us in connection with forms of society representing the stages through which the older parts of the country have already passed. We could find to-day vast tracts of territory in which society is on the stage of organization which existed along the Atlantic coast in the seventeenth century; and between those places and the densest centers of population in the East we could find represented every intervening stage through which our society has passed in two hundred years. This combination of heterogeneous stages of social and political organization in one state is a delicate experiment; they are sure to contend for the mastery in it, and that strife threatens disruption. As I believe that this view has rarely received any attention, it is one of the chief points I have wished to make in surveying the advance of social and political organization in this country.

The Federalists opposed the creation of frontier states which should share, on an equal footing in some respects, with the old ones in the federal Union. They thought that the wishes, tastes, interests, and methods of the two classes of states would be inconsistent, that they would clash, and that the things which the old states held dear would be imperilled. This view afterwards became a subject of ridicule. New states were not new very long before they became old; they filled up with population, acquired capital, multiplied their interests, and became conservative. It seemed an idle and pedantic notion that there could be any political difficulty in the combination of new and old states; the more we got in, the bigger we grew — and that was the main point. Then again all political struggle centered in the struggle of North and South for supremacy in the Union; the other elements which were included in the struggle have blinded us to the fact that that was the real character of it — a struggle for supremacy in the Union. Just as certainly as you have a unit-group inside of which different elements can be differentiated, just so certainly will those elements strive for the mastery; it is a law of nature and is inevitable. In the Constitutional Convention of 1787 the one great question was: If we have a union, who will rule in it? It was not until equal representation in the Senate was agreed upon that union became possible. Then the great division was between large states and small ones. The resolutions of '98, by Virginia and her daughter, Kentucky, were aimed at a Yankee President and his supporters, by whom Virginia would not be ruled. As soon as the system was in full operation, the alliance of Virginia and New York attempted to control it; they threw the Federal party and the East out of power,

upon which you find New England going over forthwith
to secession and disunion. Then, as the new states
came in, the divisions of the old ones sought their
alliance. The coalition of the South and West in the
'20's could not be consolidated because the new states
came in so fast. The slave states and the non-slave
states then became the most clear, important, and positive differentiation there was. With the census of 1840,
however, it became clear that the slave states could
not retain the proportional power and influence which
they had had in the confederation; and it was their
turn to become disunionists. Fifty years of our history
have gone into that struggle, for it is not more than
well over now. Meanwhile other great interests have
been neglected and great abuses have grown up unnoticed: war taxation and war currency are still here
to plague us. Our people have come out of that struggle
with a great confidence that nothing can ever again put
the Union at stake. Let us not make that error. The
Union is always at stake. Instead of being a system
which can stand alone and bear any amount of abuse,
it is one of great delicacy and artificiality which requires the highest civic virtues and the wisest statesmanship to preserve it. It will be threatened again
whenever there is a well-defined group which believes
its interests jeopardized inside the Union and under the
dominion of those who control the Union.

At the point which we have now reached the whole continent has received a first occupation and settlement;
and from now on the process will be one of consolidation and condensation. This will raise the organization over the whole country. That process cannot go
on too rapidly at the present stage, for the more rapidly
it goes on the quicker it will tide us over the dangers

in which we find ourselves — dangers due to the great differences in the social and political organization which now exist. In all the past the *rapidity* of our growth has been one of our best safeguards; no state of things has existed long enough to allow people to understand it, to base plans upon it, and to carry them out, before the facts have all changed and frustrated all the plans. There have been plenty of presidential aspirants in the United States who have found that four years was a long time to bridge over with combinations based upon the assumption that circumstances in states and sections would remain that long unchanged.

There has been, however, another and apparently contradictory evolution side by side with the one already mentioned, and it is the combination of the two which has given to our history its unique character. The public men of the Revolutionary period were not demo- crats — they feared democracy. The Constitution- makers were under an especial dread of democracy, which they identified with the anarchism of the period of 1783–1787. They therefore established by the Con- stitution a set of institutions which are restrictions of democracy. They did not invent any of these institu- tions, for all of them were already familiar in the colonies, being of English origin and developed and adapted to the circumstances here. Their general character is that while they ensure the rule of the majority of legal voters, they yet insist upon it that the will of that majority shall be constitutionally expressed and that it shall be a sober, mature, and well-considered will. This constitutes a guarantee against jacobinism. Now the whole genius of this country has been democratic. I have tried to show that its inherited dogmas and its environment made it so inevitably. Down through our history, therefore, the democratic temper of the people has been at war with the Constitutional institutions. When the Constitution was established there was no such thing as universal manhood suffrage here; the suffrage was connected with freehold in land. This restriction, measured by the number of people it excluded, was a very important one. It was not until after the second war with England that a movement towards universal suffrage began in the old states; then it ran on with great rapidity until universal suffrage was established in them all. The democratic temper also seized upon that device in the Constitution which was the most positive new invention in it and which was developed as a safeguard against democracy, *viz.*, the electoral college, and turned it into a mere form through which the voters should directly elect their own President. The same sentiments called forth an unwritten law that the President should serve only two terms and has always loudly favored one term. Perhaps, since the great precedent was the purchase of Louisiana by Jefferson, democracy ought also to be credited with forcing an unwritten addendum on the Constitution that the federal government could buy land. Democracy has chafed, at one time and another, against the veto of the President, the power of the Senate, and, above all, against the prerogatives of the judiciary — all of which are institutional checks on democracy. The most recent effort in the same direction is the plan to nominate senators by party convention and to compel the legislators to vote for the candidates thus set before them. No one will deny, moreover, that a democratic spirit has been breathed through all our institutions, has modified their action and determined their character. Opinions would differ as to whether its effect

has always been good, but I doubt if anyone would deny
that it has sometimes been good.

We see then, in our history, that neither have the
Constitutional institutions and guarantees proved a
cast-iron jacket in which to enclose our society and
prevent its changes, nor, on the other hand, has democracy been able to override the institutions and render
them nugatory. On the contrary, our institutions as
they are to-day are the resultant of a struggle between
the two — a struggle accompanying that expansion
and intensification of the organization which I have
aimed to describe.

Here, then, is an extraordinary phenomenon: an
advance of the organization and an advance of liberty
too, or, to speak more accurately, an advance in the
organization with a transformation in the conception
of liberty and the widest possible expansion of that
liberty. While the discipline and constraint of the
institutions have been exerted to reduce anarchistic
liberty, they have enlarged and created civil liberty,
or liberty under law. These two notions of liberty are
totally different from one another. We are suffering
from the fact that in our current philosophy, even
amongst educated people, the notion of liberty is not
sufficiently analyzed and this distinction is not sufficiently understood. Here has been a society advancing
with the greatest rapidity in the number, variety,
complication, and delicacy of its interests; yet it has
at the same time opened the suffrage on gratuitous
terms to all adult males, and granted them access to
every public office, with corresponding control over all
societal interests. Where else in history have all adult
males in a society actually possessed political power,
honors, and emoluments and at the same time been sub-

ject to no responsibilities, risks, charges, expenses, or burdens of any kind — these being all left to the educated and property classes? Where else has it ever been possible for a numerical majority to entail upon a society burdens which the minority must bear, while the aforesaid majority may scatter and leave the society and trouble themselves no further about it? The men of the Revolution never could have imagined any such state of things. In 1775 the convention of Worcester County, Massachusetts, petitioned the Provincial Congress "that no man may be allowed to have a seat therein who does not vote away his own money for public purposes in common with the other members' and with his constituents'." [1] That was the prevailing doctrine everywhere at the time, and yet within fifty years the evolution of civil institutions, instead of realizing that doctrine, produced the state of things which I have just described — and that state of things was produced contemporaneously with an integration of civil institutions, an elevation of the authority of law, and a sharpening of social discipline.

Now the current opinion amongst us undoubtedly is that the extension of the suffrage and the virtual transfer of the powers of government to the uneducated and non-property classes, compelling the educated and property classes, if they want to influence the government, to do so by persuading or perhaps corrupting the former, is a piece of political wisdom to which our fathers were led by philosophy and by the conviction that the doctrine of it was true and just. There were causes for it, however, which were far more powerful than preaching, argument, and philosophy; and besides, if you will notice how hopeless it is by any argument

[1] Massachusetts Journals, p. 651.

to make headway against any current of belief which has obtained momentum in a society, you will put your faith in the current of belief and not in the power of logic or exhortation. You will then look at the causes of the current of belief, and you will find them in the economic conditions which are controlling, at the time, the struggle for existence and the competition of life. At the beginning of this century it would have been just exactly as impossible to put aristocratic restrictions on democracy here as it would have been at the same time to put democratic restrictions on aristocracy in England. Now the economic circumstances of our century which have modified the struggle for existence and the competition of life have been, first, the opening of a vast extent of new land to the use and advantage of the people who had no social power of any kind; and, second, the advance in the arts. Of the arts, those of transportation have been the most important because they have made the new land accessible; but all the other applications of the arts have been increasing man's power in the struggle for existence, and they have been most in favor of the classes which otherwise had nothing but their hands with which to carry on that struggle. This has lessened the advantage of owning land and it has lessened the comparative advantage of having capital over that of having only labor. An education has not now as great value to give its possessor a special advantage — a share, that is, in a limited monopoly — as it had a century ago. This is true in a still greater degree of higher education, until we come up to those cases where exceptional talent, armed with the highest training, once more wins the advantages of a natural monopoly.

Hence it is that the great economic changes I have

mentioned have produced the greatest social revolution that has ever occurred. It has raised the masses to power, has set slaves free, has given a charter of social and political power to the people who have nothing, and has forced those-who-have to get power, if they want it, by persuading and influencing those-who-have-not. All the demagogues, philosophers, and principle-brokers are trying to lead the triumphal procession and crying: "We got it for you." "We are your friends." "It is to us that you owe it all." On the other hand the same social revolution has undermined all social institutions and prescriptions of an aristocratic character and they are rapidly crumbling away, even in the Old World, under the reaction from the New.

If now we put this result together with what we had reached before, we find that the advance of the social and political organization which should have been attended, according to all former philosophy, by greater social pressure and diminishing prosperity for the masses, although it has indeed been attended by lessening of the old anarchistic liberty, has also been accompanied by the far more important fact of enormously enlarged social and political power and chances for the masses. The world has passed into hands of new masters, and the all-absorbing questions for mankind and civilization now are: What will they do with it? How will they behave? Already in this country, and in all others which have adopted democratic forms, successive elections show a steady movement towards throwing out men of well-defined convictions and positive strength on either side, so that parliamentary institutions seem to be clearly on the decline. In every great civilized country, also, political parties are breaking up and are losing their character as groups of persons holding common convictions on questions of general policy. Their place is being taken by petty groups of representatives of certain interests. The more we enlarge the sphere of government, the more true it is that every act of legislation enriches or ruins those who are interested in some branch of industry; such persons say, therefore, that they cannot afford to neglect legislative proceedings. The consequence is the immense power of the lobby, and legislation comes to be an affair of coalition between interests to make up a majority. If that goes on, its logical and institutional outcome must be that the non-possessors, if united, must form the largest interest-group, and that they will then find that the easiest way ever yet devised to get wealth is to hold a parliament and, by a majority vote, order that the possessors of wealth shall give it to the non-possessors. This program has already been proposed and adopted and strong efforts are on foot to organize the parliamentary groups on this basis so as to put it into action.

We have abundant facts at hand to show us, also, that the higher the social organization is the more delicate it is and the more it is exposed to harm upon all sides and from slight influences. A great, complicated, and delicate social organization presents a vast array of phenomena of all kinds, many of which are paradoxical and contradictory in their relation to each other. The analysis of these phenomena and the interpretation of them is the easiest thing in the world if we go about it with a few so-called "ethical" principles; but if we approach it with any due conception of what it is that we are trying to do, we find it the hardest mental task ever yet cast upon mankind. We boast of our successes in science and art; but those successes have brought about a social organization and produced social problems which we cannot evade, and if we do not solve them aright, we may ruin all our other achievements and go down to barbarism again.

Here I find myself on the verge of prophecy and so here I arrest myself. The political prophets of our country have always been either optimists or alarmists. I should not be willing to be either. The optimists scoff at all warnings and misgivings; they think we need not trouble ourselves to think or take care, and they exhort us to go ahead, encouraging us with familiar phrases and commonplaces. I have suggested that we need to be prudent, to listen to reason, to use forethought and care. Social and political crises are sure to arise among us as they must in any human society — we have had enough of them to convince us that they will come again. I have suggested also that our political system calls for more political sense, sober judgment, and ever-active prudence than any other political system does. It also forbids us to do many things which states of other forms may undertake. It is especially incompatible with our form of democratic republic to charge the state with many and various functions, for our state should be simple to the last possible degree. It should handle as little money as possible; it should encourage the constant individual activity of its citizens and never do anything to weaken individual initiative. But the tendency to-day is all the other way. Our state should have as few office-holders as possible. The stubborn dogmatism of the old Jeffersonians on these points showed that they had stronger sense of the maxims necessary to maintain the kind of state they liked than anybody has nowadays; to suppose that these maxims are inconsistent with strength of government, in the distinct and exclusive field of government, is to give proof of a very shallow political philosophy. They are the conditions of strong government in purely civil affairs, for the more outside functions a state assumes the more it is hampered in its proper business. Furthermore, our federal state cannot enter on a great many enterprises which imperial states under the monarchical or aristocratic form have been wont to undertake; it cannot embark on an enterprising foreign policy or on conquest or on annexation without putting its internal equilibrium at stake. This is because of its peculiar structure and principles. We may see, however, strong symptoms amongst us of all the old ambitions, the thirst for bigness and glory which have cost the people of Europe so dearly, and we hear all the dogmas of militarism once more brought to the front as rules of our policy. Here are things which call for something very different from heedless optimism.

The alarmists, on the other hand, have against them the immense vigor of this society, its power to react against calamity and to recover from errors. Alarmist predictions of the past have all been proved utterly mistaken. You can find such predictions scattered all the way along: in 1800, when the Federalists gave way to Jefferson; at the Second War; all through Jackson's time; at the Mexican War; at the Civil War — and it may be some encouragement to the timid to ask whether, at those crises, there did not seem to be as good cause for alarm, albeit a different one, as seems to exist now. It is evident that if George Washington and his contemporaries had tried to anticipate our problems and to solve them for us in advance they would have made ridiculous blunders, for they could not possibly have foreseen our case or understood the elements which enter into it. Let us be very sure that if we try to look forward a century we are making just the same kind of ridiculous blunders. We cannot make anything else. One of the chief results of our historical studies is to show us the repeated and accumulated faults and errors of men in the past. You will observe that the common inference is that we, since we see the errors of the past, are perpetrating none in our own schemes and projects; but this is the greatest fallacy there is (and there are a great many) in our historical method of social study. The correct inference would be that we too, if we plot schemes of social action which reach beyond the immediate facts and the nearest interests, are only committing new errors, the effects of which will be entailed upon posterity. The reason for this is that the future contains new and unknown elements, incalculable combinations, unforeseeable changes in the moods, tastes, standards, and desires of the people. If we look back to Washington's time and see what changes have taken place in all these respects, then we may look to the future in full confidence that such changes will go on in the next hundred years.

These changes are what have turned the terrors of the alarmist to scorn. Certain it is that the Americans of the nineteenth century have been far happier, as a society, than any other society of human beings ever has been. They have been shielded from the commonest and heaviest calamities and have been free from the most vexatious burdens of human society; except at certain periods, taxation has been light and military duty an amusement; they have inherited a great untouched continent, with powers of science and art, for taking and using it, incomparably superior to anything ever possessed before by men. Very few of them apparently have understood or understand their own good fortune and its exceptional character. If all conditions should remain the same and the population go on increasing, the exceptional conditions would pass away and our posterity would have to contend sometime or other with all the old social problems again. The conditions, however, will not remain the same; they will change, no doubt in the direction of still greater and better chances. This fact is what gives the optimist his justification and makes his reckless blindness appear to be the shrewdest foresight. Furthermore, the problems which sometimes appal us nowadays are not peculiar to America; they are quite as heavy and as knotty in England, France, and Germany as they are here. In many points we are further on towards a solution than those countries are: we have better social defences from behind which to meet the dangers; and they do not come upon us, as they do upon the nations of Europe, mixed up with militarism, with the relics of feudal institutions, and with the traditions of absolute monarchy.

And now my task is done if, by a discussion of the teachings of our history, I have contributed to a better understanding of present facts and forces; for the highest wisdom and the most patriotic devotion to our country which we can manifest lie in the faithful performance of present civic duties and in diligent efforts to accomplish the tasks which lie immediately before us. We may be very sure that a succeeding century will take care of itself; also that it will not be able to take care of us. All the energy we spend, therefore, in preparing for it is worse than thrown away. It will be useless for its purpose and it will be abstracted from what we can spend on our own problems, which are big enough and hard enough to require all the energy we have to deal with them.

MEMORIAL DAY ADDRESS

MEMORIAL DAY ADDRESS

[1872]

A TIDE is rising in modern history which reaches one
after another of the institutions, beliefs, and traditions
which we have inherited from the past. As it touches
the bad ones, they crumble, one after another, and fall
beneath its waves. Some call this tide "revolution."
They see only its destructive side and its iconoclastic
spirit and as they watch its advance, they fall under its
fascination. The demon of destruction which lurks in
every human breast is aroused and men are eager to participate in the work of overthrowing and destroying. It
is true, indeed, that this new movement has several times
manifested itself in revolution. It did so in England;
it did so in America; and it did so in France; but the
thoughtful student of history will see in these manifestations no reason to "glorify revolution." He will
rather see in all such internecine strife the sad side of
human nature. He detects only the mad passions of
men: on the one hand fanatical devotion to effete institutions and rotten traditions and on the other side the
senseless love of ruin. He will tell us that if this is the
true manifestation of the so-called modern spirit, then
an enemy to civilization is abroad on the earth compared
with which the barbaric lust for destruction of the Huns
and Vandals sinks into insignificance.

But, in fact, the new movement is not simply destructive; it has also its positive and constructive side; it

pulls down only to build better. It bears a freight of
new ideas, doctrines, and institutions, rich with fruits
of peace, joy, and prosperity. Its violent manifestations
are only the fight which it has to wage for its birth-right.
It is true, indeed, that the blood which is spilled upon
its garments leaves deep stains; nay more, that those
stains must be washed out in long suffering and patient
toil and steady devotion to duty before the movement
can renew its march. The fight is never over when the
banner is furled and the arms are returned to the arse-
nal. On the contrary, that is just when the fight begins
— a new fight and a hard one; not a fight of guns, but
of ideas; not of artillery, but of discussion. The warfare of the battle-field only secures freedom of discussion
and tames the party which sought to cut it short by an
appeal to arms. Then arises a new question: whether
those who won the victory under the inspiration of
physical combat have the patience, the tenacity, and
the self-denial to secure its fruits by establishing and
spreading sound principles, by founding and fostering
good institutions, and by engrafting upon the culture
and civilization of their country the new convictions
which they have won. To destroy old traditions is
easy, but no nation can do without traditions unless
it is willing to become the prey of demagogues and
mountebanks and to chase every day a new chimera.
But traditions must be cared for through a tender
process of germination until they take root and
acquire vitality and that is a labor of time, patience,
and self-sacrifice.

Ten years ago this tide of modern history reached to
one of the inherited institutions of this nation. Foremost in many respects as we were in our sympathy as
a nation with all the new ideas and institutions, we yet

had in our midst an institution which represented and rested on the grossest falsehood invented in the past — perhaps we had even developed the wrong into phases more revolting than it had elsewhere attained. With a social and civil system which was democratic from its broadest principle to its slightest development, we yet had an institution whose essential spirit was aristocratic. With a mercantile system running to excess even in its application to all the relations of life, according to which services rendered commanded a pecuniary recompense, we yet had a system of labor within our national frontier under which one set of men did all the work and another set of men took all the pay. All history might have taught us that inconsistencies so gross could never endure; that a united nation never could be built out of elements so discordant, producing a grotesque civil, social, political, and mercantile monstrosity. Under the influence of modern inventions which were rapidly uniting us as far as space and time were concerned, it was inevitable that sooner or later this alternative must come to a decision; either the attempt to form this people into one homogeneous nation must fail or else the discordant elements must be eliminated. The enactments on which the existing status was based might avail to this extent, that the changes could not be wrought out without a frightful convulsion, but they could not avail to prevent the decision of the alternative. The modern doctrines of equality, justice, and right reason, as practical principles on which governments ought to be based, had wrought upon the consciences of our people until a majority were hostile to one of our inherited institutions which enjoyed the sanction of law. It was only another phase of the modern revulsion against all forms of privilege and caste, which had already pro-

duced so many crises in Europe. Our turn had come.
We had been foremost in accepting the modern principles; we must now put our institutions into complete
consistency with them. Here, as elsewhere, the advocates of the abuse sought the arbitration of force and
the first consequence of the new convictions was a bloody
and desolating war, but the subsequent consequences
have, I believe, been such as to educate and develop the
nation. The destructive feature was first manifested,
but we are now going through the constructive developing and consolidating movement. Let us see if this is
not so.

It is easy for us now to look back and philosophize
upon the events, but at the time none of us were so
wise. One thing only the popular mind did discern, and
discern clearly, even in the midst of the storm, and that
was the main gist of the question at issue. The people
did see that it was a question whether we should form
one homogeneous nation, or whether the discordant institution should be maintained.

With the decision of that question the nation was
born; or, perhaps I should say, attained its manhood.
For the life of this nation up to that time had been a
kind of boyhood. We had rollicked in the exultation of
youth. We were conscious of vigor and freedom. We
knew few of the burdens of national life. We had no
powerful neighbors to impose fear upon us. We were
not entangled in any weary diplomacy. We had the
sea between us and our enemies and we did not feel the
burdens of national defense. We had no old traditions
to cramp us; no vested interests to respect; no complicated rights to fetter our movements of public policy.
We were an experiment and we rejoiced in the evidences
of our success. We undertook other experiments in

social, civil, and political matters, whose apparent reck-
lessness struck older nations aghast, but which we did
not fear to make because we were confident of our power
to recover from failure. Our relations were free, our
powers were abundant enough to endure waste. Withal,
we could not find opportunities to manifest all our
strength. We could only promise to do and assert
our ability to do, and this exposed us to malicious interpretations. In all this we see the indications of
youth, of inexperience, of exuberant spirits, of overflow-
ing power.

But the convulsion through which we passed ten years
ago had the effect upon us as a nation which a grave
trial has upon a man: at one step he passes from youth
to manhood. He comes to know the world in which he
lives. He appreciates the earnestness of life. His confidence in his own powers may be no less firm, but it
is far more sober. He does not tempt the trials of life.
He no longer seeks opportunities to waste his energies
for the mere sake of exercising them. He husbands his
powers and settles down to a less romantic, but far more
efficient method of undertaking and working. So it
was, I say, with this nation. War had been to us a
tradition of glory. During a long peace, interrupted
only by a slight foreign war, a generation had grown
up which had no knowledge, from actual experience, of
what war is; but to the Americans of this generation war
is a lurid glory. *We* never can deceive ourselves as to
what it means. It brings to us no poetry or romance, but
we have seen the spectre face to face and have recognized
its true features. We are yet so near to it that our exultation is dimmed in tears and when we turn our memory back to it, we cannot tell whether a sob or a cheer
will burst from our hearts. War, to our generation of

Americans, is a grim necessity to which sober men may be driven in the last extremity to ward off violent hands from all which makes life valuable, and no flowers of rhetoric can make us see in it anything else than the dire necessity of a peaceful citizen when his life, his family, his fireside, and his country are in danger from the rage of a misguided foe.

The war taught us also the value of moral forces in national life. We were in danger of falling into all the vices of a long and lazy peace. Our interests were centering in mercantile and industrial pursuits until it seemed that, as a nation, we might hold no cause worth the injury which must result from an interruption of industry. It seemed that our country might come to mean to us only a territory teeming with wealth for which we desired to scramble without interruption. Patriotism was a virtue which languished for want of exercise. It could no longer live on the story of great deeds done by a former generation, for the love of country, like every other love, grows by what it demands, not by what it brings; those who love their country are those who have paid for it, not those who have enjoyed its blessings after it was bought. But the great crisis of our recent history offered to our people an ideal good. It held up before the mind of the nation a good to be won which was worth more than gold or raiment. It called them to win for their children another inheritance than lands or stocks and that was the inheritance of a nation which should be to them a true nursing mother by its traditions of labor, patience, suffering, and self-denial. The people responded to the call. They proved to all the world and to themselves, which is far more important, that they could understand such a call, that they could appreciate a higher and ideal good, and that they were not yet altogether given over to the desire for material prosperity.

The war also taught this people what a nation is. A nation is not a certain extent of territory on the earth's surface; nor is it the mere aggregate of the persons who may live within a certain territory. A nation is a community of various ages, occupations, talents, and circumstances, but all united in a common interest. It is a unit which has organic life. It is enduring in its existence, spanning over individual lives and generations. It accumulates the contributions of various individuals and of various generations and it brings them all to the service and benefit of each. It is, therefore, in the strictest sense, a common-wealth, in which each participates in the prosperity of the whole and all suffer through the misfortune of one. It brings down from generation to generation the accumulation of art, science, and literature and its store of these treasures should be a steadily increasing one. It brings down the public buildings, the machinery of government, the stores of defensive means, the galleries of painting, the museums of art and science, the libraries, as a continually increasing endowment of posterity. Moreover it cherishes traditions which, if they become petrified, form a prison-house which must be broken, but which, if they are fresh, living, and flexible, are the framework of society. For instance, the rights of conscience, the equality of all men before the law, the separation of church and state, religious toleration, freedom of speech and of the press, popular education, are vital traditions of the American people. They are not brought in question; they form the stock of firm and universal convictions on which our national life is based; they are ingrained into the character of our people and you can assume, in any controversy, that an American will admit their truth. But they form the sum of traditions which we obtain as our birth-right. They are never explicitly taught to us, but we assimilate them in our earliest childhood from all our surroundings, at the fireside, at school, from the press, on the highways and streets. We never hear them disputed and it is only when we observe how difficult it is for some foreign nations to learn them that we perceive that they are not implanted by nature in the human mind. They are a part and the most valuable part of our national inheritance, and the obligation of love, labor, and protection which we owe to the nation rests upon these benefits which we receive from it.

We have learned, I say, in these last ten years, to appreciate the idea of a nation and its value as a unit and as a commonwealth. We have also reached the determination that we, the people of the United States, will be a nation, not a chance aggregate of adventurers in a new country nor a confederation of jealous and discordant states, but a union and a unity, holding as municipal rights those things which are truly limited and local and by which no jealousies are aroused, but maintaining pure our sense of a true national bond embracing all as far as the national name extends.

We have also obtained clearer views as to the way in which a nation is to be formed.

1. The first necessity for a nation is a homogeneous population. The nations of Europe generally start with this condition satisfied, and it is only when, by foreign conquest, they absorb foreign elements that they experience difficulty in this respect. In general they embrace within a certain area persons who speak a common language, cherish the same traditions, have the same manners and customs and, in many cases, hold the

same religion. But we have a chaotic society and a conglomerate population. Europeans, Africans, and Asiatics meet with the aborigines of this continent in our population. We have every diversity of race, nationality, language, manners, customs, religion, traditions, and character. To form a nation, we must mold these elements into a certain measure of similarity and conformity. The divisions which are based upon the circumstances of foreign countries must be left behind. The jealousies of race and the hatreds of sects and the bitterness of parties which have sprung up in foreign lands are no heritage of ours. They are curses which must not be transplanted hither. The divisions, factions, and cliques which take their names from the origin of their members in foreign countries must be dissolved in the new bond of American citizenship. The institutions, traditions, social and civil forms which are known as American are what have made this country a more desirable residence to many persons than the land of their birth. They are welcome to the great American nationality, to which many of us are only new-comers, but it is certainly no unfair demand to ask that they shall come in order to be Americans and not in order to find in the new world a new arena for the strifes which desolate the old. Such a disposition on the part of all to merge sectional, national, and other partisanships in the new nationality is a prime necessity if we are to form a nation.

2. It is only a development of the same idea to say that, in order to have a nation, we must have homogeneous institutions. We have already noticed how incongruous the institution of slavery was in our civil and social system, and we have observed that that incongruity led to a crisis in which the question at stake was

nothing less than this: whether we should be a nation or not. It is an instance of a general law. The nation, as we have defined it, an organic unit, a commonwealth, a true educator and benefactor, cannot attain to the harmony which is its law of life unless its institutions are similar, harmonious, and compatible. They need not be uniform, for local circumstances will give them local color, but they must not be discordant. The relations of the general government to the state governments cannot be one thing in one section and another in another, if we are to solidify into a nation. If a man reared in Maine imbibes certain ideas of the right of free speech, and, on going to Florida or California finds that the exercise of that right puts his life and liberty in danger, he will not feel that any true bond of nationality unites those localities. If it is a principle which is recognized almost universally throughout the country that our soil and our institutions are open to all men who choose to come here and practice industry in peace, then any section which limits this principle by hostility to a single race impairs, in so far, the development of a true nationality. If monogamy is rooted in our civilization and lies at the lowest foundation of our social structure, then polygamy, if practised amongst us, is a foreign and disturbing element. Those who practise it may be amongst us but not of us. They cannot form with us a homogeneous nationality. We are not wise if we apply force to compel unformity in these respects, but we ought to understand the task which lies before us and the ends towards which we have to strive, and we must seek to accomplish them through the propagation of sound doctrines and general enlightenment.

3. This brings us to another necessary condition for

a nation, a condition which, in order of thought and of importance is first of all, that is, that the people shall have a fund of common convictions, common principles, and common aims. The institutions of a country are only an embodiment and expression of the national faiths. We, for instance, as a nation, believe that every man has a full right to make the most of himself and that the commonwealth will gain by making the most of every individual born within its limits. Our common schools are an institution framed to give practical efficiency to this conviction. In a country or section where it is believed that one portion of the community are born to menial offices and that the commonwealth injures itself by educating them to be dissatisfied with their position, you will find no common school system. We believe also that the truth in regard to any matter whatsoever is most likely to emerge from a free discussion. We know that much will be said in such a discussion which will be crude, much which will be foolish, and perhaps some things which will be wicked and malicious. We nevertheless have faith in freedom. We trust it, and a free press is an institution which is a natural product of this conviction. In countries where such faiths are wanting, we meet with censorships, restrictions, and limitations. One part of the population undertakes to decide for another part what things are healthful and true. So, universally, the institutions of a country are the embodiment of its faiths. Moreover every law which is passed is an embodiment of a certain theoretical principle which is believed to be sound. There is a philosophy of some sort at the bottom of all legislation, whether it be the polished philosophy of the schools or the rough and ready philosophy of men of practical experience. We take private property for public uses because it is believed right and just to do so. We punish criminals because we believe in the theoretical doctrine that a man forfeits his right to life or liberty if he misuses his powers to the injury of his neighbors. We interfere with the freedom of purchase and sale of certain articles on grounds of public policy. Thus, as we say, all our public acts represent popular opinion, that is, the beliefs which the people cherish.

It follows from all this that if we are to be a united and harmonious nation, it is of the first importance that we shall be united in our convictions on those fundamental principles which underlie our jurisprudence, our legislation, our education, and our diplomacy. We must be agreed as to whether we will seek in our diplomacy petty advantages and jealous self-interest or whether we, as a nation, will contribute to the widest good of humanity; whether our motto shall be to see that our country is always right or to stand by our country right or wrong. We must be agreed as to the ends to be sought by government, whether they are the broadest national prosperity or the satisfaction of factions and parties. We must agree in our estimate of the true province and scope of legislation, whether men can be made good and rich by law or whether the true principle of strength be reluctance of the commonwealth to interfere further than is absolutely necessary with individual enterprise and the individual conscience. Our faith in the value of training and culture must be unanimous. We must esteem care and painstaking and thoroughness and industry in every department of life, and we must so esteem the authority of knowledge, experience, judgment, and sound reason as to be willing to defer to it. We must also be reasonably unanimous in regard to the highest interests of man, the relation of this life to immortality, and the moral obligations which depend on that relation; and we must agree in our estimate of the value of conscience in all human affairs. These are only a few of the broad and fundamental principles which underlie human affairs, unanimity in regard to which is necessary in a body of men who aspire to form a nation. Men will always differ in regard to the particular application of these principles to especial cases, and therefore parties will always exist, but these principles underlie all parties and are essential to the unity of the commonwealth.

Here, then, we have an outline of what a nation is, what is requisite to its formation, and what is required for its permanent prosperity—matters which the events of the last ten years have brought into new prominence and new interest. We count them into the results of our great civil crisis. It gave us a feeling of unity and nationality, it gave us a history, it vindicated us to ourselves and to posterity as a people who could understand and respond to an ideal good, and it fixed our attention on the conditions requisite to the development and establishment of a nation.

Far be it from me to glorify war. We need only estimate our position to-day in order to see that the evil results of the war are not confined to the destruction of property, the loss of life, and the crippling of industry. There are other results directly traceable to war: diminished respect for law, love of arbitrary processes, respect for force, and a tendency to sacrifice principle to a narrow expediency, which awaken our anxiety and demand our efforts to counteract them. In view of these evils and dangers we cannot glorify war. It is a harsh experience, full of the education and full of the evil which inheres in all adversity. One thing only we do say, and we say it with full confidence in looking back on our own great strife: there is one thing worse than war and that is peace in the face of men with swords drawn on behalf of injustice and wrong. War, in its way, and peace, in its way, are parts of that great discipline of adversity and prosperity by which God makes men and nations strong.

These are the thoughts which seem to me to be in place on our "Memorial Day." A nation's civil holidays are an epitome of its history. We have a day on which we celebrate the nation's birth; it surely is well that we should have a day on which we celebrate its coming of age. But when we meet to-day, our minds do not revert to the glory of victory; they dwell rather on the memory of a grand duty nobly done. We do not celebrate amidst the booming of cannon or the noisy mirth of a popular holiday; we keep the day sacred to a pious duty in memory of those who fell in the great struggle. How could we be merry when every mind runs over its list of relatives and friends and when each recalls those in his own circle of acquaintances whose lives were full of promise of blessing to their country, but who to-day are not? The sun shines for us, and we laugh and are gay and the world goes on its course of business and pleasure, of joy and of enterprise, and still the memory of the lost ones when it revives is bright and keen. Above their graves we turn back to the retrospect and renew our vow that they shall not have perished in vain. We see now, as they could not see, all the extent of the cause for which they died and we resolve that the nation for whose external union they died shall be a nation indeed. We will carry on that moral regeneration and union which is still necessary to consolidate their work. We will establish the foundations of the nation in firm convictions and true principles; we will build it up on strong institutions and noble traditions; and we will consolidate its heterogeneous elements into a harmonious nationality.

Neither are we met to-day to exult over the defeated party or to keep alive the rancor of civil strife. That phase of this celebration is fading — happily fading out of the public mind. Rather, now that the heat of the conflict has subsided, we see distinctly the sad mischief of civil strife. The blows which we struck were blows at our own body; the wounds which we gave left scars upon ourselves; the destruction which we wrought fell upon our own interests. This is the fatal character of all civil strife, that the one commonwealth suffers the losses both of the victors and the vanquished. The names of places which we inscribe on our monuments are not those of a foreign foe; they are our own and a part of the inheritance of our children. Fifty years hence, when your sons visit Richmond and Charleston, they will hardly be able to find a rebel or the son of a rebel there. They will find a new race, energetic, patriotic, and American, a race of colonists and immigrants from the North and from foreign lands, cramped by no inherited crime, warped by no false traditions, and demoralized by no discord between conscience and social institutions. They will smile at the old folly and they will not meet with a frown the sons of the victors. Already the movements are in progress which promise to rescue the South from the unprincipled adventurers who have profited by the transition period, and to bring it into political, social, and industrial harmony with the rest of the nation. Already nature spreads her healing hand to conceal the physical scars which war had made. The trees spring again on the devastated hillside. The sod spreads over the half-buried cannon-ball. The shrubs and bushes obliterate the lines of the entrenchments. The industry of man assists in the same work, and new industry and new achievements spring up on the ruins of the old. It is not the province of Memorial Day to reverse or retard this process and by tearing open again the old wounds to rescue anger and hate from oblivion. Its province is to keep alive in the hearts of the people the meaning and value of the nation, the price which it cost, and the memory of those who died to purchase it. When men go to war for glory, let them have their reward. Pay it in the booming of cannon, in the blare of trumpets, and in the tinsel and trappings which perish in the using; but when men go to war for duty, let them also have their reward. Pay it in a new devotion to the duty for whose sake they fell; pay it in a nobler zeal in behalf of our rescued country; pay it in a loftier wisdom in public policy which shall destroy abuses before they grow so strong that it shall cost the blood of your sons to root them out.

FOR PRESIDENT?

FOR PRESIDENT? [1]

[1876]

On returning to town last Saturday, and looking over
the file of the Palladium, I found a letter by "Enquirer"
in Thursday's issue which I may assume, without much
danger of error, to refer to me. I find nothing discour-
teous or improper in the inquiry for whom I shall vote
for President, and what my reasons are, if anybody
cares to ask. I have never made any announcement of
my opinions and intentions because it was not for me
to assume that anybody cared about them, and also
because my course was not, and is not yet, so thoroughly
satisfactorily clear before myself that I care to bring
my opinion voluntarily before the public. However,
now that I am asked, I will reply.

I want to premise one thing. My first responsibility
is to the University, and I propose to be true to that
before anything else. I shall not compromise that for
political influence, and if, as "Enquirer" says, a student
and teacher of political science may fairly be asked to
give his opinions and his reasons, it is also true that a
man who occupies a university chair must be careful,
in political activity, whether he pulls down the university or pulls up politics. I have, therefore, carefully
limited my practical action in politics to such duties as
are incumbent on *every* citizen, such as will not interfere with my university duties, and such as an independent scholar can pursue without any selfish interest
or danger to that broadest influence which he ought to
seek to obtain. I therefore write now the simple, frank

[1] New Haven *Palladium*, September 11, 1876.

opinion of an independent man, whose ambition and career lie entirely inside the sphere of the university teacher. Such a man is bound to be honest, dispassionate, and unprejudiced; to seek no friendships and fear no enmities. His opinion, if it is worthy of himself and his position, must be calm, broad, fair, and sincere. I shall aim in the present statement to fulfill this requirement and not to gain any other point.

I observe that most of the public discussions turn upon the antecedents, the acts, and the characters of the one and the other party. Those considerations have no force at all for my mind. I know my neighbors: one of them is a republican by habit and the other a democrat by habit, and neither of them can define his party name. The population is very equally divided between those who are ranged under one banner and those who are ranged under the other. When, therefore, I read the descriptions that party newspapers and party orators give of the opposite party, I look around me for the demons who seek the national ruin and I do not find them. I find neighbors, some of whom are under one banner and some under the other, but in their general tone, and will, and intention, those of one party are just as good and just as bad as those of the other. Especially when I remember that the social distribution of the two parties in the northern states is exactly opposite to what it is in the southern states, it seems to me that the national parties are very equally adjusted in regard to the social, intellectual, and moral elements which they contain. Now an historian, or a foreigner, reading the accounts which the parties give of each other, must infer either that these accounts are all false and that they simply constitute a depraved method of electioneering which obscures the issues and prevents the people from really using sound judgment, or else that they are all true, in which case the people of the United States are so unpatriotic, corrupt, disloyal, unjust, murderous, and venal that it makes little difference what is the result of any political struggle. And if we assume the standpoint of either political party and accept as true what it says of the other, then one-half of the population of this country are scoundrels so lost to honor and patriotism that no mere political victory could prevent bankruptcy in the national morals. If it is true of either party that no reform can be expected of it, then reform is impossible for the nation, for one-half of the people are at least indifferent to it. I discard all this argumentation, therefore, as the kind of appeal to passion and suspicion which befogs judgment. I regard the good sense, sound patriotism, and correct intention of the masses of the people in either party as substantially equal. I regard the evil elements in the parties as substantially equal, and I turn for my grounds of judgment to the considerations which I think genuine.

I find these in *men*. I cannot trust a party; I can trust a man. I cannot hold a party responsible; I can hold a man responsible. I cannot get an expression of opinion which is single and simple from a party; I can only get that from a man. A party cannot have character, or conscience, or reputation; it cannot repent, nor endure punishment or disgrace. I know very well that we are in the habit of predicating all these things of parties, but I should think our experience had offered the fullest proof that we cannot properly predicate any of these things of a party, except in a broad, half-metaphorical sense, under which all the sharpness and efficiency necessary to practical politics are lost. The proof is, at any rate, satisfactory to me.

The answer will probably here be made that the party elects the man, forms his "backing," will control his policy, and will not be ignored. I beg to call attention here to the illustration offered of the mischievous ambiguity in the word party. I have been speaking of parties as great bodies of voters, but those who present this objection mean by parties the group of professional politicians who control party machinery. In regard to parties in that sense I can only express my opinion, without entering on any accurate measurement of the heaps of dirt which each has piled on the other, that I, or any other similarly situated private and independent voter, have nothing to choose between them. I therefore pay little heed to platforms and letters; I have been deceived by them until I have lost all confidence in them and regard them much as I do sensational advertisements.

I look at candidates, and if the point be urged about the "backing" of each of the men now before us, I will state just how that appears to me. I have no information other than what the newspapers have given us all. From their story I do not see how any one can feel respect for the candidature of Governor Hayes. It appears that Mr. Cameron was piqued because some members of his delegation violated a sacred political tradition and did not throw the state vote as a unit, and he therefore refused to give the state vote as a unit for their candidate at the decisive moment. The senatorial aspirants could not see the prize go to either one of their own number and agreed only that it should not go to Blaine. These two things combined gave it to Hayes. At the time I expressed the opinion that this course of events, when one reflected that business in hand was the selection of a chief magistrate of the

nation, was a "farce." I did not then, and do not now
deny the *possibility* that Hayes may be *the* man for the
crisis. I cannot deny the possibility that, if you shake
up the names of eight million voters in a box and draw
one by lot, you may get the one out of the eight million
who is best fitted for the Presidency; but we are assumed
to be rational beings, making a selection on rational
grounds, and I think we did ourselves little credit on that
occasion in that point of view. Some of the gentlemen
there came home rejoicing and triumphing over the party
machine; they defeated the machine in its first intention, but it doubled upon them with its well-known
suppleness and activity. Mr. Hayes seems to be the
creature of the machine, and to have no other public
claim to the Presidency. He must feel that his selection is arbitrary, that he has everything yet to do to
justify public confidence that he is the recipient of an
"honor." He cannot act with the assured independence
of a man who has advanced by well earned steps, to whom
the Presidency comes as the highest trust at the end of a
career, to whom it is less an honor than a recognition and
concession. If "backing" gives control, I should think
that he was subjected to his backing from the outset.

I am well aware that Mr. Tilden has no long career
of public service behind him and that the theory of our
political system, as I have hinted at it, is not thoroughly
fulfilled in him. It is a profound and melancholy reflection, well worth every man's consideration, that our
public service does not furnish a number of tried statesmen from whom to select. I restrict myself now, however, to the *choice* which is the only practical question.

Mr. Tilden's nomination was opposed by all the worst
elements of his party and was supported by as honest,
pure, and intelligent men as ever led in any political

convention in this country. Many of them were young men, representing the hope, strength, faith, and purpose of the younger half of this generation, to which I turned long ago with all my confidence for the national future. I believe that few men now over forty-five appreciate the wide divergence of their political faiths from those of the men now under forty-five. Mr. Tilden's nomination was wrested from this convention by the conviction that he was the real leader of the party, the representative of its strength, the champion of its best principles, and the embodiment of its hope. The party came to him in that sense and took him for its chief because he was its head. That this was not purely and consistently and thoroughly true, belongs to the nature of all political parties and does not invalidate the criticism as a broad and sound one on the action of the convention. It appears to me, therefore, that Mr. Tilden's relation to his party is that of such dependence only as properly exists between leader and followers.

The question of the currency, to me, stands before any other. We must all grow better together. The sovereign's conscience is always hardest to move. He blames his ministers, his army, his people — anybody but himself. It is so also of the sovereign people. We are just now treating some of our old idols very harshly, and we are slow to learn that, if we govern ourselves and have our own way, we must blame ourselves for results. If we are to have any reform which shall be real, it must begin and spread far in the minds and consciences of the sovereign people. We must have a finer honor, a higher tone, a severer standard, a more correct judgment about ourselves. The sovereign people must recognize their own errors and follies and shoulder their own blame; they must repent and amend, discard false

notions, accept true ones, and so put the latter in practice as to engender a sound public opinion and an
incorruptible public morality. As a political measure to
help bring this about, I place the restoration of true
value money first of all.

It appears to me that Mr. Tilden has shown a more
correct, detailed, statesmanlike knowledge of the evil,
the remedy, and the process of cure than any other
public man who is eligible. I say *statesmanlike* knowledge, because I mean to distinguish between a lecture
on political economy which would be suitable for me,
and the program of a statesman which is what we want
from him — a distinction which has rarely been observed in Congress or in the Cabinet.

I am, of course, utterly opposed to the repeal of the
resumption act or any part of it, and I disapprove of
any concession on that point, in form or substance, by
Mr. Tilden or anybody else.

I know that the soft-money democrats have claimed
that Mr. Tilden has surrendered on the currency question, and the republicans have hastened to accept their
authority as conclusive on that point. Mr. Tilden's
opinions on this point are not new, nor were they first
placed before the public in his letter, but if he does not
in that document lay down hard-money doctrines, then
language has no meaning, and I could not express hard-
money doctrines myself. The soft-money men have,
within a year or two, begun to use some hard-money
phrases in forced, artificial, and impossible applications;
they find those phrases in Mr. Tilden's letter, and that
is the ground on which they claim his surrender.

Mr. Hayes has made a very distinct avowal that he
will resist the repeal of the resumption act unless something better is put in its place, and if he is elected I shall

certainly await with generous confidence a fulfillment of that pledge. The difficulty is just the one which seems to me radical in his candidature. He may do what he says he will; I am not held to say that he will not. I say only that when I have an act to perform I must look for measures which have been tested; when I want work done, I must look for an agent in regard to whom there is some record, some ground of belief in his ability and fitness. Between two candidates, one of whom is recommended to me on the *opinion* of his friends, the other of whom has a record of action and achievement under my knowledge and inspection, my most rational expectation of such a performance as I desire attaches to the latter.

I may be told, here, that the President cannot resume specie payments. He certainly cannot do more than his constitutional share. We are now talking about the election of a President for so much of the matter as belongs to him, and the objection is not in point. How much, at any rate, he can leave undone we now see by facts before us. I never judged the resumption act favorably; it did not seem to me to make practical provision for the requisite financial measures. Others, whose opinion is worth far more than mine on a point of law, agree that it is practical in respect to the means it provides; but the administration has not taken those means and nothing has been done. If we get a President who knows what to do, and how to do it, and who has the will to do it, it will be our own fault if we do not elect a Congress to co-operate with him.

I put next in this canvass the matter of administrative reform. Mr. Tilden has been governor of the state which has led in the demoralization of our politics since the beginning of the century. He has had the hardest position for beginning reform, perhaps, which there is in the Union; but he has made, at the risk of his own political fortunes, the only positive and successful steps towards it which I know of in the country. The newspaper exposures of the Tweed ring would have made no more impression on that body than the pattering of rain on the hide of a rhinoceros, and the members of the ring would to-day have been flaunting their stolen wealth in the face of the public if Mr. Tilden had not reduced their guilt to an arithmetical demonstration, available in a court of law. The Canal ring fight is known to everybody. The governor of New York cannot put a man in a state prison because he is convinced that he has stolen public money, and if the judicial system of New York is such that conviction and sentence cannot be secured, it is the judicial system which the people have given themselves by their representatives. If they reform themselves they will raise their standard of fitness in candidates for the legislature. New legislators will make new laws and judicial systems. Public administrators, if dishonest, will then find a surer path to the penitentiary, and their number will diminish; but I do not see how this sequence can be started anywhere but at its beginning.

I have in mind, however, not only these "reform" efforts, but also administrative reform. I will take a single case which floated in a paragraph through the newspapers, occasioning, so far as I ever saw, very little attention, but which had an immense effect on my mind and which I have often urged in private conversation.

It was stated that the politicians of the southern tier of counties of New York were bitterly hostile to Governor Tilden. The reasons were given, two in number: (1) Mr. Tilden had refused to remove the re-

publican superintendent of the asylum at Elmira in
order to appoint a democrat; (2) Mr. Tilden had removed, for cause, the corporation counsel of Elmira, who
was a democrat, although the common council of city
was republican and could elect a republican successor.
These were good grounds for the opposition of the
"politicians," but they were an imperative demand
on me, if I was an "Independent" and meant what I
had been talking about for years, to give him my full,
hearty, and efficient support, if it ever came in my way.
This was not popular reform; it was administrative
reform of the hardest kind. All question of motives,
of affiliations, of party antecedents, falls to the ground
when I see a public officer doing just what we want done
and what we have been vainly begging some public officer
to do; and when I see him engaged in a desperate fight
on account of it, I care nothing for any such objections.
My business is to give him recognition and support,
and when we want a man for a larger sphere, I know of no
one more fit, or from whom we can, with more confidence,
expect what we want. As for motives, I can judge a
man's motives only by his acts; I am tired of being asked
to believe that a man who has committed some rascality
had nevertheless a good motive, and that a man who
has done well had only a selfish impulse. That Mr.
Tilden is politician enough to be available is only an
advantage, since we cannot get an angel with a flaming
sword; and I think that we independents have cast
worse reproach upon ourselves than our most sarcastic
critics, since we have failed to seize upon a chance which
offered itself to our demand and have chosen to trust
to a groundless faith and a hope for which we cannot
give a reason.

In this latter light I must be allowed, without offense,

to regard the support of Governor Hayes. It may be accepted upon the testimony of his friends that he is a gentleman of integrity, high character, and spotless honor. Beyond this, however, when the question arises as to whether he has the independent judgment, the original force of mind, the staying-power, which are wanted in the next President of the United States, neither his friends nor any one else can say more than "we believe" that he has. That he has not the wide experience requisite is certain. I repeat what I am not held to say that he has not the former qualities — perhaps he has them. The point is, if I am asked to vote for him, that I have a right to demand to know that he has them, or else, as between him and another who has given guarantees, sound judgment forces me to choose the latter. I received a letter a while ago from a friend of Governor Hayes, who declared that Governor Hayes was a very modest man whose modesty prevented him from accepting the United States Senatorship. I quote it as an instance of what seems to me wrong reasoning on these matters. If Governor Hayes is such a man as is now claimed, it seems to me he is just the man we have sadly needed in the Senate for the last few years, and if he refused to go, he turned his back on the call of public duty. I do not deny his right to refuse, although in general I hold it sound doctrine that a man of good health and independent fortune ought to serve the state when duly and honorably selected; but *if Mr. Hayes was ever to be a candidate for the Presidency*, he ought to have pursued a public career in the subordinate places which opened to him, he ought to have allowed us to see him in those places, and he ought to have made a record on which we could form a judgment to-day and not be thrown on the say-so of his friends. If he is to be elected, I shall certainly not prejudge him nor allow any prejudice to arise in my mind, but when I look back on former cases in which the campaign enthusiasm has surrounded an untried man with a halo which has subsequently faded into something worse than obscurity, my imagination refuses to act.

Another point in this canvass which very deeply interests me is the condition and future of the South. The campaign seems to be turning more and more to that issue after all, and it seems to be found that distrust of rebels and the old war spirit are still so strong as to be the best available campaign capital. If that is to be so, then I must take sides against any further administration of the affairs of the South by the North acting through the general government. I have had occasion within a year to review the whole history of reconstruction. The effect upon my mind has been shame and blame to myself for the share which I, as a republican, have had in helping to build up the worst legislation of the nineteenth century. I have been shocked to realize by what successive stages we have erected here a system of restrictive and coercive legislation which very few northern republicans know in even its broadest features; and I can only recognize in disorder, riot, misrule, irresponsible official tyranny, and industrial loss, the results which have followed everywhere in history from coercive legislation enacted by one community against another. The republican candidate for the Vice-Presidency devoted his letter of acceptance almost exclusively to the Southern question. He believes that the Southern States are not civilized up to the standard of the Northern States, and he wants to bring them up. I agree with him that they are on a lower grade, but I submit that it is not his business nor ours

to civilize them by any political measures. Communities
do not take kindly to that kind of school-mastering, and
I see in such a spirit only a threat of further interference, further coercion, further resistance, and prolonged
trouble. The Southern States have on their hands a
race problem of the first magnitude; they will have all
they can do to manage it, if they are left free under the
natural social and economic laws. They think, generally, that a black man is not the equal of a white man,
which is not an essential question in the problem; but
the Northern communities, a thousand miles away, insist
that they shall first change their minds on that dogmatic
point, and proceed to try to coerce their opinions. I
think that Southern people are unwise and narrow in
very many of their notions, but the only practical
question is how to deal with erroneous opinions. Can
we ever coerce opinions? Do we not all know rather
that if we leave unwise men to pursue their folly, their
own experience will teach them, but that if we attempt
to impose contrary opinions, we shall only lead them
to cling to their errors as the most sacred faiths? I,
therefore, desire now, as regards this political question,
that the South be left to work out its own social problems under no arbitrary political coercion, but simply
under the constraint of social and economic forces. I
want the Northern opinions kept to their own sphere of
action, and the local self-government left free to act in
the South under the plan and intention of our Constitution, without which the Union is impossible. If the
Union is really secured and is to last, it must do so under
peace between its parts and not under war, either military or political. I therefore condemn the attempt to
revive and use the old war passions, suspicion, dread,
or hostility. When it is done by demagogues I perceive

in it only their natural and disastrous activity; but when it is done by men of principle, who have some knowledge of history, of constitutional law, and of the science of government, I see in it only a proof of how hard it is to resist the current of party opinion, and the consistency of political passion. As for dread of the Southern influence in the general government, I would rather trust to-morrow, either on pecuniary or political questions, to a Congress made up entirely of ex-Confederates, then to one made up of such men as the Southern republican representatives have been since reconstruction. The man who won more of my respect than any other man in the last Congress was Randall Gibson, a democrat and an ex-rebel; if the South has any more such rebel brigadiers I would like to help get them back into politics, especially now that General Butler is going down to fight them.

Finally, in regard to another matter which I have very much at heart, but which is hardly an active issue in the campaign, whatever hope there is for free trade lies in the election of Tilden.

I have not written this to convert anybody, or do anything but state my opinions and feelings fully. I therefore add, with perfect frankness, that there is much in the canvass which I do not like and which makes a decision difficult. I find that this has been the case with independent men in almost every election since that of John Adams. In this case I find it very hard to vote for a Vice-President whom I think unfit for the Presidency, should he be called to it. Moreover, I cannot be thoroughly satisfied where any floating doubt remains in regard to the life-long uprightness of a candidate, but I shall try, even here, to keep my judgment clear. I cannot be carried away by the hot and exaggerated assertion of a campaign charge whose injustice is apparent in its form of statement, which I am not competent to investigate, and which cannot be properly tried by anybody. I cannot be affected by a charge which is no charge, but only a challenge to a man to divulge his private affairs. Above all I shall not commit that folly into which some, trusting in the moral fervor of the Independents, seem anxious to drive them, to hang an important political decision on disapproval of the course of conduct adopted by a man at one or another point of a long business and professional career, to the disregard of all the properly political considerations involved for the present or future. If, then, a decision is forced upon me, I simply judge, on all the information I possess, that Mr. Tilden has more knowledge, ability, skill, and will to do what I want to see done in politics, than Mr. Hayes. Nevertheless, I am not called upon to bind or pledge myself in any way, and I hold myself free to take any course which may, upon further information or reflection, seem best. However the election may result, I shall be guided in my relations to the next administration entirely by its performances in regard to the matters I have here discussed.

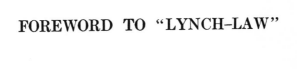

FOREWORD TO "LYNCH-LAW"

FOREWORD TO "LYNCH–LAW" [1]

[1905]

FEW people are able to read about lynch-executions, with atrocious forms of torture and cruel death, such as have occurred from time to time within ten years in this country, without a feeling of national shame. It is necessary that facts should be known and that public opinion should be corrected as to the ethics of that mode of dealing with crime. Lynch-law is a very different thing where laws and civil institutions are in full force and activity from what it is where they are wanting. It is not admissible that a self-governing democracy should plead the remissness of its own selected agents as an excuse for mob-violence. It is a disgrace to our civilization that men can be put to death by painful methods, which our laws have discarded as never suitable, and without the proofs of guilt which our laws call for in any case whatsoever. It would be a disgrace to us if amongst us men should burn a rattlesnake or a mad dog. The badness of the victim is not an element in the case at all. Torture and burning are forbidden, not because the victim is not bad enough, but because we are too good. It is on account of what we owe to ourselves that these methods are shameful to us, if we descend to them. It is evident, however, that public opinion is not educated up to this level. The reader of the present book will learn very interest-

[1] By James Elbert Cutler

ing facts about the causes alleged for lynching, and about the public view of that crime. Many current errors will be corrected, and many notions which are irrelevant, although they are popularly believed to be germane and important, will be set aside.

FOREWORD TO "THE ANTHRACITE COAL INDUSTRY"

FOREWORD TO "THE ANTHRACITE COAL INDUSTRY"[1]

[1901]

THE anthracite coal industry ranks as one of the most important in the United States, not so much on account of its magnitude as on account of its peculiar position in our industrial system, and the great number of social and economic questions which cluster around it. It is a limited natural monopoly. It is an extractive industry, the stock of which is exhausted as it is exploited. All the facts which can be learned about it are, therefore, as interesting to the investor as to the economist and geologist. The amount of supply, and the length of time before it will be exhausted, are matters of public welfare. Economizing of the supply and improvement of the methods of working, therefore, interest us all. The policy of management of the industry has turned upon a series of most interesting and important changes in labor supply, modes of transportation, aggregation of capital, and legislation. Therefore we have here a most instructive history for the statesman and man of affairs. The industry has also been the arena of many experiments in labor organization, and of many industrial wars over wages, hours, rules, methods, etc. It brings into co-operation a variety of interests, mining, transportation, banking; and the suodivision of interests is such that the industry, as a whole, is a cluster of interests which it is no easy

[1] By Peter Roberts

[387]

matter to bring into harmony. The miners form a community which is to a certain extent isolated and peculiar. It is not easily acted upon by currents of thought which are strong in the rest of the state, and it is, at the same time, open to agitation and internal commotion and strife, or to temporary fits of feeling and irregular notions. Hence arise peculiar and important social phenomena in mining towns where laborers of different nationalities are assembled. The position of women and children, the relations of marriage and the family, the condition of churches and schools, all tend to become anomalous, and strange or hostile to our civilization.

INTRODUCTORY LECTURE TO COURSES IN POLITICAL AND SOCIAL SCIENCE

INTRODUCTORY LECTURE TO COURSES IN POLITICAL AND SOCIAL SCIENCE

[1873]

THREE things are necessary for a student who is to acquire intelligently a new branch of knowledge under a teacher. First, an idea of the importance of the subject; second, an idea of the method of the teacher; and third, some notion of the outlook, that is to say, of the thing to be acquired. I propose in this lecture to give a program of the year's work in this department, as well in the graduate as in the undergraduate schools, and my aim is to supply as well as I can the three requisites mentioned.

There is a necessity for such a lecture in this department, which does not exist in any other. Almost everyone has some idea of the range, meaning, purpose and method of the sciences which are taught in a university, but I doubt very much if there is any but the most vague notion in the popular mind of what is meant by political science, in either its narrower or its wider significance. It is not generally understood what it aims at, how it teaches, what its methods are, nor what guarantee there is for its results. Let us try first to arrive at a conception of these points.

You are aware that the civilization of mankind has proceeded by stages and that its course has been one of development and progress. This progress has been from the simple towards the complex. Institutions have been multiplied, functions in the body social have been divided and subdivided, interests have increased in number and have been more and more interlaced with each other, classes and professions have arisen which were formerly unknown. We can no longer divide society exhaustively into upper, lower, and middle classes. In this country, at least, such a division would have no meaning. Government has passed through successive forms and stages, which we generally regard as successive improvements, until now government is a complex machine, with numerous departments, diverse organs, complex functions, and above all an abstraction called law which determines the method of operation of all the parts. A nation is no longer a horde of individuals following the command of one man. It is a vast organism. Its members are endowed with free will to determine their own acts in accordance with their own wishes. They undertake independent enterprises of wide scope; they select their own combinations into which they enter; they form their own opinions of what is wise and right and true. They find in all this that they are inextricably entangled with each other. Society is solidified and bound together by these numerous bonds, and we find that it is of the utmost importance to us that our neighbors, as well as ourselves, be wise and prudent, for we see that their folly or wisdom reacts upon us as ours upon them. We can no longer appeal to some supreme ruler to make others do what they ought to do in the interest of all. We must get together and by common consent agree upon what we will do, what concessions we will make to the common interest, what efforts we will contribute to the general welfare. We can no longer get the social body regulated by instructing a prince or a few ministers; we must mold public opinion — this new power until recently unknown as a social force, but now seen to be the great engine which controls the whole. So too we find that the government, however free may be its form, inherits traditions and bears names of authority. Power of control must be lodged somewhere, at least as a reserve for those cases in which malice, evil, and passion raise their heads. But those who are clothed with this power undergo an inevitable temptation to abuse it. They have an opportunity to exert upon the social body a power not justly theirs as individuals. They may use this influence selfishly for themselves or their favorites. For the more completely we popularize a government, the more we trust it; we put our interests of all kinds at its mercy. Hence it occurs that the government, either ignorantly from want of knowledge to use the great powers it possesses for the general good, or with corrupt motive, inflicts harm upon the citizen. It is, therefore, necessary for us to agree what powers we will give to the officers of government, and what restrictions we will put upon them. Our determinations in regard to these things — what we will do and allow to be done, or what we will not do or not allow to be done by each other; what things the government shall do or shall not do on our behalf — constitute the body of our laws. Still again: when the mass of the population governs, an important question arises as to how its will is to reach an expression. An opportunity offers itself for manipulating this body in order to make it do what a few desire that it shall do. Every such body is subject to manipulation and any clique, party, or corporation which has a definite object which it pursues steadily and energetically, is able to lead the mass of uninstructed or indifferent citizens.

This is especially the case with regard to party government — and no other kind of government is possible, so far as we can yet see, in a republic. The party tends to become a unit inside of the nation. It acquires vested interests, traditions, history, glory, all of which give it momentum. It is able to carry measures under the party name irrespective of their wisdom. It is able to cover up and conceal wrongs under the mantle of past achievements. Its watchwords and its slang acquire infallible authority. When a party has reached this stage, it is a valuable piece of property. It is like an army trained and disciplined to obey orders without asking questions or making objections. Then the question is, who is to command; and a man or a clique who holds the authority over it can do with it what he chooses. It is a machine all finished and oiled to work smoothly and it obeys as well one hand on the lever as another.

Hence arise a mass of questions as to the means to be used for securing a true, spontaneous, and original expression of public opinion; and the answers to these questions are not always laws, though they may require that authority, but they are political usages applying to the constitution of party committees, the authority of caucuses, the rules of the primary meeting, the binding force of party nomination, and also the forms of legislative procedure.

You see then that in our modern society changes of immense scope have been made in the fundamental principles of the social order. All traditions of government and society have been called in question and put on trial. New interests, new institutions, new faiths, new conceptions of life have arisen within two or three centuries. Industry and commerce have changed their form, education has been revolutionized, the press has come into being. Now the question arises as to what regulations we shall adopt for the constitution of the social body under this new state of things. The traditions and usages of past ages are broken, or at least discredited. New conditions require new institutions and we turn away from tradition and prescription to re-examine the data from which we may learn what principles of the social order are *true*, that is, conform to human nature and to the conditions of human society. This inquiry embraces political economy, or the science of wealth, as well as comparative politics, jurisprudence, international law, the theory of the state, the theory of government, and the history of all these. This is political science in its widest sense and this I propose to make the subject of my lectures to the graduates during the present term. I call it the Encyclopædia of Political Science, borrowing the name the Germans have given to it. It treats of the divisions and subdivisions of the science and of their relation to each other, serving to map out the whole field, giving a brief description of each part, and preparing the way for further intelligent study of details. I desire now to show what the immediate, practical, and specific importance of political science is for us Americans of to-day, assuming the existing constitution as permanent and not subject to question.

Here I meet with an embarrassment which oppresses every teacher in the same situation. On the one hand is my obligation to truth which compels me to speak fully and boldly in regard to our national affairs at the present moment, and on the other hand is my duty as an instructor of the young men of the country to train them to respect the institutions and the government of their native land. I should be glad to do justice to the latter duty. I consider it a sad thing that the favorite subjects for college exercises should be the corruption and misbehavior of the public men of the country. I dislike to hear the government of the country referred to in terms of commonplace contempt by young men who, by reason of youth, ought to be ultra-patriotic, if anything, and yet I cannot rebuke it because I know how much ground there is for it. I dislike to hear politicians sneered at and the career of politics tossed aside as if it were the career of a swindler, for I hold politics — or, if we must abandon the degraded word, statesmanship — to be the grandest calling open to men; and yet, if a young friend of mine goes into politics I feel misgivings for his future, not lest he may not get rich, for that is probable enough, but lest he may lose the manliness and honor of a gentleman and may acquire the character of an intriguer and a gambler. But my duty to scientific truth is here paramount to all others and the degraded state of American politics and public life is the evil with which I have to deal. I can no more avoid describing it than a physician lecturing on pathology could desist from the description of a loathsome disease. I desire only that I may not be ranked amongst those dilettante politicians and essayists who sneer at everything American as a means of showing their elevated culture, nor with those flaccid cosmopolitans who boast of being superior to narrow claims of nationality and who certainly do their duty by no nation.

The American Constitution, at the time at which it was formed, embodied the most advanced doctrines of political science which had then been developed. The courage with which the men of that day grasped these advanced principles and embodied them in their new scheme of government excites admiration and astonishment. During the first years of our national life the few limitations on popular sovereignty which the Federal party had retained were overthrown. Since that time we have added nothing to the world's knowledge or experience of political science. It has, on the contrary, been demonstrated in our history that representative government is, as yet, by no means perfect, but that much yet remains to be done to elaborate a system of such government which shall be efficient and shall be guarded against evils — evils which, though different in form, are as grievous as those which are incidental to other forms of government. We have seen the departments of the government degenerate, the judiciary forfeit the respect of the people, the legislature fall under the manipulations of the lobby, the executive transgress the bounds of its authority to interfere in local affairs, the machinery of parties get into the hands of a set of men without character, who make a living which they could earn in no other way by low political intrigues. We have come to regard the touch of politics as carrying contagion to religion, to education, to every interest which it touches, and yet, under our system of government and society I beg you to notice that we cannot separate politics from one or all of these things. Our politics are our public life. Our society is and must be and ought to be nothing but our politics. We have brought state, government, politics, down into every man's keeping. We have developed a civilization in which no man and no interest stands alone, and our political life is in and pervades all our national life to bring either health or decay. It must touch everything. Those things which we try to keep aloof from it are languishing on account of their separation from the real vital pulse of the nation. Our religion is dying out because it is divorced from the living interests of the na-

tion. Our educational institutions are far short of what
they ought to be because they cannot be entrusted to the
care of the state, and, on the other hand, our educated
men miss their share, their due influence on the public
life of the nation. They are regarded almost like foreign intruders on that field. What then? Ought we to
commit these institutions to the state as it is? We dare
not and cannot. The fate of the churches which have
made this alliance and the shameful history of the agricultural college land-grants forbids it. We must, however, understand that the regeneration of our political
system is on that account only the more imperative and
that we must seek its regeneration by returning to first
principles and applying them with scientific rigor. I
propose to give a course of lectures on the political
and financial history of the United States, in which I
shall try to set forth the mistakes of which we now see
the fruits.

I hasten on, however, to speak in a similar brief manner of the department which now more especially demands our attention — political economy. This branch
of political science has at present the most vital importance for the American people. I measure its importance
not by the stir which it is now making in party politics,
for that is slight enough. A languor and apathy have
settled upon the people. This is a remarkable phenomenon, but I suppose that it may be a nervous reaction
after the period of war and reconstruction, similar to
that which overcomes an individual after a great nervous
excitement. A movement has indeed originated in the
West from which something may eventually come,
though as yet I see in it no signs of that sober desire to
investigate causes which must precede any successful
attempt at cure, nor any of those plans and methods of

action which alone lead to correct and beneficial results. But it is the duty of this chair to measure national needs by a knowledge of the national status, not by public sensations, and I affirm that the questions on which our national future to-day depends are questions of political economy, questions of labor and capital, of finance and taxation. The fruits of the Civil War did not cease when the armies disbanded. It left us with financial and industrial legacies whose fruits, as every student of political economy and social science knows, are slow in ripening; and they contain seeds of future and still more disastrous crops. No man can estimate these long following results. No man can tell what social, moral, and political transformations they may produce. There is no field of activity which now calls so urgently for the activity of honest and conscientious men as the enlightenment of the American public on the nature and inevitable results of the financial and industrial errors to which they are committed. I do not indeed expect that this continent is to become a wilderness again. I would not exaggerate. I know that a people can and will drag on a slow existence under the most unfavorable social, political, and industrial circumstances, and I know that the resources of this continent are such that we may waste and squander recklessly without feeling those bitter consequences whose healing function it is, in the moral order, to warn and convince us of mistakes. But the duty of the economist is not simply to learn how to avoid waste of what has been won but to learn the laws by which there may be no falling short of the utmost that might be attained; and the duty of the social scientist is to teach that moral and social deterioration follows inevitably upon economical mistakes, whether, looking to our general ratio of physical comfort, it

may be said that we can afford to waste or cannot.
This continent has never been used economically for
production in the sense above described. It has always
fallen far short of the development of which it has been
capable under the circumstances of any given time, if it
had been used according to the best economic knowledge
of that time. Perhaps this is true now more than ever.

The patriotism with which the American people submitted to the burdens of taxation and paper money, believing them to be necessary parts of the evil of the
War, is deserving of the most enthusiastic admiration.
It serves only to deepen the sadness with which the
economist must declare the conviction that the paper
money never was a necessity, never could in the nature
of things be a necessity any more than it could be necessary for a physician to poison a patient in order to
cure him of fever or for a man to become bankrupt to
escape insolvency; and also this other conviction, not a
matter of science but of history, that the necessity for
taxation has been abused by the creation of a protective
tariff which increases the burden which it pretends to
carry. These two subjects, money and tariff, will be the
subjects of my lectures during the present term. I say
money because I intend to treat the subject exhaustively
and to bring the paper money into its proper connection.
Next term I hope to offer to the graduate students a
course on finance and taxation, treating those subjects
with more independence of actual circumstances, and
according to the principles which science dictates.

Now as to the method which I pursue. I say nothing
here of the conflicting schools, the historical and the philosophical, into which political scientists are divided.
The philosophical or *a priori* or speculative method is
perfectly legitimate. I was glad to see that Professor

Tyndall, a year ago, vindicated the deductive method even for the physical sciences. This method is the prerogative of genius. But the inductive method, though slower and more commonplace, is far more sure and convincing. The only real antagonism of method is between the scientific and the traditional or dogmatic. Here I take sides decidedly. I have no confidence in any results which are not won by scientific method and I leave aside all traditional and dogmatic systems as scarcely worth noticing. I insist upon strictness of definition, correctness of analysis, precision in observing phenomena, deliberation in comparison, correctness of inference, and exhaustiveness in generalization. These are what constitute the scientific method as applied to diverse subjects. I vindicate for this department of study the character of a true science — not of a closed and finished science but of a science true by virtue of the methods by which the truth is discovered. We shall find the data of our study to some extent in history and statistics, for I think that it is here that we must look for the facts upon which a true science of politics and political economy is to be built; but our history and our statistics are, as yet, by no means in the form of perfection which is required by the economist if he is to build his science upon them. We shall not therefore shun the *a priori* process where we are thrown upon it as our only resource, and in discussing the details of practical politics, many of which are unprecedented, we shall have recourse to considerations of expediency as the true rule which governs such matters.

My course for the present year, then, involves for the seniors the study of political economy, with especial reference in the lectures to paper money and tariff. In our English text-book these things are curtly dismissed

as covered, as indeed they are, by a few common sense
reflections. As these, however, are living questions
amongst us, I must subject them to full investigation.
In the second term we shall study the science of government and the theory of the state — political science in its
narrower use. In the third term, international law. To
the graduates I offer a course this term on the Encyclopædia of Political Science as the basis of a knowledge of
the whole subject. In the second term I shall lecture on
finance and taxation, this being really a continuation of
the lectures on political economy, and in the third term
on the history of politics and finance in the United
States. In future years, as the University course develops, I hope to take up other branches of the wide
department which has been entrusted to me here and
gradually to win for this chair the influence which belongs to it as the chair of political science in the first
university of the republic. My aim will be to give to
those who visit this university faith in science, in
thought, in training as applied to politics. I desire to
use the opportunity given me to furnish the country
with citizens of sterling worth, and to give to the professions men whose public influence will tell in the cause
of liberty, industry, and honesty. I hope that those of
you who become lawyers will learn how to legislate
far-sightedly for the permanent welfare of a free people,
not to follow the clamor of a noisy faction. I hope that
those of you who become editors will learn to wield
honorably the immense power you will enjoy for the
instruction and molding of public opinion. I hope that
those of you who become clergymen will teach that
no one can be a righteous man in our time and country
unless he is also a faithful citizen. I hope also that the
career of politics may open in the future in such a way

as to tempt the ambition of the best youth of the republic. Republics learn only by experience, but the bitter
experience will not be wanting. The men of this generation are not doing their duty by the men of the next.
They are putting off hard duties and are shirking responsibilities and are relaxing the political virtue of the
country. In one way or another the results will inevitably come. When they come, I am of opinion that the
American people will find that it does not pay to be
ruled by small men. They will look about in their need
for men who know what ought to be done and how to do
it. It is my duty here to try to provide that when such
a time comes the men may be ready; and to you I say
that, whether you are in the ranks of the citizens —
where you will need to know how to choose your leaders
— or whether you are called to fulfill the responsibilities
of office yourselves, the course of study upon which we
now enter deserves your most careful application.

SOCIOLOGY AS A COLLEGE SUBJECT

SOCIOLOGY AS A COLLEGE SUBJECT[1]
[1906]

When I looked over the program of this meeting I chose to speak in the discussion on this question because it is the one that interests me most. I hope that in the course of the discussion we shall develop some useful suggestions in regard to it. The fact is, it seems to me, that to-day there is nothing more important for all young men to learn than some of the fundamental notions of sociology. I use the term now in the broad sense of a philosophy of society, the synthesis of the other things that we sometimes include under sociology; and it seems to me that in all the public discussion that is going on and in the matters that nowadays seem to interest people more than anything else, what they need is some sound fundamental notions that a sociologist might give them.

For instance, everybody ought to know what a society is. "Society" is a word that has a great many different uses. It is very much confused by these different uses; and at the same time a society is the fundamental thing with which sociology is concerned. The social sciences are all of them connected with particular details of social life, and if people could get an idea of what a society is, and perhaps still more exactly what it is not, it would correct and define a great number of false suggestions that nowadays perplex the public mind.

Then, again, it is most important in regard to a society that it shall be publicly understood what you

[1] *The American Journal of Sociology*, Vol. XII, pp. 597–602.

can do with a society and what you cannot do with it. People who know what a society is, and what we can do with a society by our best efforts, would know that it is great nonsense to talk about the re-organization of society as a thing that people are going to take in hand as a corrective measure, to be carried out by certain social enterprises so called. What we try to do, and what we want to try to do in class work, is to give the young men and young women (where the latter are concerned) a sound idea of some of these fundamentals, that would stop them from going over into a false line of effort and thought.

Now, it seems to me that in doing this one thing what we want to do is to get down to facts; and we ought to stick as close to facts as we can. I don't mean statistical facts, but I mean the realities and the truth of the life around us, the life that is going on, the motives of the people, their ideas and their fallacies, the false things on which they pin their faith, and so on. And the facts all show that there ought to be understood by students of sociology all fundamental facts about society, about what it is, what is possible in it, what is not possible in it, and so on. We have our work at New Haven so organized that we try to have the students take courses in ethnography and some related subjects which are of a fundamental character and which form a stock of knowledge that a student of sociology ought to have. If we do not do this, sociology becomes a thing up in the air. We have a lot of abstract definitions and abstract notions that may, of course, have some philosophical value or psychological truth; but the student starting out from them is in great danger, at any rate, of going off into the old-fashioned methods of deduction from these broad notions that he starts with, and the whole thing becomes lost in the clouds. That seems to me the greatest danger that sociology nowadays has to encounter. If we allow it to become foundationless — I mean in regard to the real facts — and make it a matter of thought and deduction, we cannot expect that we shall have great effect on public opinion; we cannot expect that people will pay very much attention to us or care much about what we say. The only way to get an influence that we want and that we think we deserve is to keep sociology directly and constantly in touch with common everyday life and with the forms of the social order.

If I were a man forty years old, and were beginning to be a professor in one of our American colleges, I should think that the opportunity to take hold of a department of sociology, and give it shape and control its tendencies, lay down its outlines, and so on, was really the most important thing that a man nowadays could undertake, because of the tremendous importance of these social questions that are arising. There cannot be any doubt of it, and I, at any rate, am perfectly convinced that within the next twenty-five or thirty years the questions that are going to shake American society to its foundations are questions of sociological character and importance. Some have already been referred to; such, for instance, as this race question that has been rising and getting more strenuous every year. It has got some truth at the bottom of it, if we can get at it; in the end it will have to be settled from the merit that is in it, and it is the sociologist who will have to find the truth that is in this matter. Again, such questions as are involved in conflicts about capital are unlimited in their influence on the welfare of the American people. And if I were at the beginning of a career, instead of at the end of it,

I should think there was nothing that was better worth work than to get into the minds of the young men some notions that were sound in regard to such fundamental matters. Then in regard to this matter of divorce and the way in which it is acting upon the American people; it is a question that ramifies through the whole society and even the most dithyrambic of our orators have never gone beyond the truth of the importance of this matter to the American people.

My opinion in regard to this is that the way to build a science of sociology is to build it on the same fundamental methods that have proved so powerful in the other sciences—I mean the more or less exact sciences. We cannot pretend that we can ever make an exact science of sociology. We ought not to try. We haven't got the information, and I don't know that we ever can get it in the accurate, positive shape in which it is ascertained in the exact sciences. We are all the time dealing more or less with propositions that under certain circumstances will have to be modified. They are valuable, they are important, but more knowledge, more information, may force us to modify them. That will not do any harm. There have been sciences that have had a long and useful life, although they remained in that form. I don't think that is a fundamental difficulty, but it is one that we want to overcome so far as we can. We ought to be truly scientific so far as possible. We ought to use positive and well-tested methods and we ought not to trust any others. The methods that we use ought to be such as would be regarded as valid at any time and anywhere, on any subject.

Now if the young men are to be trained in this, you have got to bring them up to it by a study of a positive character that deals with facts and information. We have thought that ethnography was at any rate one of the very broadest of these subjects. The books on sociology all refer constantly to certain things as true with regard to primitive or uncivilized people, and we ought to have a stock of knowledge about such matters that is firm and well-learned, so that the students know what we are talking about. They would know at once if all the things as asserted are actually and positively true. Then there are the economic courses: as has been well said, they have important limitations, but they furnish a convenient and practical introduction to our line of study. Again there is the great field of history; that furnishes us a vast amount of our material—the material on which we base our deductions and generalizations, so that a student who is going to be a sociologist never can know too much history. And if history is taught well and according to modern ideas and methods, it furnishes a very good introduction to sociological study.

Well, I myself am about at the end of it; only one or two more years remain, and I am most interested now to know what can be done for the sake of the future, for those who will come after and take up the work and carry it on. I hope we shall get up a discussion here — if necessary, a quarrel — which will develop ideas about this matter that will help. Somebody asked me last evening if this was going to be a gay discussion, and I said it had possibilities for a very gay discussion; and, Mr. Chairman, it is what I hope we shall have in the remainder of the session.

THE PREDICAMENT OF SOCIOLOGICAL STUDY

THE PREDICAMENT OF SOCIOLOGICAL
STUDY [1]

DURING modern times science has gradually gained the mastery of one after another of the great departments of human interest. As yet its dominion is imperfect and disputed, but it is gaining ground every day as the authority to which we must all look for truth about the earth, human life, and the nature and destiny of man. As fast as science gains dominion it displaces arbitrary and personal elements. It gives correct notions of causation and so dispels superstition; it drives out transcendentalism, mysticism, and sentimentalism from every interest over which it obtains dominion. But science has not yet extended its domain over the social interests of mankind. Sociology is a science which has yet to come into being, and it is as yet only the name for an outline which we have to fill up by a long and laborious investigation.

If, as we well know, biology and its cognate developments are yet in their struggling infancy, how much more is sociology new and tentative. Yet if we can train a body of men to study it we shall undoubtedly win advantages as great as science has produced in any department which it has yet conquered. Let us now consider the sort of thing which the advance of science must drive out of sociology.

There are no topics which are more constantly discussed than social topics. Everybody has views about social questions; and these views are generally crude. That, however, does not prevent them from being freely

[1] For approximate date, see preface.

put forward.   Every one gets some experience of society and has an opportunity to make some observations of social phenomena.   I believe, however, that any one who studies sociology will be very loath to give opinions on social topics which lead him far away from the most primary facts and doctrines of political economy or the simplest maxims of statecraft.   We do not indeed lack those who are far more ambitious.   I am not quite sure how much is intended in that clever satire, "The Revolt of Man," when the women who have come to rule the world and have destroyed civilization and lowered the population, are represented as chiefly interested in politics and political and social economy.   If it means that people who are fond of talking a great deal in proportion to the working and thinking they do, are prone to pitch upon social and economic topics, there is a great basis of truth under the satire.   All the world-reformers, the philanthropists, the friends of humanity, and in general the class of those who are anxious to mind their neighbors' business, pitch upon sociological topics with especial avidity.   It is a broad and expansive sensation to feel one's self telling one's neighbor how he ought to live.   It must be sublime to have the consciousness that one is capable of setting the world straight.   A religious teacher, who speaks in the name of a creed of religious dogmas, does not believe that he is speaking for himself, but thinks that he is bringing a message of authority to a world lost and blind in the midst of perplexities; but one who speaks only in the name of an ethical philosophy or a sentimental desire for reform has no standards or guidance whatever.   The orthodox preacher may insist strongly on the authority and absolute value of his message, but the *a priori* philosopher can only establish arbitrary points of departure and arbitrary deductions.

The preacher may be easily set aside if his authority seems to be destitute of foundation; the philosopher is certainly only entangling himself in a maze of rhetoric and metaphysics. The old biblical system unquestionably contained a sociology. The religion of the Jews and that of the Christians reaches out to the dimensions of a cosmic philosophy; it contains a whole system of natural philosophy, of the state, and of society, as well as of the church; it embraces, in short, the whole life of man in its scope and interest. So far as I know, that has been the case with all of the great religions; each one of them contained all things necessary to human life, the center of the system being in the religious bond or the religious consciousness. Modern science also embraces in its scope all human interests — all those at least which are limited by this world. These two systems cannot come to an adjustment and division of territory without many collisions and much friction. Now, however, there comes the metaphysician, the ethical philosopher, the sentimentalist, the man who wants to make everybody happy, the reformer, and the friend of humanity, and they all seek to conquer the domain which religion has not yet lost and science has not yet gained. Hence it is that sociology is to-day torn and distracted amongst them all and that science seems, as yet, to have but the smallest share in the treatment of social issues.

A consequence of this state of things is that sociology is dominated by all the evil forces which ever harm any subject of human interest. There is a kind of transcendentalism in regard to social matters which is cherished by a certain school. Often the least experienced students are captivated by subtleties of this kind. The most round-about discussion, or the one which treats phenomena by reference to unimportant incidents and accidental coincidences, is pursued by preference. The whole discussion of social topics is conducted in a vein of sublimated and over-refined speculation. Of course the effect of holding this standpoint is that phenomena are not observed and that facts are left out of account.

Closely allied with this way of looking at sociological questions is one which is rather mystical than transcendental. There are German writers who are very fond of this mode of viewing society. Their influence seems to be spreading. They generally confuse political economy with sociology, and then give us a mystical political economy which is made to cover more or less the whole domain of sociology. The influence of this school is spreading both in England and America. Our American students go to Germany and, returning, need to prove that they have gained something by it. They undoubtedly do gain more than one can estimate and in a great variety of ways, but they feel bound to vindicate the specific instruction which they have received lest it might seem that their foreign study had not been necessary or advantageous. The particular effect produced is that the science of political economy, the art of government, and morals are confused together to the great disadvantage of all. Occult relations and laws are devised, and the path of social growth is held to lie in the cultivation of certain soul-states in the individual.

Then we have a certain peculiar dogmatism in sociology. Men who are eminent in other branches of science and who would vigorously resent any intrusion of dogmatism into their own departments will not hesitate to dogmatize in the most reckless manner about sociological questions. The reason is because they have never yet learned to think of social phenomena and laws as subject to the same point of view and modes of thought as natural and other sciences.

Then there are the sentimentalists, who are the largest class and who make the easiest work of social questions. In the study of the individual organism we know that normal physiology presents the greatest difficulties and is the essential basis for a correct study of diseases and remedies. We also know that popular knowledge of physiology is meager in the extreme, while popular notions attach almost entirely to diseases and to remedies. The same is true of society. The study of the structure and functions of the organs of society is long and difficult, and we have, as yet, accomplished very little towards it. We can hope to accomplish much only by a long study of history and a careful examination of institutions. I venture to say that no study except the highest mathematics has ever yet made such demands on the human mind as are made by sociology. We cannot make an experiment in sociology because we cannot dispose of the time, that is, of the lives of a body of men and women. We have to carry in mind a great number of variables, to weigh their value, and to deduce their resultant, although for many of them we can find no unit of measurement or comparison, and although we have no notation to help us. I think that we shall have to adopt some of these methods of the other sciences sooner or later, but at present I see no means of advancing sociology save by the cultivation of a trained judgment through the careful study of sociological phenomena and sequences.

Under these circumstances the student of sociology as a science will necessarily feel great timidity about all generalizations. There are so many more things that he does not know than there are which he does know,

that he never feels ready to close the case and advance
to a decision. There are so many components whose
value he can only measure approximately that he cannot
feel sure of his result.

This state of things, however, is precisely made to fit
the sentimentalist. Here we have before us social diseases, and we see a great number and variety of social
phenomena which are disagreeable and shocking to our
sensibilities. Some of them are appalling. In the city
of New York and in any other great city, we can find
representations of every grade of. barbarism from the
bottom up. We think of the primitive man as a strange
creature of passion and impulse, but there are social
groups amongst us consisting of persons who have grown
up without discipline and who are similarly primitive and
barbarous. About all of civilization which they have
caught is the fashion of wearing clothes. The primitive
man made women do all the work; but there are plenty
of men in modern civilized society, especially in the
great cities, who do the same. We can find slavery,
caste systems, serfdom, and feudal relations represented
in scarcely disguised forms in the midst of any great city
of to-day. We can find fetishism and every other form
of religious superstition represented; likewise polygamy,
polyandry, and every other form of sex relation. It has
been said that the human animal runs through, in˜em-
bryo, the whole biological development from which the
human race has sprung and contains within himself all
that development in an accumulated form. Something
of that sort is true about society; our society to-day
contains fragments of the whole history of civilization,
accumulated and consolidated into the great existing
fabric.

Hence it is a great mistake to think that we have left

behind and sloughed off all old things. We have not. We carry with us survivals of all the old things. Sometimes those survivals appear to be clogs upon us; sometimes they seem to be stepping-stones by which we rise higher.

But now observe what a grand chance of error is offered to any one who goes out to look around upon our civilized society of to-day and to say how it pleases him. Of course he sees the most grotesque contrasts side by side. If we begin to boast of some of our triumphs, we do not finish the boast before some one of these contrasts bursts into view like the face of a grinning demon rising to deride us. If our social observer has imbibed the humanitarian sentiments which are afloat in our most refined society and if he looks at the horrors, cruelties, and sufferings which underlie our society, he cries out in dismay. He does not know that he is looking at a feeble reflection of the only scene which this earth presented to the sun for thousands of years. He does not see that the wonder is that we have gained a certain peace and security for a part of the human race, not that there yet remain at the bottom of society vast realms of misery and strife.

Of course the sentimental observer, terrified at the disease, is in haste for a remedy. The first step is to make a diagnosis, which is done by fastening the blame on some things or some persons. Let me repeat that the real marvel is that civilization has triumphed so far that, in three or four great civilized nations, a few million people can so far control the condition of existence that they can live their lives out in peace and security. One of the commonest and most baseless popular notions is that all men could be or ought to be to-day on that same status and that there is blame to be dispensed if they are not.   A little reflection will show that it is quite impossible for all to have the best there is.   No doubt all the social force in the world is exhausted in sustaining human society at its present level.   That force is not all employed as economically as it might be; far from it. But that only throws us back on our true point of view and of effort, *viz.*, to make the wisest use of what we have — to improve our institutions and advance the arts as a means of increasing our social force and to trust to this increase of power to advance civilization.   Even then, however, we must understand that some men will absorb to themselves any gain we make and will thus prove themselves the best men.   In fact, the advance which we gain, instead of saving and raising the miserable and pitiful victims who are at the bottom, may possibly crowd them out of existence entirely.   For instance, if we break up one of the slums of a great city and disperse its poverty-stricken, vicious, and criminal inhabitants who might have festered there for a long time yet, we force them out into open contact with society where they are soon crushed by the competition of life or by the machinery of the law.

Such a line of thought as this, however, is never pursued by the sentimentalist.   Seeking a diagnosis of the social evils which he perceives, he notes the preponderant importance of capital in modern society, and he notes the struggle of interests which is involved in the whole structure of our modern industrial system.   I have tried elsewhere to show how it is that capital is the backbone of all civilization, and that higher and ever higher organization is essential, as the number of men increases, for the human race to keep up its advancing fight with nature.   Consequently the struggle to get capital, to keep it, and to use it, is and must be one of the leading phenomena of society. The moralists and philosophers sneer at the struggle for wealth and criticize it, and still it goes on. The moralists and philosophers might do a great deal to make the struggle for capital more intelligent, but to try to preach it down is like telling men not to live; and to try to set limits or bounds of any kind to the accumulation of capital is simply telling men not to live as well as they can. We always come back to the same point: restraint or diminution of capital is a reduction of civilization.

The case is no better if we try to regulate in any way the struggle of interests under liberty. The sentimentalists are always greatly outraged by the notion of the survival of the fittest which is produced by liberty. If we do not like the survival of the fittest, we have only one alternative and that is the survival of the unfittest. If A, the unfittest to survive, is about to perish and somebody interferes to make B, the fittest, carry and preserve A, it is plain that the unfittest is made to survive and that he is maintained at the expense of B, who is curtailed and restrained by just so much. This process, therefore, is a lowering of social development and is working backwards, not forwards.

These points of criticism show us what we have to think about the attempts of the socialists and sentimentalists to attribute the dark phenomena of our society to capital or to liberty of organization, and of their proposals, by way of remedy, to assail property and liberty. It is only a commonplace to say that all human institutions and arrangements are liable to abuse and that we must keep up a constant warfare with selfishness and greed whenever they show themselves. That necessity will never be done away with while the world stands. Selfishness and greed will

change their forms and lines of operation as changes
occur in the industrial system and in the organization
of society. To check the development of society in
order to prevent selfishness and greed would certainly
be preposterous.

Passing by others who dabble in social discussions, I
will notice, finally, the poets and the novelists. The
influence of the latter, in our day, is very great. About
all the information which certain people possess on social
questions comes from the novelists. They give us
pictures of society either as they see it or as they want
to see it. Their presentations are as fragmentary and
disconnected as paintings hung in a gallery. At best
they are kaleidoscopic and have no cohesion but that of
an arbitrary symmetry. They deal by preference with
that sociological subject which stands first in importance, the family, including marriage, paternity, and
divorce, and also the relations of love and courtship.
It is significant of the effect which the novel has produced by its treatment of these things that they are
all regarded with a certain levity; we know, however,
that they surpass all others in weight and importance.
Consider the notions about love which are spread abroad
amongst our young people by the novels of to-day.
Those notions are purely conventional and artificial. I
do not, of course, mean to argue that the old-fashioned
plan under which the parents selected husbands or
wives for their children was wiser than our methods of
to-day, though we might well ask whether the old plan
made any more unhappy marriages than are made
to-day. But if young people are taught that love is a
kind of disease which may be caught or may not, like the
measles, that it comes only once in a life-time, that it is
a passion which ought not to be controlled by reason or

duty, that it is a law to itself, and so on, then it is not strange that families are broken up and lives are blighted later on. We can build nothing strong on passion. We build strongly only when we build on duty.

Nor can the novels be thought much more fortunate in their teaching about the relations of parents and children than in what they say about love and marriage. We stand here midway between the old doctrine that the parent had all the rights and the child all the duties, and the new doctrine which is that the child has the rights and the parent the duties, but that the child owes respect, deference, and obedience where he meets with affection and care.

Enough, now, has been said to show that what we need in this department, confused as it is by old theories and new, by old traditions and new fashions, by old creeds and new philosophies, is a scientific method which shall descend to a cold clear examination of facts and build up inductions which shall have positive value. That is what sociology attempts to do. If we can trace the evolution of society from its germ up to its present highest forms, we may hope to identify the forces which are at work in it and to determine their laws. We can disabuse our minds of arbitrary codes and traditions and learn to regard society as a growth under law. We may then hope to understand what we see about us, and if remedies are either desirable or necessary, we shall stand some chance of selecting them intelligently.

MEMORIAL ADDRESSES

MEMORIAL ADDRESSES[1]

ADDRESS OF OTTO T. BANNARD,
YALE, 1876

As one of the very early students of William Graham Sumner in Political and Social Science, I may be permitted to speak briefly — not as a scholar or economist — just as one of many who sat at his feet and never forgot, who listened and read and always rejoiced at meeting him. He was a great central figure and a large part of Yale, and Yale without Sumner taxes the imagination of us older men. He was a University Keystone not to be removed, and he will continue in our thoughts and in our life as long as we who knew him live.

Without any national official position, he was a national character. His subjects dealt with national policies and current events and his views were sought even by those to whom they were unwelcome. Oddly enough, no matter how unyielding his opposition, he generated no personal rancor, for it was self-evident that he was the apostle of truth, and interested only in the correctness of the conclusions. There was no vanity in the argument, no conscious pleasure in the words. He had the constructive faculty, and his logic was merciless, and as unanswerable as a problem of Euclid, because human nature, expediency, local environment, and the compromises of government by party had nothing to do with abstract essence of truth. One late evening in his library, as a senior, I timidly questioned him as to the anti-Chinese sentiment in San Francisco and I shall never forget his impersonal demoli-

[1] Delivered June 19, 1910, in Lampson Lyceum, Yale University.

tion of every argument against the admission of the Chinese. The human rivalries of workmen were not to mar the comprehensive chart of the world studied as a whole. To a teacher, fundamental propositions must not be affected by local color.

Truth was a world-wide proposition founded on the testimony of the ages, and any community which found it useful to vary these laws for purposes of revenue, growth, or government would do so at its peril and with full notice.

And so Sumner convinced us and we students scattered from New Haven and drifted where we might, free-traders to the core — and economically sure of it until, later, contact with the world began to modify our ideas, adapting them to the local needs and conditions of some small industry in which we were trying to survive. We found pure economics somewhat theoretical and that many men must be consulted as to how governments may obtain revenue. In life few can have all they ask, and we ventured occasionally to take a liberty with a verity to meet an exigency, to clothe as it were a too naked truth.

The world happened to be already populated and must be operated by human beings. If we could begin anew it would be as he said, and as far and as fast as possible his laws must be arrived at, for fundamentally he was always right. Live and let live had nothing to do with truth as he taught it.

We never forgot what he said or how he said it or the tones of his voice or his gestures. They were stamped into our minds by his powerful, incisive personality and his rare gift of expression and illustration. He was a wonderful teacher without the slightest unpleasant accompaniment which some teachers have with unwilling students. Against our will we became willing and eager, and we liked him and would follow him wherever he led, and if we wanted a cut we cut some other recitation. Sumner's was not drudgery; it was stimulation.

And he was so extraordinarily clear and practical and nothing of the metaphysician. He never preached for the sake of preaching. He was no crusader from habit or for effect. Take it or leave it, he presented what he knew.

And then the division would be dismissed from the class-room, and a remarkable transformation take place. This man of iron would step from the platform, the atmosphere still charged with his electricity, throw his cape over his shoulders, and at once become the most friendly, kindly, genial, generous, human, and sympathetic of companions, the best of good fellows. He was only cast iron when he was denouncing economic enemies. He had no others.

His duty was to teach truth and to lead, and never was there a more exalted teacher nor so valiant a leader. After thirty-five years we find his truths chiselled in a rock and we see him now and forever in clear outline against the sky, high and strong and true.

ADDRESS BY HENRY DE FOREST BALDWIN, YALE, 1885

WHEN I was an undergraduate we were lately launched upon a new epoch. The world had been assimilating Darwin's "Origin of Species" about twenty years. The intellectual world was looking at things from a new point of view. Tradition was less sacred, authority less compelling to us than it had been to our predecessors. We revered and admired the old men, but they did not altogether meet our needs. The college had not then departed very far from the old curriculum which characterized institutions of learning for the three or four previous centuries. From all I can learn, there has been more change in the college curriculum from 1880 to the present time than took place from the foundation of the college to the time when I entered it. We were looking for a teacher who we felt could free himself from the old ways of thought, and whom we could rely upon to speak boldly, honestly, and clearly from the new point of view. We found our intellectual leader in Sumner. He did not appear to be afraid of talking over our heads. We felt he was giving the best he had to give, and that he believed what he taught. We knew he was devoting his great talents to us and had stores of wealth to give us, if we chose to listen to him. As a scholar he asked no quarter from an antagonist. As a teacher he did not ask blind acceptance of his ideas from his pupils. He stated his views without any concessions to make them acceptable to his hearers and without any attempt to hide a weak spot. His method of teaching called for an exercise of his pupils' critical capacity.

He had a striking way of putting things which made them stick. I remember once there was under discussion the subject of socialism. In dismissing the class Sumner said: "If any of you are ever in a community where a committee runs the whole thing, take my advice and get on the committee." Nearly twenty-five years afterward I was sitting in Cooper Union, New York, enjoying the interesting experience of hearing a prospective candidate for President of the United States questioned by an audience politically, although not personally, hostile to him. He was asked some question about socialism, and he replied that he did not know very much about it; that he had read a book on it and had come to the conclusion that it involved having everything run by a committee, and that he preferred not to live in a community where a committee ran the whole thing — unless he were on the committee. I then realized that Professor Sumner had repeated himself at least once, and that the result of his teaching had not been entirely lost, even though it had not made a democrat of this distinguished Yale graduate.

I hear it said that many economists question some of Sumner's conclusions. I do not care very much how you professional economists now look upon his views of the wage-fund theory or of any other particular economic problem. I do not mean to imply, by that, that it is not important that such questions should be thought out right. But I am sure that the most important thing we got from Professor Sumner did not lie wholly within the limits of the particular subject he was teaching us. He gave us a point of view with respect to the individual's place in the political and industrial community. He warned us to allow for bias. He implanted in us certain fundamental notions which I for my part have never been able to get away from. A few years ago I came across in a lady's drawing-room his great work on "Folkways." I read it with delight, not only for what it gave me that was new, but also for what I found in it that awakened old memories. I continually ran across various expressions and thoughts which I recognized as old friends; thoughts which had influenced my whole intellectual life; in many cases thoughts of which I had forgotten the source and had, perhaps, foolishly believed them to be the result of my own reflection. I realized then more than ever before what an influence Sumner had been in my life.

While I was an undergraduate, there was going on in the country a trend toward the democratic party. Sumner's sledge-hammer blows in the cause of free trade and sound money, as well as his general treatment of economic subjects, were a powerful influence in that direction. His advocacy of the causes which so many younger men hoped the democratic party would represent added interest in his personality and made him to a greater extent the subject of discussion. It also led some of those who came from stalwart republican homes to withhold themselves, to a certain extent, from the full benefit they might have received from his leadership; for the normal man holds his politics like his religion, and treats with suspicion any one who undertakes to subject them to intelligent examination. A few of these obtained the attendance of a Pennsylvania professor to deliver a lecture or lectures on protectionism. This turned out to be a good thing, for the contrast was marked.

But Sumner's influence on the tariff and sound money was not confined to undergraduates. The New York Free Trade Club, and later its successor, the Reform Club, which for many years constituted the center of agitation against protectionism, were largely dominated by men who had come under his teaching and influence in one way or another.

The absence of the qualities which make the successful politician was as marked in Sumner as was the presence of those qualities which make the scientific man and teacher. When men seek to attain political ends they necessarily look for allies; and if they are opposed to those in power they cast their eyes on the discontented, the unsuccessful under the present régime, and bid for their support by offering what they believe will prove attractive. Political affairs are necessarily a series of compromises. The need of allies to make a majority prevents logical progress, and in political life an old evil is rarely eradicated without the planting of some seeds of a new evil. The politician must be a compromiser. Sumner was no compromiser. I heard him once speak of himself as a popular agitator; but his agitation consisted in pointing out to his fellow-citizens the folly of what they were doing. I do not believe he ever undertook to tell them what they should do. He never set up to be a statesman. Certainly he never attempted the politician's rôle, which is quite apt to be to point out to a part of the people how they can collect some unearned advantage from another part of the people.

Sumner continually called attention to the difference between the task of the political economist and patient

student of the industrial and social consequences of
certain courses of conduct, and the task of the statesman. He used to insist that there is no "ought" in
political economy; that it is neither the study of the
question of Christian charity, nor of morals, nor of
statesmanship. These other subjects are well worthy
of study, but he could see no gain in mixing them with
the study of political economy. There flourished during
his time many statesmen who believed themselves
possessed of some happy thought which, if put into
operation by legislation, would ameliorate the lot of
mankind and change our social condition. There were
also men calling themselves political economists who
believed they saw the one thing needful as a cure for all
poverty, discontent, and unhappiness. These he called
"Prophets." Such people have always been assured
of a following. Our great political parties have often
been dominated by their ideas. Sometimes we hear
that probably our national existence or, anyway, our
prosperity, is due entirely to the beneficent operation
of the protective tariff, and to perpetuate it was justification enough for saddling the country with the
demoralizing, not to say expensive, pension system.
Again, we hear that all will go well if the government
will only give us the blessings of free silver coinage, or
government ownership of railroads, or prohibition of
the traffic in liquor. Against all such short cuts to
welfare Sumner poured out his scorn. He had no
place in such company. He laid the emphasis not on
what the state or the individual ought to do, but upon
the need of a careful inquiry into the consequences for
the community and individuals of proposed actions
however well-intended.

There is frequently drawn a distinction between

democrats and "real democrats," or, as it is sometimes phrased, "democratic democrats." Sumner was a real democrat, a real apostle of democracy. But it was not in a party sense of the word that he was a democrat. He had faith in the possibilities of a true democracy, — as he expressed it, a society based on contract as distinguished from a society based on status. His democracy was of the kind that asked for each man a fair field and no favor. He would let the individual reap where he had sown, and suffer for his own vices, slothfulness, or stupidity. He was against privilege as wrong economically, as wrong morally, as against justice, against progress, against human welfare, and against civilization. He was as much opposed to those who would array the House of Want against the House of Have as he was against the beneficiaries of a protective tariff. He pointed out that "the real danger of democracy is that the classes which have the power under it will assume all the rights and reject all the duties — that is, they will use the power to plunder those who have," and he could see no difference between the poor plundering the rich and the rich plundering the poor.

If, as is sometimes said, faith in democracy is waning, it is doubtless due to our failure to be true to the democratic principles of equality and liberty. Sumner tersely and vigorously pointed out wherein that failure consists. He strove against the two strongest tendencies which have undermined our democratic faith — protectionism which has created a privileged class among the wealthy, and humanitarian social theories which would create a privileged class among workingmen and among the lowly and poor. He scornfully says that A and B, the reformers and the philanthropists, undertake to decide what C shall do for D, D standing for the poor man and C, for the Forgotten Man, the man who pays. He saw the great net gain in the destruction of the ancient privileges of the old classes of society. He combated the tendency to fasten upon our social institutions new privileges which must inevitably create new classes. The European aristocracies always recognized some duties attached to their privileges by immemorial tradition and custom. The privileged classes which *we* are creating have no traditions and recognize no absorbing personal duties to society. They are as self-centered as corporations. Sometime this country may wake up and realize that the things Sumner specifically attacked — protectionism, trades-unionism, and the doctrine that it is beneficent to devise means to distribute among the poor the proceeds of taxes collected from the rich — perpetuate the same kind of injustice and inequality which characterized the feudal system and constitute the great dangers to democratic institutions. If, ultimately, the people of this country renounce the temptation to establish privileged classes as a part of our political and industrial policy, we shall owe a great debt to Sumner, who led, away in advance, against such tendencies.

In the comments that have been made since Professor Sumner's death, I have seemed to feel a suggestion that in his last years he felt some disappointment that he had not observed more tangible results in our national policy of his vigorous teaching. I cannot but believe that this has been assumed as something that might be the case rather than an impression gained by those intimate with him. His self-imposed rôle was that of a critic who called attention to the need of

subjecting plans for political and social amelioration
to scrutiny and investigation. It involved a life-time
of running counter to popular tendencies. The man
who adopts this course can never expect to attain a
popular following such as comes to the man who advocates a happy thought which is believed to lead to
prosperity and contentment. He attacked privilege,
and naturally the Interests tried to destroy him. He
told his contemporaries they were pursuing false and
wasteful methods. They disliked to listen to him.
When the whole country was laboring under delusions
with respect to protectionism and bimetallism, he stood
boldly for free trade and sound money. He turned not
aside to ride on the wave, but headed straight for his
mark, sturdily stemming wind and tide, and no one
better than he knew that he could not expect popular
applause, or better realized that his achievements
could not be measured in the coin with which the
politician or the demagogue is paid. Like most philosophers who are not more politicians than philosophers,
he must wait for the full results of his efforts from the
work of his many pupils whom he started upon courses
of correct thinking. The seeds he planted by his long
years of teaching and by his writings we may hopefully
expect to bear a substantial fruit in the strenuous
times we must all anticipate in the immediate future.
As was said of Socrates, he was more useful in devoting
his energies to teaching the youth than if he had tried
to rule the state.

It is not at all unlikely that the strongest advocates
of Sumner's political philosophy will soon be found
among the very class which looked upon him as its
enemy when he denounced protectionism.

ADDRESS BY ALBERT GALLOWAY KELLER,
YALE, 1896

> Great in council and great in war, . . .
> Rich in saving common-sense,
> And, as the greatest only are,
> In his simplicity sublime. . . .
> O voice from which their omens all men drew,
> O iron nerve to true occasion true,
> O fall'n at length that tower of strength
> Which stood four-square to all the winds that blew!

THE loss which Yale has suffered in the retirement and death of Professor Sumner is one which no one of his colleagues can contemplate without a sinking of heart. We have needed him all this year; we could face our crises of the future with more of equanimity if his presence supported us. For almost forty years Yale has had the devoted service of a great man and, what is more, of a natural leader of men; his strongly molding hand has shaped to an extraordinary degree the destiny of the academic world in which it fell to him to live and work. We younger men are told that at a crisis the leadership has been wont to creep into his hand as by some inherent urge. Such men are rare in academic circles and our sense of loss is correspondingly heavy. It is what we pay for having had him — and the price is not too great. Yale could not have become what she now is if he had not been hers; all of us should rejoice that Sumner lived and labored here. It should be our object in this memorial meeting to strive to temper our sense of loss by recalling what he was and what he did for Yale and for us all. Sumner's great intellect and his loyal love have been built into the structure of Yale just as his mind and character have entered into the formation of what we call the Yale type of man; and just as his ideas have gone to constitute many a block (perhaps unlabelled) in the framework of the social sciences.

Sumner would have been the last man to admit the truth of what I have just said, though I fear no contradiction in the saying of it; for he was a very humble man and esteemed his services very lightly. He took no pains to attach his initials to the work he did; and I firmly believe that the grand ovation of last June, and the many cordial letters that came to him last summer were a great and touching surprise to him. He told me that he was moved to tears as he stood on the Commencement platform, and added that the world was treating him very well. So, I say, he would have set aside what I have said of his abiding influence on Yale and Yale men and science. But it is the unseen things that are eternal. They may be unidentifiable in their details; they may be impersonal — but therein is revealed their kinship with what is elemental.

However, not everything that is "seen" is bereft of lasting memory; it is part of our purpose in being here to-day to recall those more definite temporal things about which human affections twine more tightly, perhaps, and upon which the memory rests more tenderly, than could be the case with influences of a more general nature. If we are talking of claims to immortality, what more cogent claim can be set up than the abiding and indefinitely fructifying influence of a powerful and deep-hearted personality? To-day we are recalling the splendidly human Sumner, and it is my privilege, as a younger man and colleague, to speak of his life and work during his latter years.

It is here that we younger men are met by the insistent pity of our elders who reiterate that we did not know the real Sumner — him of the pitched battle — the Sumner who found ordinary prose too feeble a medium to express his views about "the ——ism which teaches that waste makes wealth," and so broke through into that truly classic dialogue between the discoverer of natural resources and the Congressman. "Where," they ask us, "is the latter-day creation fit to stand beside *The Forgotten Man?*" To this friendly patronage the answer of the younger generation might be: "We envy you your experiences with the younger Sumner. It must have been wonderful to see him in his prime. But you do not cause us to regret that we came later. We cannot conceive that that earlier stage could have matched the ripe wisdom and sagacity, the comprehensiveness and perspective of Sumner's later phase. Splendid as Sumner's political economy may have been, it was but a preliminary study to his science of society; compelling as was his sympathetic sketch of the type of man who minds his own business, it was but a detail in comparison with his treatise on the matrix of human institutions in general — "The Folkways."

In these later years, Sumner's personality was disclosed to us, in contra-distinction perhaps to the experience of our predecessors, not so much (so to speak) in "severalty" as collectively or communally. We did not recite to him, — there was no give-and-take with its abrasions, often remembered with peculiar delight, and its beneficent blood-lettings. Sumner lectured to us; but there was no foolishness about it. We were ruled from the revolving chair in Osborn Hall as if we were a division of twenty instead of one many times that number. We daily made haste to transcribe, in the few moments he gave, our most intimate thoughts on the "lesson of the day." After a few awe-inspiring cases of confiscation, we brought no more newspapers — his pet aversion — into the lecture-room. When the daily tests had been collected, Sumner lectured the rest of the hour; and the sensation was to us as of the opening of long and orderly vistas. What we had learned unintelligently seemed to fall into its natural and inevitable sequence with the obvious realities of life. In short, though the term "personality" is a trite one, we felt the force of a personality so dauntless and dominant that there was no escape or evasion.

It is perhaps futile to attempt to analyze the impression Sumner made upon us. Someone has well said that he possessed an incomparable combination of manner, matter, and method; but for many of us at least the compelling influence lay outside the *matter;* and Sumner never held very much to conscious *method.* One who reads over his old note-book on the Science of Society sometimes cannot see just why the course laid hold of him so strongly; but then he closes his eyes and recalls the *manner* of presentation — the long forefinger uplifted, the authority of a face whose very ruggedness was not a matter of lines without, but rather of straightness, of undeviating and uncompromising honesty and sincerity within — and the spirit re-enters the dull and boyish pencillings, and all is explained. That was why he compelled us to think, to accept or to resist, it mattered not which; no "copious shuffler," no half-scholar, no shirk or mere pleasure-lover, no man who had not grappled with the grimnesses of thought, could thus, apparently without conscious effort, have compelled our intellectual homage. One reflects upon his old note-book again, and presently he sees that there was yet something more in the case — call it method, if one will, it was yet a living demonstration of the method being the man — and that was the simplicity always characteristic of Sumner and his work. No long words where a short one could be found, and no wastefulness even of the monosyllables; crisp, curt sentences as devoid as possible of latinity; no ideas so lofty and tenuous as to be incapable of full comprehension by the normal, healthy, youthful mind. The intellectual draught he reached us was so clear in its quality that sometimes, in retrospect, it looks as if there were nothing there at all. The ideas in the old notes seem so familiar as to be almost axiomatic; and yet, if we reflect upon them, we realize that they came to us first from Sumner and that they are in our notes because we hurried to get them down as being so new and grand to our youthful minds. Now they are part of us; for Sumner is living in us all and in those whom we shall influence, as he is living in this college, in whose service he found no labor too great — nor yet too small. He disciplined us and chastised us, and we return thanks for it; he opened our minds, taught us to detect and hate humbug, to trust to the truth, and to be faithful to duty — and for that we tender him our enduring reverence. The simple fidelity of a powerful man is an abiding treasure of remembrance, and a bracing one.

But I am privileged in being able to speak of Sumner as I could not have spoken if I had not remained at Yale and been closely associated with him for some years. Perhaps the most impressive thing about the man is that one straightway forgets his intellect and work when one is led to contemplate the union of austerity and tenderness which made up his character. If he has any enemies now living I am sure they would all agree that, for a mortal man, Sumner had about him nothing that was *small*. To those who knew him well it seemed that he must possess an almost intuitive sense of rectitude; for as his unrivalled mental acumen and common sense were wont to pierce so keenly the husks that surrounded any intellectual issue and to adjudge it according to its merits in its more than local setting, in like manner did his delicate sensitiveness to the quality of a moral issue serve as a sort of touchstone for those privileged to know him well. One man brought close to him in the physical weakness of his latest years has said that he had never known a woman with finer feeling. Nothing mean or low could thrive in his presence. But the steel of his character was not so delicate as to snap or to lose its cutting edge in the rudest of combats; he was "great in war." Sensitive of soul and strong of heart, his voice was one "from which their omens all men drew."

But I turn to the actual labors of the latter years. Some people have believed that when Sumner retired from the field of political economy, his career was thus practically closed. No greater misapprehension could exist. From the outset, Sumner's interests were never confined to political economy [1]; there is now in the University a professor of prominence in another line who has told us that way back in the seventies Sumner came

[1] These volumes of essays present an abundance of evidence bearing on this contention, with which the author of this address was not acquainted in 1910. — The Editor.

near to making an anthropologist out of him. When Sumner left political economy to others he freed himself to pursue his life-interest, awakened first by Herbert Spencer, in the science of society (or sociology, in the Spencerian sense of the term). His achievements in political economy were of a nature to secure wide repute, and his only public utterances of note during the ten or twelve years succeeding his withdrawal from political economy gave no special warning that the mode of his activity had changed. The last fifteen or more years of his life were divided between the classroom and the study, and it was only with the publication of "Folkways" that the results of his last and richest period began to appear.

In 1899 Sumner began to write what would have been his *magnum opus* on the Science of Society; and he had written a very considerable mass of manuscript, when it began to be borne in upon him that there underlay his whole conception of the evolution and life of human society a certain unifying and basic idea—and that this must be developed before the main treatise should be pushed to completion. In tracing the evolution of the several social forms (the industrial organization, marriage and the family, religion, government, and so on) he had observed that they all went back to an origin in popular habit and custom; that these conventions and habitudes formed the "prosperity-policy" of the society practicing them; that they exercised a coercion upon the individual to conform to them, though they were not codified by any authority — though their origin was lost in the mystery of the far past. He saw that some explanation of the nature of these "folkways" formed for him the indispensable preliminary to the analysis of the various forms of the societal institutions which came out of them. And so he set the bulky first manuscript of his Science of Society aside and devoted many months to laying bare the rock upon which he planned to build a science of society or sociology that should not be, as much so-called sociology is, a by-word and an object of merriment to scientists in other fields. This was the origin of that notable book of 1907 concerning whose grave importance to all succeeding scientific study of human society there can be no two opinions. Since the publication of "Folkways," in whose preface Sumner announced his forthcoming Sociology, the eyes of all social scientists, and of many others, have been turned toward the aging savant with feelings of anticipation and of impatience. With the personal grief over his loss there has been mingled not a little of professional chagrin over the fact that the book of his life had not been completed. But it does not lie in the intentions of those who were near to him either that he shall be deprived of the scholarly renown which is rightly his, or that a science upon which all too many cranks and weaklings have wreaked their insidious vocabularies and vaticinations shall be robbed of the support of one whose common sense and hard-headedness were sufficiently developed to balance off a praetorian cohort of the feeble-minded.

For a younger scholar and colleague, association with Sumner during these last years has been the experience of a life-time. The beginnings of special study with him were not fraught with any very perceptible modicum of care-free browsing along rose-scented paths of learning. He was the most discouraging of men until some purpose and much industry had been disclosed. He rowed the would-be swimmer out into the open sea, put him over head-first, and then pulled for shore without looking back, or at least without letting us see him do so. Demanding so much of himself he carried over the demand to his charges — he himself had learned since middle age eight European languages in addition to the Hebrew, Greek, Latin, French, and German which he already possessed. Respecting the method of acquiring a reading knowledge of some out-of-the-way language he used to say briefly: "The way to learn a language is to sit down and learn it." He drove us on with resolute hand, and we did not always realize that his stress was nicely gauged for the particular stage of greenness and foolishness through which we chanced to be passing.

But the man grew upon us, and the wisdom and justice of his demands became ever more apparent. How could we resist the wealth of sense in his three queries about a piece of work: What is it? How do you know it? *What of it?* He was intolerant of the man who could not say what he had in mind, clearly and plainly, for he thought involutions and vagueness betokened lack of accurate understanding; he had no use for the man who knew, but didn't know why he knew; but above all he abhorred random fumbling over matters that seemed to him to have no relation to the vital issues of life, or to be by their nature not susceptible of scientific investigation. Let those who are familiar with academic production say whether that question: What of it? is not eternally pertinent!

Now all this looks very hard and stern, and it often seemed so; but it was a nipping and an eager air that swept the intellectual heights which Sumner frequented. If you took him for your guide there could be no lagging;

and above all there must be no whining, for he could stand almost anything else rather than that. He did not wish you to take even your legitimate castigation from his own hand, lying down. But presently those of us who emerged from the ordeal found a metamorphosis in our relations; instead of the austere, uncompromising propulsion we found an indulgent, unassuming, loyal, warm-hearted friendship. The fellowship of learning took on for us a new meaning when we found this great scholar, for whose power and erudition we had so profound an awe, assuming that we were all on a par and taking us into his confidence and listening to our views as if they were really worth anything. We now see how he overlooked our lapses into foolishness, even when it meant boredom for him, as it often did. And then came the time when his interest reached out and he took within his ample affections those who were near and dear to us. Indeed it has seemed to us sometimes as if the focus of his interest had moved over to the younger generation, for Sumner's love of children was almost a passion in his later years. The orator at the last Commencement said splendidly of Sumner: "His intellect has broadened, his heart has mellowed, as he has descended into the vale of years." But I do not know that one could subscribe entirely to that second clause. A heart so great and warm and human as that which Sumner revealed cannot be of any place or time or age; it must have been there from the beginning. All this gentleness was present while yet the joy of battle had not cooled. His was a Roman soul among us, and its essence was strength. Strong in mind, strong in will, strong in sentiment — a big, strong, human, soul. Yale and Yale men are rich in his life. We

have had Sumner and shall always have him.   We all
need this thought to temper the sense of his loss and the
concern for a future without him.   His service will be
more deeply missed and valued as time passes.

> O fall'n at length that tower of strength
> Which stood four-square to all the winds that blew !